Praise for *By Faith, Not By Sight*

"Scott is a brilliant example of achievement in spite of adversity. His passion, faith, and sheer talent shine in this book. Read on and prepare to be affected, effected, and forever changed. We were!"

ALICE AND SHERYL COOPER,
SOLID ROCK FOUNDATION

"This book is full of surprises. It is so much more than a book about someone who refused to let blindness stop him from finding his own song. It goes far beyond his amazing success on *American Idol*. It's not even a book about someone who has continued to overcome obstacle after obstacle. This is a book about the power of love to transform every life, every day, if we dare to believe. It inspired me, I believe it will touch you deeply too."

SHEILA WALSH,
BEST-SELLING AUTHOR, SPEAKER, AND ARTIST

"If you watched Scott MacIntyre compete on Season 8 of *American Idol*, you might think you know his life story. But you only know a small part of it. There is much more to tell, and now Scott has done just that, in his new book, *By Faith, Not By Sight*. He holds nothing back, discussing in intimate detail what it is like to be visually impaired, to love music, to fight a life-threatening illness, to live alone in London, to compete on *Idol*, and to find the love of his life. There are lots of surprises, lots of laughs, and lots of tears. This is also the story of a loving family, one you'll want to be a part of when you read Scott's inspirational and revealing autobiography."

FRED BRONSON,
MUSIC EXPERT AND JOURNALIST, *BILLBOARD* MAGAZINE

"Scott captured our attention the moment he walked on the *American Idol* stage. There was a warmth and sincerity about him that drew us in. I think more than a few calls were made from the Smith house in support of Scott! What we've seen on camera just scratches the surface. Scott's moving story will inspire everyone who reads it."

MICHAEL W. SMITH,
GRAMMY-AWARD WINNING SINGER/SONGWRITER

By Faith,
Not by Sight

By Faith,
Not by Sight

*The Inspirational Story of a Blind Prodigy,
a Life-Threatening Illness, & an Unexpected Gift*

Scott MacIntyre

with JENNIFER SCHUCHMANN

THOMAS NELSON
Since 1798

NASHVILLE   DALLAS   MEXICO CITY   RIO DE JANEIRO

Published in Nashville, Tennessee, by Thomas Nelson. Thomas Nelson is a registered trademark of Thomas Nelson, Inc.

Page design by Mandi Cofer.

Thomas Nelson, Inc., titles may be purchased in bulk for educational, business, fund-raising, or sales promotional use. For information, please e-mail SpecialMarkets@ThomasNelson.com.

Scripture quotation in chapter 5 is taken from THE ENGLISH STANDARD VERSION. © 2001 by Crossway Bibles, a division of Good News Publishers.

Scripture quotation in chapter 34 is from the Lexham English Bible, Second Edition. Copyright 2010 Logos Research Systems, Inc. All rights reserved.

Library of Congress Cataloging-in-Publication Data

MacIntyre, Scott, 1985–
  By faith, not by sight / by Scott MacIntyre.
    p. cm.
  ISBN 978-0-8499-4721-6 (hardcover)
  1. MacIntyre, Scott, 1985– 2. Singers--United States--Biography. I. Title.
  ML420.M1384A3 2012
  782.42164092--dc23
  [B]

                                 2011053186

Printed in the United States of America
12 13 14 15 16 17 QG 6 5 4 3 2 1

Contents

Competing Realities

If an illusion's all you really are
It's all a big mistake
'Cause dreams are what we're living on
And it's the reason hearts will break.

—from "Sweet Dreams," Scott MacIntyre

"I don't feel very good."

I dropped the cup, spilling the water on the floor. The nurse tried to help me, but I had become unresponsive. When I couldn't respond to her questions, she began frantically pushing buttons on the machine and trying to adjust the tubes. It was immediately obvious to my parents that she couldn't figure out what to do. They could tell something was terribly wrong as they watched the nurse's demeanor grow more panicked. Another nurse came over to help.

"He's coded," the first nurse said.

Mom, who was already standing close to my bed, moved in closer. She didn't know exactly what had happened, but she knew it wasn't good.

The nurses continued to talk among themselves.

"Check his vitals."

"I can't get a reading."

"BP?"

"Falling."

Mom started praying out loud. A social worker suddenly appeared by her side, as if she had been notified of an impending crisis. Mom looked to Dad for help. He was sitting about ten feet away from her on the other side of the bed. With all of the medical people moving around, she couldn't see his face at first, but as more people rushed toward the bed and Dad stood up to make room for them, she finally got a glimpse of his expression. He was staring at me with horror in his eyes.

By now, loud alarms were beeping and everyone in the room knew something terrible was happening.

The nurse in charge of the ward rushed around the corner.

"His blood pressure's falling and we can't stop it," one of the nurses told the charge nurse.

"Lord, protect him!" Mom prayed out loud. "Please protect Scott."

The charge nurse took my vitals and then adjusted some of the controls on the dialysis machine. Using a syringe, she inserted medication into the lumen. A tense minute passed while everyone waited to see what would happen.

～

Two and a half years later
April 8, 2009

I knew what was at stake.

I was in the bottom two. After the commercial break, Ryan Seacrest would announce which one of us had the lowest votes and that person would be going home.

The commercial break ended, and it was time for the announcement. America had cast thirty-four million votes for their favorite idols, and I had the lowest total. The difference in votes between the next closest contestant and myself was infinitesimal—less than one-tenth of one percent. But standing on the *American Idol* stage, I didn't have the luxury of worrying about the difference in votes. I was going home.

Unless . . .

Season eight of *American Idol* was the first time the "judges' save" had been introduced. The save gave the judges veto power over the votes. Regardless of the vote total, the judges could use the save to keep a contestant in the competition for at least another week.

Singing was the only thing that could possibly save me now. I needed to give my last song everything I had in hopes that the judges would use their one and only save. My fate was in their hands. If they chose to use it, I stayed. If not, I was headed home.

I would be singing for my life—my life on the show, and the future of my life in music.

Even Ryan Seacrest, the ordinarily enthusiastic *Idol* host, seemed subdued as he handed me the microphone. I took it from him and licked my dry lips. Everything was riding on the next two minutes. Ryan introduced the song, and as the first notes of my music played, I decided to just let go of everything I'd been thinking about and be present in the moment.

On cue, I opened my mouth and started singing.

Immediately I realized there was a huge problem—the sound in the monitors wasn't working! If I couldn't hear myself sing, I had no way of knowing whether I was on key or in time with the music. *How could this be happening?* Everything I had was riding on *this* performance.

As the song continued, I chose to do the only thing I could—keep singing. Instead of worrying about what I couldn't hear, I decided to focus on the meaning of the lyrics. I sang with all the depth and passion that burned inside of me. I sang like no one was listening and everyone was listening. By the time I finished, I had no idea how well I had done or how it sounded to the audience, but I knew I had given it everything I had. It was an emotional performance, and I felt that I had laid my heart on the line.

Now it was up to the judges.

The heat from the lights warmed my face as I stood center stage with Ryan. I tried to catch my breath. Earlier in the show, the judges had indicated they might be inclined to use the save. Each breath came fast and shallow as I waited for the judges' decision.

Ryan pushed the deadlocked judges for an answer—two wanted me to stay and two were ready to send me home. Then I heard Simon Cowell's clipped English accent, and I turned my head in his direction. I wanted to look into his eyes for a sign of what was to come—to prepare myself for what he would say—but that wasn't possible.

"Scott, someone's got to make a decision here and I'm going to say . . ." I held my breath as I waited for Simon to finish his sentence. My heart raced, and shouts of "Save him!" from the audience grew louder. I felt like I was hanging over a precipice dangling from a frayed rope.

"It's the end of the competition. Sorry."

Simon's words were like knives that cut the rope and then plunged into my heart. That was not what I expected to happen. I was stunned and confused.

I nodded and swallowed hard.

"Thank you, Simon," I said, and I meant it.

Suddenly everything seemed to speed up. I was powerless—stuck in a free fall toward a very dark pit but too shocked to do or say anything to stop it. I waited for the inevitable crash and the pain that would surely follow. "Scott

MacIntyre, ladies and gentlemen," Ryan said. The audience roared with applause and cheers (later I learned they had given me a standing ovation). "We will certainly miss you on this show," he said, hugging me. But even as I hugged him back, he kept things moving along, "We're going to take a look at Scott's journey on *American Idol*. Roll it!"

A montage of video clips began to play on the screen, and I heard my voice say, "I hope I can be an inspiration to a lot of people."

I wanted to grab the moment and hang on to it. I wanted to stretch it out, to breathe deeply and inhale my final minutes on the *Idol* stage. But time moved too fast for me to catch it.

I heard *Idol* judge Randy Jackson say on the video, "Every time you sing, I can see the passion pouring out of you, how much you love this, and how much you want this." Next a female voice said, "You move mountains when you step on that stage." It was judge Kara DioGuardi. She was new to the judges' table—the first judge known for her songwriting abilities. As a songwriter myself, I respected her greatly. Her words were followed by Simon's distinctive voice: "In a sea of forgettable people, you're the only one I am actually going to remember."

I wanted to yell, "Stop! Wait! Let's take this a little slower." I wanted to hear everything they said—ponder it, think about it, treasure it—but I couldn't wrap my mind around any individual comment on stage or on the screen.

Instead I went through the motions of thanking the other contestants and smiling in the general direction of the cameras. The video montage finished and Kris Allen, another contestant, put his hand on my shoulder. Somehow, that comforted me. I waited for Ryan's final words to end the show, but instead, he said, "Before we say goodnight, Paula, I know you want to have the last word."

That had never happened before. Every other elimination show that season had just ended without any further comment. I strained to hear what I couldn't see. "On behalf of the judges," Paula Abdul said, "I just want to say you've been an inspiration to the entire world through your commitment and your talent. We all watch *American Idol*, so as an audience, we get to witness unique and gifted artists—such as you, Scott—realize an incredible dream . . . You are one classy gentleman. God bless you. And we love you."

And it was over.

CHAPTER 1

Obstacle Courses

I've been in places where my life couldn't be better
Just to see myself slip back into the dark

—FROM "THE GOOD, THE BAD, THE UGLY," SCOTT MACINTYRE

Thursday, May 12, 2005

The worst day of my life began as the best day of my life.

The alarm went off, and I threw back the covers, leaped out of bed, and jumped on my brother, Todd, who was sound asleep in his bed.

"Wake up! Wake up! Wake up!" I said, pushing him until he finally rolled over.

Satisfied that he was now awake, I reached across his bed to open the blinds. The sun hadn't been up long, but enough Arizona sun filled the room to prevent Todd from going back to sleep.

"What time is it?" asked Todd.

"It's time to get up," I said, jumping up and down and clapping like a seal. It's this thing I do when I'm so excited, I can't contain it. I knew it would make Todd laugh.

Todd chuckled. "What are you doing?"

"I can't help it. This is going to be the best day ever!"

In a few hours, I would be graduating from college. My peers, all dressed in their caps and gowns, would be seated in chairs on the floor of Sun Devil Stadium. Admiring friends and family would be in the stands looking on. I would have a seat of honor on the raised stage. I couldn't help smiling as I thought about all the things I'd overcome to get to this point.

Because I had ben born blind, my parents had to fight to get me the education they wanted for me, and eventually they chose to homeschool. Until my college admittance exams at age fourteen, I'd never taken a standardized test to know how I compared academically to my peers. But now, at age nineteen, I was graduating summa cum laude with a bachelor of music degree in piano performance. I had been selected as a Marshall and a Fulbright scholar, two

1

prestigious awards that would pay for me to continue my academic pursuits in the coming fall at Cambridge University in England. In addition, *USA Today* had recognized me as one of the top 20 undergraduates in the nation in their All-USA College Academic First Team.

Though I had never expected those honors, I had worked hard for them. I'd spent the last year filling out applications, writing essays, and interviewing for the scholarship programs. The interviews were the most rigorous part—I had to be prepared to discuss any topic imaginable and be able to defend whatever I said. There are times in life when we work hard, but regardless of our hard work, we don't see the fruits of our labor. But this time, on this day, I would have a bountiful harvest.

Before the graduation ceremony, I would be one of several guests honored by the president of the university at a brunch. Afterward, the dean of the College of Fine Arts would hold a dinner in my honor. And if that wasn't enough, in a few hours, I would be the featured graduation speaker at Gammage Auditorium for the College of Fine Arts diploma ceremony. I had worked so hard, and despite being blind, I had overcome many obstacles. Now my life was coming together in the most fantastic way.

My dreams were coming true.

~

As I waited for my turn at the podium, adrenaline pumped through my veins. I tried to remain focused. I'd been in the audience at Gammage Auditorium countless times during my four years at ASU—usually to see touring productions of Broadway musicals. But now, much like at the main graduation ceremony earlier that day, I was seated on stage next to the dean. A few weeks earlier, I'd been on the stage to perform Beethoven's Second Concerto with the ASU orchestra after winning a competition. I knew the auditorium and its acoustics well. Designed by Frank Lloyd Wright, the round building had a proscenium stage and three tiered balconies that held three thousand people in terra-cotta cushioned seats.

I listened to the polite applause as each of the speakers ahead of me finished, and I noticed how the acoustics sounded different on stage than they did in the audience. As if warming up for a concert, my fingers silently danced on my knees, occasionally getting caught in the folds of my graduation gown. Whether it was excitement, nerves, or habit from so many piano performances,

I was barely cognizant of what my fingers were doing. When I played piano for large audiences, I was eager to inspire others through my music—I let the piano say the things I couldn't. But today there wouldn't be a Steinway to hide behind. There would be just the microphone and me, and I would have to do my best to inspire my fellow graduates with only my words.

My pulse quickened and I quietly cleared my throat. At nineteen, I was three or four years younger than most of the other graduates. I'm sure some of them thought I was still a kid who lacked life experience. But life had taught me that no matter who we are—young or old, rich or poor—we all have dreams and we all face obstacles. *And* we all have a choice as to how we will handle them. Pursuing big dreams in spite of tremendous obstacles was something I felt comfortable speaking about.

But perhaps I should have practiced my speech more?

Because of my blindness, I didn't use note cards. I had to memorize every word. I had intended to spend more time practicing out loud the day before, but we had been too busy. Friends and relatives were driving or flying in from as far away as Canada to attend my graduation and to celebrate with a party at our house. All morning, as we prepared for the festivities, the phone had rung with people wanting to confirm times and locations. Then, when Mom left to pick up a few last-minute items, I went with her so I could stop by the doctor's office and retake a blood test. One of the scholarships I'd won required proof from the winning candidates that they were healthy enough to travel and live abroad. The physical had been done weeks earlier, but last week the doctor's office called and said my creatinine level had tested high at 3.8.

"It's probably just a fluke," the doctor said. "I'm not worried. He's nineteen. Even people in their forties and fifties don't have levels higher than a 1.5. Unfortunately, I can't clear him medically until we get him retested. Just stop by the office at your convenience and we'll take care of it."

With my senior piano recital, finals, and graduation preparations, I hadn't yet had time to get by his office. So along with picking up the fruit trays, extra paper products, and dozens of maroon and gold balloons, a stop at the doctor's office was just one more thing that prevented me from practicing the speech. But ready or not, there was nothing I could do about that now.

I closed my eyes and said a quick prayer for my speech—not only for my delivery to be smooth, but for God's love to show through it. I obviously couldn't discuss my faith during this speech, so I just prayed that his love would be completely evident through my heart and personality. And I prayed that I would be a blessing to those who heard me speak. As I finished my prayer, I heard the dean finish my introduction.

"Please welcome Scott MacIntyre."

I stood up and took a deep breath as the dean guided me to the podium. I placed my hands on both sides of the heavy wooden frame so I knew I was squared off and facing the audience. An orange glare from the lights hit me in the face and confirmed I was in the right place. The applause slowly receded. I heard the low buzz of the air conditioning system. Worn chair springs creaked throughout the auditorium as people shifted in their seats. Somewhere in the back, a child started to cry.

"When I first discovered I had congenital blindness and that this would limit my abilities in certain aspects of life, I saw a significant choice before me. And I continue to make this choice daily. Would I stop believing in myself, become indifferent, and lose hope of living a meaningful life? Or would I dare to dream that someday, though the road may be laden with obstacles, my abilities would outshine my blindness?" I paused briefly. The auditorium was silent. I could feel the crowd looking at me. "By the same token, will each one of you stand in doubt and succumb to your own fears? Or will you embrace all that life has to offer?"

I spoke with confidence. I knew each person in the room had doubts and fears. Though each of our concerns may be different than our neighbor's, the fact that we have them unites us in a kind of anxious human bond. There was no shame in that, as far as I was concerned. In the past, I'd had momentary doubts and lingering fears. But I'd also found that when I let go, when I gave my concerns to God, his presence and assurances became more real to me. It was my dependence on him—and not in my own strength—that helped me progress toward my dreams.

I continued with a quote from Göethe, the brilliant German author: "'Concerning all acts of initiative (and creation), there is one elementary truth . . . the moment one definitely commits oneself, then Providence moves, too. All sorts of things occur to help one that would never otherwise have occurred. A whole stream of events issues from the decision, raising in one's favor all manner of unforeseen incidence and meetings and material assistance, which no man could have dreamt would have come his way.'"

Many people talk about going to college, but I reminded the graduates that they were there because they had committed to their idea. As a result, they could now choose from opportunities they otherwise never would have had.

"Many times, the first step is the hardest to take. Our dreams seem so distant, and our initial efforts do not often reap the results we expect. This is why it is important to focus on long-term goals and not get caught up in the immediate consequences of taking a chance."

Again, my own life had taught me that well. Without the ability to see, every step forward was a chance. A chance to fail, but also a chance to succeed. And I had succeeded. I could feel the energy in the crowd increasing as my words connected with them. Nineteen years old and blind, standing on the stage, I was the best example I could offer for what happens when you take the risk to follow your dreams. I had been told that my life had already inspired many people, and it was my prayer that I would continue to inspire those who needed it most.

"When you truly believe something is possible," I said, "then, if in reality it is, it will come to pass."

I finished with another quote from Göethe: "'Whatever you can do, or dream you can, begin it. Boldness has genius, power, and magic in it. Begin it now.'"

To my surprise the audience exploded in applause. I bent down to pick up my cane, and Mom was there to guide me to a seat in the audience with the rest of the graduates. As the applause continued, she said, "They're giving you a standing ovation." Before taking my seat in the front, I turned toward the crowd, smiled, and nodded in the general direction of the audience.

As I sat down I felt a huge sense of accomplishment—partially for just making it through the speech without messing up, but also because I felt that I'd really connected with the audience. It was the capstone of a very exciting day for me. The standing ovation was a wonderful send-off from ASU, and I hoped to work hard and earn more of them in my future.

I had big dreams. Ever since I could remember, I wanted to go on tour and share my music in concert halls and arenas. It's not that I needed crowds to validate me or my music; it was just that there was something so communal about being the one to create the music that lifted a crowd to its feet. I couldn't imagine a dream bigger than leading that kind of emotional experience.

Looking into my future, it was easy to dream big—big things were already happening. During the previous few years, I'd had opportunities to play with the ASU, Phoenix, and West Valley symphonies, and I knew that more opportunities were on the horizon. Also during that time, I had been part of a singing quartet with my mother, sister, and brother, and we'd recently released a CD. That would give me even more opportunities to travel and perform, but that wasn't all. Although I was classically trained in voice, two years earlier I'd released a CD of inspirational songs, and recently I'd taken an interest in pop music. I was working on my first pop album and planned to release it during the next year. And in the fall, I would be attending Cambridge University in England to get my master's degree in musicology.

As the audience's applause finally died out, I realized that the life I'd always dreamed about was starting now.

~

The graduates, who had been so contained during the ceremony, commenced to celebrating. Hundreds of families erupted through the exits in a controlled chaos. I could hear the cheers and the shouts of congratulations, and I could sense the hugs and enthusiastic handshakes. Everyone seemed to be talking at once. The celebratory mood was contagious and only seemed to grow as Mom escorted me out of the building to where the rest of my family stood waiting.

"You did great!" Mom said.

"I was so proud of you," said Dad, putting his arm around my shoulder.

Other family members echoed their words. "You did a really good job!" "Congratulations!"

The plan was for Mom to take me to the dinner the dean was throwing in my honor, while Dad, Todd, and Katelyn, along with my grandpa, Poppy, would head back to the house to begin final preparations for my graduation party. The rest of our friends and relatives would return to their hotels to rest and change clothes before meeting us at the house.

We tried to head to the parking lot as a group, but moving through the crowd was slow going. People kept stopping us to congratulate me. I stopped to talk with everyone and to shake hands and take pictures. While all that was going on, Dad's cell phone rang.

"Can you hold on a minute?" he said into the phone. "I need to step away so I can hear you."

Dad sometimes had to take work calls during family events, but there was something in the tone of his voice that concerned me. Though he had stepped away from the crowd, I could still hear bits of his conversation.

"What does this mean?" he asked. "How soon do we need to do something?" It sounded serious.

"Scott, come here and take a picture with Poppy," Mom said.

I moved toward the sound of her voice. I stood where Mom told me to, and someone took my hand and pointed it in the direction of the camera so I'd know where to look.

"But what can you do to fix it?" Dad asked as cameras clicked.

"Scott, Walter Cosand is here to see you," said Mom.

I walked toward her and heard the familiar voice of my piano professor. Walter Cosand was a formal man but in a friendly sort of way. Always humble, the cadence of his speech was thoughtful, as if giving great care and consideration to every word. After four years of studying with him, I knew the man very well, and I respected him greatly. He truly believed in my potential, and there seemed to be a glow about him when he told other musicians about me.

"Thanks for coming," I said, holding out my hand.

"Well . . . great job, Scott!" he said.

I knew that he was very proud of all that I had accomplished and was excited about my future. We chatted briefly about our summer plans and then he left.

Mom and I took off for the car. The crowds had thinned, and in the distance, car doors slammed and graduates whooped and hollered as they left the parking lot. Dad was ahead also, and I realized he was still on the phone. From the sound of his voice, I knew whatever it was, it was bad. Mom knew it too. The closer we got to him and the car, the faster she walked. But I slowed down, as if I had a premonition that everything was about to change.

No one was whooping and hollering anymore; the other graduates had all departed for parties and bright futures. In the distance I heard the solitary click of high heels on the pavement. And then a car door opened and shut. The car drove away. Dad ended his call, and everything was very quiet.

"Who was that?" Mom asked tentatively.

"I don't know how to say this," he replied, his voice cracking.

And then, before he could tell us anything else, *I knew*. Somehow, I knew.

The joy of the day was instantly gone. It was as if a speeding car had hit me and slammed me to the ground. The sensation was immediate and physical. I struggled to breathe.

"That was the Mayo Clinic. Scott is very sick."

"What?"

"His creatinine levels came back high again. His kidneys are failing. It's very serious."

"But the doctor said it was just a fluke. They said the test was wrong." The tremor in Mom's voice sent cold shivers through my body.

"The second test came back and they're sure. It's stage four renal failure."

I heard Mom gasp, or maybe it was me—my hearing started going in and out like a faulty speaker. I'd been surprised when the initial test results had come back high, but the doctors had assured me that it was nothing, and I hadn't thought about it since.

"The doctor wants to see him first thing in the morning."

"What does this mean?" I asked, my voice coming out calmer than I felt on the inside.

"He's not sure," Dad said. "We'll find out more tomorrow."

I was stunned. My stomach turned and my face grew hot with the realization that I was sick. Very sick. But it was almost impossible to believe. It was as if I'd just walked off the stage of my college graduation and my parents told me I was adopted. It was unfathomable and went against everything I thought I knew about myself. I couldn't be sick; I was healthy and felt great. I had a life that was just starting, and I had dreams that were coming true. *How could this be true?*

For the first time that day, I realized that I was no longer in control. The plans I had for the rest of my life had all been tossed into the air like graduation caps.

Just an hour earlier, *I* was the one who encouraged my fellow graduates to pursue their dreams regardless of the obstacles. But one walk across the parking lot had changed all that. Now all of my dreams were at risk, and the obstacle seemed insurmountable.

CHAPTER 2

Blindsighted

My sight's not quite the same somehow
I've never seen the world the way I see it now
—FROM "THE GOOD, THE BAD, THE UGLY," SCOTT MACINTYRE

Mom slid the key in the ignition, and I looked in her direction. "Let's just get through this day," she said gently, the quiver in her voice betraying the resolve in her words. "We're going to enjoy dinner with the dean, and afterward, we'll have fun at your graduation party. You've worked really hard for this." She turned on the engine and put the car into reverse.

I leaned my head back against my seat. Mom's decisiveness reassured me. Although the news that my kidneys were failing was unfathomable and devastating, there wasn't anything we could do about it right then. Besides, there was a room full of people waiting for me (including the dean, several other dignitaries, and many financial supporters and arts patrons).

Though those people were gathering to show their support and celebrate my accomplishments, it was my mom who'd always been my biggest supporter. Being on the dean's list and graduating summa cum laude, being named "Outstanding Graduate," and receiving the Marshall and Fulbright scholarships—those validated Mom's hard work as much as they did mine. Throughout my life she had always been my primary teacher and advocate. When the experts told her she didn't know what she was doing, she continued to fight for what she believed was right for me. Whatever came next, I knew she would be there for me because she'd been there from the beginning.

~

"He's not acting like a normal fourteen-month-old," Mom had told the pediatrician during one of my regularly scheduled appointments. "I don't think he can see me."

Mom described how the doctor then pulled out his light and looked into my eyes. "Everything looks good. His eyes are a nice crystal blue. They're very clear and they move together. He's fine."

"But he doesn't lock eyes with me. And when I smile at him, he never smiles back."

"He's your first child. I understand that you're overly concerned. That's normal. But he's fine. Just try to relax and maybe have your husband take you out to dinner so you can get a break."

A few months later she tried again with another doctor, and the result was the same. "He's a healthy boy. You just need to stop worrying so much. Just go out to the mall with your girlfriends."

My mom is an intelligent woman, and she isn't an excessive worrier. She tried not to be insulted. She also tried to believe the doctors when they told her there was nothing wrong. However, the signs only increased. It soon became obvious that I couldn't see what other children saw.

In the visually impaired community, "blind" can mean many different things. On one end of the spectrum are people who can't even detect light; their whole world is dark. At the other end are those who are considered "legally blind." Though they are considered "blind" for purposes of receiving disability benefits, many legally blind people can see with the aid of corrective lenses. A normal visual field is 180 degrees. With corrective lenses in their good eye, a person could have up to twenty degrees of vision, or have a visual acuity of 20/200, and still be considered blind as defined by law. Often, legally blind people can even drive a car.

I was nearly one and a half years old before a doctor finally confirmed what Mom already knew—I was blind. But no one could tell her where on the spectrum I fell. So at the request of the doctors, my parents continued to take me to specialists to try to identify the cause of my blindness. Often that meant expensive tests that weren't covered by our insurance. Over a period of about eighteen months, many specialists ran tens of thousands of dollars' worth of tests, some of which were pretty traumatic. One test required them to shave my head in spots so they could attach electrodes. Other tests were even more invasive.

I was about two and a half years old when a doctor wanted to do an electroretinography, or ERG, to detect abnormalities in my retina. After dilating and numbing my eyes with drops, the doctor tried to insert a metal speculum to force my eyes open. By then, I was crying hysterically and fighting him every time he tried to touch me.

"We're going to have to give him a sedative," the doctor told Mom.

"I'm not comfortable with giving him a sedative just so he can take a test," Mom said.

"Well then, our only option is to put him in a straitjacket and tie him down to the bed."

"Can I just try to talk with him?"

"You can try, but I've never seen that work."

But Mom insisted.

"Scott, honey, I need you to calm down," Mom whispered in my ear. "The doctors are going to test your eyes. If you can just be still for a few minutes, then we can finish and go home." She continued to speak quietly to me until I relaxed enough for the very surprised doctor to go ahead with the procedure.

The next step required the doctor to attach an electrode *to my cornea*. It was like a metal contact lens, which they placed directly on my eye. The other end of the electrode was placed on my skin. Then he flashed lights and measured the results. Looking back, I'm glad I was born blind. If I'd actually seen someone attaching the electrode to my eye, nothing Mom said would have calmed me down. But because I couldn't see it and because I trusted her, I didn't freak out.

Unfortunately I didn't respond to the flashing lights, so there was nothing for them to measure. Despite the lack of findings, the doctors persisted. And even though she was now pregnant with my brother, Mom continued to take me to appointments. It was during one of those visits that she received some very alarming news.

"I'm sorry to tell you this," the doctor said, "but a brain tumor is causing his blindness. We'll have to do more tests to confirm how big it is and where exactly it's located."

"Is it cancer?" Mom asked.

"We don't know yet."

During a tense six months of tests and contradictory results, my parents were kept in limbo while doctors searched for an answer. In March, Mom gave birth to Todd, and to everyone's relief, he was born healthy and fully sighted (though they didn't confirm that until later). In June, I turned three years old, and a few months after that, the doctors finally concluded that the cause of my visual impairment was not a brain tumor. And it wasn't anything else.

I was just born blind.

Despite Internet reports that I have Leber's congenital amaurosis, I don't.

I've never actually received a conclusive answer to the cause of my blindness. My official diagnosis was "congenital blindness." Of course, *congenital* just means "from birth."

Knowing that I just had a visual impairment and not some life-threatening illness, my parents chose to move forward and not look back. They gave up searching for a cause. Instead, they wisely focused their time and energies on helping me succeed at all the things I *could* do rather than worrying about the things I couldn't. But seeds of doubt about traditional medicine and a healthy skepticism of doctors had been planted in my mother. That skepticism would later play a role in the medical decisions we made as a family.

I'm told the size of my vision field is equivalent to a pinhole. If a sighted person looks through a pinhole in a piece of paper, they can see; but they just can't see very much at one time. To read a book through a pinhole, a person would have to read it a letter or two at a time. If that person were to look through a pinhole to see a picture hanging on the wall, they would have to scan the entire canvas a quarter of an inch at a time. They wouldn't be able to see the whole scene at once unless they were standing really far away from the picture. That pinhole is my viewfinder to the world. But that view only allows me to see contrasts, and even then I need a lot of direct light to see them.

I have two degrees of tunnel vision, which is 1 percent of what a fully sighted person has. That means that if I hold my finger about twelve inches in front of my eye, I will have to look around until I finally see a part of my finger. If it were someone else's finger, I might not *ever* find it. But even when I finally lock on to my finger, I can only see about a quarter of an inch of it. I can't see the whole thing at once, and if I move my finger slightly to the left or right, it disappears. It's not black or blurry; it's just gone. It's like when a sighted person puts their hand behind their head—their hand doesn't get blurry or disappear into blackness—it's just removed from their sight.

I remember looking at the lower half of my brother and sister a lot, but I don't remember looking at their faces. Most of my early visual memories are glimpses of tables, desks, floors, grass, and people's feet because I often walked with my head down. For a blind person, there isn't a reason to raise your head.

Though blind people often walk with their heads down, Mom thought I could do better. After observing blind children in several different environments, she noticed that blind students often had other distinctive behaviors. For example, some blind people liked to press the backs of their hands against their eyes because, if they pressed hard enough, it created flashes of light. Others liked to rock back and forth to soothe themselves, and some even scratched themselves in public because they didn't know it wasn't socially acceptable. But Mom wouldn't have accepted those behaviors in Todd, so she decided she wasn't going to accept them in me.

One day when we were walking, I was looking at people's shoes. When no one was in front of me, I looked at the contrast between the grass and the sidewalk. Mom said, "Scott, can you look up when you walk?"

I tried it for a few minutes. "Yes."

"Try and do that from now on."

"Why?"

"That's what people do. They look up when they walk."

Later, I was talking to Mom and Dad in the kitchen, but instead of looking at them, I just stared at our beige speckled tabletop. "Scott, look in the direction of the person who is talking," Mom said. "Even if you can't see them, it helps them know that you're listening."

When she or Dad said those kinds of things, it opened up a whole new world to me. I wouldn't have known to look up or in the direction of the person talking unless someone told me. But once I was conscious of it, I did my best to do it every time.

Mom worked very hard on my table manners too. She would joke, "You can't eat like that if you're going to eat with the president someday." While I didn't think much of it at the time, her comments were actually quite prophetic.

~

We arrived at the University Club, and Mom came around to my side of the car to escort me in.

"Just enjoy the dinner with the dean. We'll talk about everything else tomorrow."

I nodded and then took her elbow and allowed her to guide me into the building. The University Club was built in 1908 and was listed on the National Register of Historic Places. With its brick exterior, sweeping central staircase, and dark moldings, it was supposedly one of the most architecturally beautiful buildings on campus.

"It's very elegant," Mom whispered as we walked through the door.

The intimate event was held in two adjoining rooms separated by double pocket doors. About thirty people were socializing in small groups in the first room when we entered.

A waiter offered me a cocktail even though I wasn't old enough to drink. I asked for water instead.

Tables had been set up in the adjoining room, and when it was time for dinner, the dean escorted Mom and me to our chairs. Reaching for my napkin, I could feel that the table had been set with luxurious linens and expensive china. The flatware felt heavy, like real silver.

The dean made a few remarks, someone made a toast, and then dinner was served. Before I knew it, I was lost in conversation, and the next hour passed quickly. It was a bit of a reprieve from thoughts of kidney failure, and I actually enjoyed talking with the people at my table. But like Cinderella when the clock struck midnight, I was yanked back to reality too soon. It was time to leave, and I thanked the people who had invited us as we said our good-byes.

The dinner had offered a dim light in a very dark hour. For a few moments, I once again felt special. People were proud of me. My hard work had been recognized. But back in the car afterward, fear and unwanted questions again hijacked my mind. I was too tired to fight them off. We drove in silence, the party looming large in both our minds.

I'd been looking forward to the party since the day the invitations went out. Everyone I loved most would be there. But now I was exhausted. My health concerns occupied so much of my mind and spirit that it was hard to imagine celebrating.

"I wish I could go home and go straight to bed."

"Me too," Mom said. "It's been a long day. If you want to cancel . . ."

Mom's thoughts trailed off and she didn't finish her sentence. We *could* cancel the party. All it would take was a phone call to the house and a short conversation with Dad, and he'd take care of it. *Maybe that would be easier.* Most of the guests were already at the house. I couldn't imagine how Dad was playing the jovial host and proud father with the doctor's words echoing in his ears. With one word, Dad could make everyone go away. We could come home and no one would be there. I could be alone with my thoughts. But then I thought about the food and decorations and how sad they would look without people enjoying them. *Coming home to an empty house would be worse.*

"I think we should go through with the party," I said.

"Okay," Mom said quietly.

But she knew as well as I did what would be waiting for us. We would walk in the door and ebullient people would greet us with shouts of "Congratulations!" and "We're so happy for you!" I pictured myself walking around our pool, shaking hands and saying, "Thank you," as friends and relatives engaged me in conversation. They'd want details about what I'd be doing in the fall.

In the fall.

Will I even be able to go to Cambridge?

I imagined describing the Marshall program to interested friends and family members while knowing that I might never get to experience it. How could I pretend to match their joy while feeling an incredible ache? The future I had so clearly embraced just hours earlier was murky and dark, and now the honors I'd received seemed meaningless, especially if I didn't have the health to enjoy them. Instead of celebrating around the pool like I had planned, I would be caught in a riptide of questions and fear.

But even knowing all this, the least I could do was try to pretend to celebrate with them. As if reading my mind, Mom spoke up on cue. "You've already done so much, Scott; you can do this too."

CHAPTER 3

The Party's Over

Do I have to be silent
Locked inside
The fears of my feelings
For the rest of my life?
—FROM "SILENT," SCOTT MACINTYRE

As soon as I got out of the car, I heard the sounds of celebration in the back-yard of our house. Music and conversation, punctuated by laughter, splashed around like water from the pool.

We walked through the front door, and Mom immediately started to pick up abandoned paper plates and half-drank Cokes. I stopped and inhaled the scent of homemade chocolate sheet cake, freshly cut strawberries, and pine-apple. As she proceeded to the kitchen, I stayed just inside the front door. Our house was laid out so that it was possible to enter without being noticed.

"Are you going to be okay?" asked Mom.

"Yes, I just need a minute."

"I'm going to go check on Dad," she said, and then she was gone.

I stood still and listened to bits of the conversations coming from farther in the house. The familiar voices made me feel bathed in love. The people I cared about most were at the party. There were friends and family from California, whom I'd known since I was very young, and friends from Toronto, where I'd lived from ages ten to fourteen. We'd been in Arizona since then, so most of the guests lived nearby. There were friends from my homeschool co-ops and friends from church. I pictured them piling food on paper plates, tossing their heads as they laughed, pretending annoyance when they walked too close to the pool and got splashed. It was easy to hear that everyone was having a good time, and it made me want to forget about my problems and share the night with them.

I put on my best smile and stepped out of the foyer shadows and into the light of the kitchen. Friends and relatives who had been patiently waiting for my arrival soon engulfed me with hugs and handshakes. Each one had something special they wanted to say. Within twenty minutes, I had thrown myself into the festivities, getting caught up in the conversations and losing myself in the celebration.

It was a beautiful night of connecting with loved ones. Though earlier in the evening I would have preferred to have just gone to bed, now I was truly thankful for the happy distraction the party provided. But it was also surreal. It was as if I was on top of a mountain, celebrating the highest my life had to offer, while at the same time, I was in the darkest of valleys. There was no middle ground. I wasn't halfway up anything. I was on the top *and* the bottom at the same time.

Hours later, the party was over. Suddenly the absence of sound in the Arizona night was deafening. Everyone was gone. Even the insects were silent. As I headed back inside, I worried about the dark thoughts that would consume me once I was alone in my bed.

I went into the kitchen for a snack. I didn't know whether I was hungry or just trying to avoid going to bed. As I picked through the leftover food, Mom, Dad, and Poppy came in through the patio door.

"There he is," Poppy said, and I knew he was talking to me. *Did Dad tell him the news?* I hadn't talked to Poppy since he left campus after my speech. He'd been busy helping Dad with the grilling, and since he was staying with us, he probably figured there would be other chances to talk to me.

Like now.

"I'm so proud of you," he said. His delight in me made me smile. Then I felt his arms around me, and I hugged him back. "This day was amazing!" he said. "Absolutely fantastic!" Poppy was so positive and overjoyed about the events of the day, I realized he couldn't have known. *Dad must not have told him.* But then, without missing a beat he said, "And it's going to be okay."

Dad had told him after all.

I heard the rich warmth and certainty in his words, as if he really did know it was going to be okay. "I sure am proud," he said again before heading off to the guest room.

I marveled at his words. He knew about my diagnosis, but that still didn't ruin the day for him. He could still relish in all the good that had happened, despite the bad that followed.

Lying in bed that night, I didn't dwell on the fear or the questions. I thought about Poppy's words and resolved that, although my health might be languishing, there was no reason I couldn't still hold on to my joy. Outside my window I heard the insects come alive, but as I fell asleep it was the afterglow of the party ringing in my ears that lulled me into dreamland.

~

Before I opened my eyes the next morning, it all came flooding back. Yesterday's nightmare was today's reality. And the reality was that I had an appointment with doctors at Mayo Clinic Hospital to find out how sick I was.

I got up and dressed slowly. There would be no dinners, no parties, and no words of congratulations to distract me. No more fanfare. No more well-wishing. It was just me, my family, and this looming thundercloud.

When I walked into the living room, I sensed that the tone in the house had changed. Todd and Katelyn sat quietly on the couch not saying anything until they heard me come in. *They know.* "I hope you get well soon," said Katelyn.

"Thanks."

I knew Mom and Dad had only told her the very basics—they didn't want to worry her, especially on her birthday. Poppy and a few close relatives had stayed to help us celebrate with her, but even without a word being spoken, I could tell I remained the center of attention.

A few hours later I sat in the back seat while Dad drove and Mom tried to distract us with some talk radio. The route from our home in Scottsdale to the hospital in Phoenix was a familiar one. We had made it many times before, but under much different circumstances.

After we moved to Arizona, it didn't take long to get involved in the local community theatre scene. Katelyn, Todd, and I did lots of local plays and musicals; sometimes we were even cast together. I was Charlie Brown to Todd's Snoopy in *You're a Good Man, Charlie Brown*, and all three of us had parts in *The Music Man*.

At fifteen I auditioned for my first professional job. A touring company affiliated with ASU and the Mayo Clinic Hospital was doing a show called *The Doctor Will See You Now*, which was about the relationships between doctors and their patients. I was paid fifteen dollars for every hour of rehearsal and performance, and there were a lot of rehearsals. By the end of the run, I'd saved up enough money to buy a new keyboard.

At the time, many of my friends were getting their learner's permits and saving money for a car. When I bought my keyboard, Mom affectionately said,

"This is your car. And it will take you places you never dreamed you could go." Sinking into the backseat, I wondered if that could still be true.

~

One of the performances of *The Doctor Will See You Now* was held in the atrium of the Mayo Clinic Hospital. The grand piano in the center of the lobby was used for accompaniment. Knowing that I played, the Mayo representative for our show told me that Mayo would likely be interested in having me volunteer to play the piano for guests and patients if I was ever interested. I had done hundreds of concerts for charity, and I loved to perform, so it only made sense for me to say yes.

After that, I came as often as my schedule allowed. The hospital's piano was a beautiful instrument with deeply resonant tones and a pleasing sound that bounced through the wide-open space. Located in the center of a five-story glass atrium, the piano would reverberate magnificently throughout the building. Even when there wasn't someone to play it, the piano's built-in player was on so the piano was always making music.

It wasn't the kind of performance where audiences stood around to listen to me play. Most of them were on their way to work or appointments, so I was always surprised when I heard a handful of people clapping after a song. Often it seemed that the number of people sitting around to listen increased the longer I played. But I didn't pay much attention to them. I was happily lost in my own little world, making music and listening to the sounds bounce off the walls like light in a hall of mirrors. Sometimes I thought about the audience in the rooms above me. Mayo believed that music was an important component for healing, so I liked to think that, perhaps in some small way, I contributed to someone's recovery. It was my way of ministering to those who were sick.

But during all those hours of playing, it never once occurred to me that perhaps one day I would be the patient.

CHAPTER 4

Piano Prelude

There's a time to try to be modest
There's a time to lay it on the line
—FROM "VALENTINE," SCOTT MACINTYRE

My first professional gig as a musician was playing keyboard for a wedding. It was the first wedding I ever attended, and I got paid two hundred dollars.

I was seven years old.

I don't remember when I first started playing piano, simply because I was playing before I had memories. My great-grandmother had died, and though she could have left her upright piano to any of her fourteen grandchildren, she left it to my mother. Mom played the piano more than her sisters and cousins did, but the inheritance was still a surprise—a surprise that likely changed my life forever.

I wasn't even a year old when the moving truck arrived from San Francisco. The men unloaded the oversized upright instrument and carried it into our tiny house in Redondo Beach, California. They maneuvered it through the narrow doorways and positioned it in our family room.

After the movers left, Mom sat down at the bench to get familiar with the new piano. She sat me in her lap facing the genuine ivory keys and then slowly touched them, pressing a few chords and playing as best she could with a baby in her arms. But as soon as she started playing, I immediately perked up. Then I reached out to touch the keys too.

Mom had observed toddlers around a piano before. She knew that they loved to slap the keys with their hands, pound the notes with their fists, and generally try to make as much noise as possible. That's why she was surprised when I pressed one key at a time and listened to each note before pressing another key. The relationship between touching the keys and the resulting sounds seemed to captivate me.

During the next few days, Mom says I insisted on touching the piano, but still only one key at a time. As a busy mother, she capitalized on my new interest by pulling my high chair up to the piano and letting me explore the keys while she cooked dinner or cleaned the house. I would entertain myself for twenty minutes at a time by just pressing those keys. As I learned to walk, I would go to the piano on my own. I could barely reach the keyboard, but I would still stretch my arms up over my head and push keys that my little fingers could barely reach.

～

I grew up listening to music. Mom always had something playing around the house. She started playing classical tapes while I was still in the womb, and after I was born she continued to play them. It was rare that I ever took a nap or went to bed at night without listening to some kind of music on my Fisher Price cassette player. Though she started with classical music, she soon added Disney tunes, praise songs, and music from *The Phantom of the Opera*. Soon I began to try to re-create on the piano the melodies that I heard on the tapes. By eighteen months, I was playing "Mary Had a Little Lamb" and other one-fingered songs.

One night when I was two, Mom and Dad were in bed watching TV when they heard a noise in the family room. Mom got up to investigate and quickly called my dad to come see what I was up to. I had snuck out of bed and was playing the song I'd just heard on the cassette she'd turned on after tucking me in. That was the first of many times that I would slip out of bed after listening to music, patter out to the piano, and try to re-create what I'd heard. Although my parents were extremely proud, that never stopped them from sending me back to bed.

By the time I turned three, I could climb up to the piano by myself. I have memories of sitting on that creaky old wooden piano bench, which we had covered with a soft sheepskin, and playing for an hour or more at a time. Mom says I would be lost in my own little world, just working out the melodies on the keyboard. One day she was cooking dinner when she peeked around the corner to see me playing with both hands. I had already advanced from one-finger melodies to three-finger chords, but when she saw me playing the melody with my right hand and the chords with my left—at three years old—she knew I had a special gift.

Mom and I also attended a "Mommy and Me" class during that time. The teacher, Diane, had worked with hundreds of preschool-age children, and Mom began telling her the things I was doing. Diane had also observed me on the school's piano and was so impressed that one day she asked me to play for the class. That was the outside confirmation my mother needed. I started piano lessons soon after that.

By the time I was four I was playing my own arrangements of songs from *The Phantom of the Opera*. I played "Music of the Night," "Think of Me," "All I Ask of You," and my favorite, the title track, "The Phantom of the Opera." I would record my arrangements on cassette tapes to give to my grandparents and Sunday school teachers as gifts. By five, a piano teacher had taught me about syncopated rhythm, and I began making my own drumbeats by exploring different kinds of sounds. In the kitchen, I would take the pots, pans, muffin tins, and the Nestle Quik chocolate powder container with the rubber top and assemble them like a drum set. I organized the items so I would have a snare drum in one area and a bass drum in another. Then I took two spoons and played them like a drum set. Sometimes Dad joined me on his guitar.

For the most part, my beginnings were classical. But a few pop artists stick out in my mind from that time. One day our car was parked in the garage and the radio had been left on. I heard a song and liked the melody so much, I went and got my tape recorder to capture it so I could listen to it again. The song was Sade's "Smooth Operator." I also fell in love with dc Talk (back when they were still doing rap music) and the song "Baby Baby," by Amy Grant, after a babysitter played them for me. While those pop songs and artists made an impression on me, for the most part, I continued to listen to classical music.

～

Our family attended a large church in Southern California, and I participated in the Christmas musical with the children's choir when I was five. We had simple choreography and some cute songs to sing. But being on stage with all those lights made the biggest impression on me. There must have been fifty light cues in the first song alone. Although I shared the stage with forty other kids, the performance bug had definitely bitten me, and I wanted more.

That Christmas, Santa brought me a Casio keyboard. I took it out of the box and the first song I played was "God Is So Good." I loved my new keyboard because it could also sound like an organ. My arrangement of "The Phantom of the Opera" had never sounded better.

One day Mom got a call from a woman who attended our church. "Diane gave me your name," she said. "We're looking for a keyboard player for the college and career group praise band. Is Scott available?"

"You realize he's only six?" Mom asked.

"Yes."

"And he's blind. He doesn't read music. He just memorizes it."

"That's fine. Can he come Wednesday night?"

So on Wednesdays, Mom and I attended the praise band rehearsals. In the beginning she just sat with me, but when they found out she could sing, they asked her to join the band. We were probably the youngest and oldest members in the history of the college and career music ministry.

I loved doing it because I loved making music. I remember the band members treating me as an equal—they gave me tapes of new music and told me what chords to play when they wanted something changed. Looking back, guess I'm not surprised. Although I was young, I was extremely serious about my music. I have recordings from that age of Mom and me playing a duet on the piano. On the recording you can hear me giving her directions on how and what to play.

"Just a little here."

"Now slower."

"Wait. Okay, now!"

Now that I'm older, I wish I could look back and get a better sense of how the other band members interacted with the six-year-old version of myself. I laugh when I think about their reaction when the leader introduced me that first night. Surely they were shocked! Fortunately I played well, and that led to other opportunities to play in the main sanctuary for services, and for other events, such as ladies' luncheons at area churches.

But the most extraordinary request to play came on an ordinary spring day. A neighbor showed up at the door, and after exchanging greetings with my mom, she announced, "My daughter is getting married in September, and I want Scott to play all the music at the wedding."

"You realize he's only six?" asked Mom.

"Yes, but from everyone I've talked to, I heard he would be perfect. Besides, he'll be seven by the time the wedding happens."

I think Mom was too stunned to respond.

Playing in a praise band with other musicians or performing for a ladies' luncheon was easy for me. But a wedding? I didn't know anything about weddings;

I'd never even been to one. But from her description, it sounded like fun, and even at that age, I always jumped at a chance to play for an audience. When I found out she was going to pay me, too, there was no question.

"I'll do it!"

"Here's what my daughter wants you to play," she said as she leaned over and handed me six sets of sheet music.

"Do you think you could make a cassette of the songs?" Mom asked. "He doesn't really read sheet music, but if you have them on tape, he can memorize them."

"Oh, sure," she said.

Soon I had a cassette filled with songs ranging from Lionel Richie's "Endless Love" to Bach's "Jesu, Joy of Man's Desiring."

I practiced the music on my Casio keyboard, which I'd be playing at the wedding. We didn't have a keyboard stand, so most of the time I just laid on my stomach and played. I listened to the recording and then played what I heard on the keyboard. Mom studied the sheet music and compared it to what I was playing to make sure I got it just right. Though I could pick out most of the chords, occasionally I'd get stuck and she would help me out. "It's an A chord," she'd say, and then we'd listen to the tape again.

Since I was homeschooled, I had a lot of flexibility in my schedule, and each day I worked to learn a little more of the music. On the first day of a new piece, I'd learn the verse. The next day I'd learn the chorus, and on the third day, I'd figure out the bridge. Then I'd put the whole song together. Mom kept me on track to make sure I had it all learned by the time of the wedding, but she never had to push me; I loved doing it and would often play the pieces just for fun.

How to play the pieces wasn't all I needed to know, however.

"When they light the unity candle, you will play 'Masterpiece,'" she said.

"A unity candle?"

"Yes. And then for the recessional, you'll play 'Wedding March.'"

"What's a recessional?"

"Well, after the wedding is over, the bride and groom walk back up the aisle followed by their attendants."

Mom had to explain how each piece was used, so if necessary, I could repeat it or end it depending on how long it took the participants to walk down the aisle or to light the candle. Since I couldn't see what was happening for myself, the plan was for her to sit near me during the wedding and discretely tell me when to keep playing, when to fade out, and when to start the next piece.

Though she never said anything to me, Mom had to know that every bride wants her wedding to be flawless. Having a blind seven-year-old musician, who'd never even been to a wedding before, was taking a big risk.

But the stakes soon got higher. Our neighbor, the mother of the bride, worked in public relations, and she decided to help her daughter get a little extra attention on her wedding day, so she called CNN.

"My daughter's getting married, and there's a seven-year-old blind boy playing the music at her wedding. Do you want to come film it and interview him?"

Soon a CNN producer called our house and spoke with Mom. After talking with her for a few minutes, the producer asked if he could talk with me. He probably wanted to get a feel for my personality and see if I'd make for an interesting profile, but at the time I didn't have a clue as to what he wanted. I didn't even know who or what CNN was.

"Hi, Scott," said the unfamiliar voice.

"Hello."

"How old are you, Scott?"

"I'm six."

"Do you like playing the piano?

"Yes."

"Can you tell me your favorite food?"

"Salmon and rice, with capers."

There was a short pause. "Okay, you can put your mom back on the phone now."

Maybe they were expecting pizza or hot dogs? But Mom often made salmon with capers, and it was my favorite.

Apparently my food choice sealed the deal. Months before the wedding, they set up a date and time to come to our house and interview me.

On the day of the interview, the CNN crew filmed me playing the old upright piano as well as my keyboard. I remember I didn't look up at all while I played. I just stared at the keys. After I played a few songs, the producer asked, "Can you play anything else?"

I was happy to oblige. "I can play 'This Is the Dungeon of Your Life,'" I said. I started playing and singing for them.

"What's that from?"

"I wrote it."

"You wrote it?"

"Yeah."

"The music or the words?"

"Both."

"Wow!"

I had no idea why he sounded so surprised. By then I had been writing songs for more than a year. I started composing music when I was five. I know lots of kids make up songs when they're young, but songwriting was a serious endeavor for me (and it still is). The songs I wrote had a structure and flow. Parts of the song related to other parts in very specific ways—a melody that stayed the same while the chords changed or chords that stayed the same while the melody changed.

The crew finished filming for the day but returned in June to film me ice-skating at my birthday party. I loved skating. It was one of the few physical activities I could do where I felt absolutely free. Usually I held hands with one of my friends, but if the rink was nearly empty, I could skate all by myself. The crew also filmed me attending a concert and doing other things around our neighborhood.

CNN's final visit was in September to tape me playing at the wedding. I was dressed in a little black tux and stood behind the keyboard because I was too short to sit.

"It's time to start the pre-service music," Mom whispered to me.

I played songs from my repertoire, including "God Is So Good," "Be Glorified," "Endless Love," and selections from *The Phantom of the Opera*.

When it was time for the mothers of the bride and groom to walk down the aisle, Mom said, "As soon as you can make it happen, transition to the processional music."

For the mothers I played "Music of the Night" from *Phantom*. When the bridesmaids entered, I switched to "Jesu, Joy of Man's Desiring," and when the bride processed, I played Wagner's "Bridal Chorus" (better known as "Here Comes the Bride").

With each new song, Mom would tell me when I needed to wrap it up. "Look for a place to end it," she'd say, and I'd find a place that made musical sense to finish the song. She also sang on a couple of the songs, and it was fun to play along with her. Mom and I worked together harmoniously until one part of the service when I wasn't sure what she was doing. As I came to the end of a song, she whispered, "Keep playing, Scott." So I started the song over. Five times I neared the end of the song, and I would hear her whisper, "Keep playing." I had no idea why I needed to do it, but I trusted her, so every time she said that, I'd start the song again.

After the wedding, several people came up to me and said, "It was so great that you kept playing even after the bridesmaid fainted."

In an effort to not alarm me, Mom never mentioned that a bridesmaid had fainted and they were reviving her. Mom didn't want to panic me, and she wanted to make sure the wedding continued as planned, so she just kept saying, "Keep playing."

A few weeks later the piece aired on CNN. My whole family gathered around the TV to watch it. They didn't show the fainting bridesmaid, but they did show me playing the keyboard. The story included footage from the interview at our house and a clip of me ice-skating with a friend (and falling down).

Robert Vito, one of CNN's best-known voices, narrated the piece. During the story, he called me a "child prodigy." No one had used that term with me before, but it was a label I'd wear a lot from then on.

Something else he said, however, got an even bigger reaction from my family. He was probably just repeating a line a producer had given him, perhaps even something I had said during the interview but was taken out of context. In his distinctive narrator voice, he said, "Scott also writes music for his family and for *girls he likes*."

My family howled after he said that, and though I laughed, too, my cheeks warmed with embarrassment. While it wasn't true at the time, in just a few more years it would be. As a teen, I would write lots of songs for girls I liked and for whom I hoped would like me back.

CHAPTER 5

Sad Songs

Who am I to sit and wonder
Wonder why I'm goin' under
It's not right to say
That all of this could happen to somebody else
When I don't even know myself
—FROM "WHO AM I," SCOTT MACINTYRE

"You need a kidney transplant," the doctor said.

Mom, Dad, and I sat in his office trying to absorb the shock of his words. I felt like a fastball had just been thrown into my gut. *A transplant? How is this possible?*

"Are you sure?" Mom asked.

"I'm sure. His most recent creatinine level is 3.5, but his first test shows it was a 3.8. That puts him in stage four renal failure."

In our family, Dad generally trusted traditional medicine. Despite a few bad experiences, he believed a medical professional's expertise held the answers for treating disease. But Mom didn't agree that they always knew best. Ever since doctors dismissed her when she sought answers about my blindness, she'd questioned some aspects of traditional medicine. As kids, we rarely got sick, but when it came to curing colds or treating an infection, Mom didn't think we had to run to the doctors for every runny nose. Instead, she would figure out how to strengthen our immune systems. Neither did she think she always had to take a doctor's advice at face value. She believed in asking as many questions as possible so she could make informed decisions.

"But he's healthy," Mom said. "He doesn't feel sick, and he looks great."

The doctor was all business. "With kidney failure, at some point he will start to feel tired and weak as the toxins build up in his blood. He's very young—typically we don't see these kinds of numbers until someone is much, much older. If he isn't feeling the symptoms yet, it's probably because of his youth. But they're coming. If we let it go, he will soon be very sick."

"How soon?" Dad asked. "He's supposed to leave in September for a year at Cambridge to get his master's degree."

"He needs a transplant in the next three months."

It felt like the air had been sucked out of the room. Tears filled my eyes.

"You'll want to start the paperwork now to get him on the national transplant list," said the doctor. "That way he'll be ready if a kidney becomes available."

I wanted to scream, *Just shut up!* I couldn't stand to listen to him anymore. He wasn't one of those doctors who tried to carefully deliver bad news. He didn't try to sugarcoat anything. It was more than I could take. I needed someone to buffer the news from me, explain it gently, and with love. But the only two people who could do that were in the room with me, and they were being hit as hard as I was.

"You're also severely anemic," he said, scribbling something on paper. "That happens when you have kidney failure."

"Just how bad is it?" Dad asked. His voice sounded weak and frail.

"He's in the worst possible circumstance he can be in." He tore a sheet off his pad and handed it to us along with another paper. "Here are a couple of prescriptions and the name of a specialist I want you to see."

And that was all. I heard the door close behind him as the doctor left the room.

~

Somehow we stumbled out of his office. The next thing I knew, I was standing in the hallway looking down at the atrium, reeling from the news. From the second floor, the atrium windows let in a lot of light. Everything was bright and shiny, reflecting nothing I felt on the inside. I leaned against the hallway wall, tears pooling in my eyes.

"I don't want a transplant."

"I don't want you to have one either," Dad said.

"You're not going to have to have one," Mom said.

By now, we were all crying in some sort of awkward group hug. "We're going to figure this out," Mom said as she wrapped her arms around me. I could tell she was brokenhearted at the thought of her son facing a major organ transplant, but I also knew that no matter what lay ahead, both Mom and Dad would bear the burden with me. Dad wept as he held us both, and I reached out to take his hand. "They told us you had a brain tumor when you were a baby and they were wrong," Mom said. "We're going to get through this one too."

Her words gained confidence as she spoke. I knew she must have felt as confused and disoriented as I did, but I appreciated her resolve. "We'll get through this. Let's just pray." So right there in the hallway, Mom started praying. "God, you are the great physician, and we come to you now and ask you to please heal Scott. Spare him from a transplant. It seems so dark right now and there are no easy answers in sight, but you are so much bigger than the bad news we've just heard. Please give the doctors wisdom, and guide us in the days ahead."

Mom finished praying and then offered Dad and me tissues as we pulled ourselves together.

The hardest part of accepting the news was the shock that it was happening at all. *I jumped out of bed happy and healthy yesterday, but now I need a transplant? How did it go from one extreme to the other so quickly?*

"We're all scared," Dad said, handing me my cane. "But we need to trust God to get us through this."

"The verse that keeps running through my mind is Isaiah 41:10," Mom said. "'Fear not, for I am with you; be not dismayed, for I am your God; I will strengthen you, I will help you, I will uphold you with my righteous right hand.'"

Mom's words helped me feel a little better. Perhaps there were other options.

We were quiet as we took the elevator down to the concourse. Then I heard the swishing of my cane as we crossed the tile floor toward the parking lot. For the first time I could remember, no one was playing the piano. Even the automated player had been turned off.

In the atrium, the healing music had ceased.

It was a sign of things yet to come.

～

After we got back from the doctor's, I went to my room and closed my door. I'm sure my family was surprised—it wasn't like me to separate myself from people. I liked being with others, and I loved being with my family. But after hearing that I needed a transplant *in the next three months*, I needed time alone to process what it all meant.

The doctor told us that kidney disease happened in five stages. As the kidneys failed to do their job, there would be an increase of water, waste, and toxic substances building up in my body, which could cause problems like anemia, high blood pressure, acidosis, cholesterol disorders, and even bone disease. The fifth stage was kidney failure—a total loss of kidney function.

I was already at stage four. Since I had no symptoms, no one was sure how long it had taken me to progress through the first four stages, and therefore no one was sure how long it would take before I reached stage five. With no known cure for kidney disease, the only thing doctors could do was search for a cause while treating the symptoms, or, as my doctor was strongly advocating, do a transplant.

I lay on the bed, my face toward the ceiling. Everything was quiet except for the mesmerizing *tick, tick, tick* of the spinning ceiling fan above me. As the doctor's words sank in, something else rose up inside me—fear.

What is happening to me? How can I fix this? There's so much I already can't do because I'm blind; now this too?

~

I had accomplished so much despite my disability, but my blindness had made my life much more difficult than it should have been. Although I hated to admit it, there were things I couldn't do because of my blindness. There were the practical things, like not being able to see when meat is done on the BBQ or change the oil in a car. But there were more personal ones, like not being able to smile back at a pretty girl because I didn't know she was smiling at me. And of course there were the embarrassing ones, like spilling my water glass at a nice restaurant because the waitress moved the goblet when she refilled it.

There were also professional obstacles that I was still trying to overcome. I would never be able to sight-read music—one of the most treasured skills of a classical pianist. That meant I could never work as an accompanist. If someone called and wanted me to play the next day or to accompany an orchestra, I'd have to turn them down. Classical music, with all of its intricacies, took longer than a day to memorize.

I had never been able to see a presentation, watch a professor draw a diagram on the board, or quickly skim through a book with my eyes. Though I loved good stories, seeing only one letter at a time made reading print extremely cumbersome. Of course there were other ways; I could use adaptive technology that helped me see a book better, I could listen to it on tape, or I could even read braille. But some things didn't have workarounds.

Like sports.

Growing up I'd done a lot of things like skiing, swimming, roller-blading, bike riding, gymnastics, and even skateboarding, but I'd never been able to play competitive sports like baseball. It was impossible for me to see a ball flying through the air or to know where to throw it. I hoped to have children someday, and it saddened me that I would never be able to play catch with my son.

But of all the insurmountable obstacles I faced while living in a sprawling suburban area, the biggest one was not being able to drive. When someone learns to drive, he suddenly has a freedom he's never had before. For the first time, he can go where he wants, when he wants, without worrying about getting a ride on someone else's schedule. Being able to drive gives you social freedom—and the ability to date.

When I wanted to go out with a girl, I had to ask my parents first. They did their best to accommodate me, but if they weren't available to drive, then there could be no date. It killed the spontaneity in asking a girl out. As a result, I never dated a girl unless I knew her well and we'd been friends a long time. Sometimes I made light of my predicament by saying, "If you drive, I'll buy." But in my heart, I knew that many guys drove *and* paid.

I knew many people probably thought differently about me because I was blind, but I learned to push through my fears, and my parents supported me. From the moment they knew I was visually impaired, I never heard them say, "Oh, he can't do that. He's blind." They certainly didn't paint a negative picture of my condition, nor lead me to believe I was inferior in any way. We knew there were obstacles—and there always would be—and I faced them every day. But we also believed obstacles had solutions. If we worked hard enough and long enough, or if we were creative enough, we could find a way to overcome them.

We'd believed that until now.

But how will we overcome this?

Uncertainty about the future had sometimes scared me. But now the thought of facing the future without being able to overcome the life-threatening obstacle in front of me left me terrified.

～

Faceup on my bed I could feel the breeze from the ceiling fan. Tears filled my eyes and slowly spread across my face. I'd spent the last nineteen years learning to live blind. And with all of my recent success and plans for the future, the pieces had finally fallen into place. But now someone had changed the puzzle.

Why God? Why do I have to go through this too? People who have kidney failure are supposed to be in their seventies or eighties. This isn't supposed to happen to teenagers!

How could this happen while I was still so young? It would have been terrible if something like this happened to one of my grandparents, but at least it would be understandable. Everyone knows that your health declines the older you get, but for a nineteen-year-old to need a transplant? It didn't make sense.

I was headed to London in a few months to get my master's degree. Opportunities were coming my way to perform on larger and larger stages. I'd been recognized nationally for my academic abilities.

I had a full social life too. I was popular. But more important, my friends accepted me for who I was. Instead of saying things like, "Scott? He's my blind friend," they now said, "Scott? He's my friend who plays the piano." That was huge for me.

But how will my friends accept this?

My family and my closest friends had come to see my blindness like I did—as a blessing. Blindness had given me an incredible gift—to see the world in ways that other people who were distracted by sight didn't. Though I didn't have my eyesight, I'd developed insight and I'd learned how to trust people at a very deep level. But over the years, the biggest blessing of my blindness seemed to be that it inspired other people. When sighted people saw what I'd accomplished, and the limitations I'd overcome to accomplish those things, they felt empowered—like there was no excuse for them to not try. My blindness gave me an opportunity to talk about my faith and encourage others to follow their dreams.

But how can I talk about my faith, or be an inspiration, if I'm sick in bed, trapped inside a failing body?

Usually I was the guy who saw a glass half full and was excited about the potential in things, but now I was having trouble even finding the glass. I had plenty of friends who celebrated the highs with me, but how many would be there to walk through the lows? I thought about the people at my graduation party the night before. *Will she still want to be my friend? Will he visit me in the hospital?*

Maybe it was my mood, or maybe I just hadn't taken that kind of inventory before, but the list of friends who would support me through something this awful seemed awfully short. Sure, a couple of friends always remembered to include me, asking if they could give me a ride, and even driving long distances to make sure I could attend events. But I could count those people on one hand. I didn't know what the future held, and neither did they. *How much support can I really expect from them?*

My family would always be there, of course, but I knew how hard it had been on Mom and Dad to hear that I needed a transplant. *How will they react as they go through it with me? Will they even understand what I'm feeling?*

I felt very much alone.

≈

From the time I was very young, I used music as a way to communicate things I couldn't say any other way. Playing the piano was my way of expressing what was stuck inside of me. While other teens slammed doors or yelled when they were upset, I released my frustration at the piano by pounding out a stormy song like "L'Orage" by Burgmüller.

Music was emotion for me. When I played, I pressed my feelings into the keys, playing louder, softer, faster, or slower depending on the mood I was communicating. I sometimes thought of the music as a movie score, swelling to increase the emotion and backing away to reduce the tension as I told my story.

Music made me feel, but I couldn't always help the *way* it made me feel.

Once my family gave me a beautiful birthday gift. It was a wooden music box with a delicate little golden movement with thirty keys. But the song that played when the box opened made a very strong impression on me. The tinkling of the pins spoke to me about a person who longed for the wonderful life he'd had before moving away. When I listened to the simple melody, I felt a sense of forlorn sadness, of a happiness that had once been and no longer was. But no matter how much I tried to explain it, my family couldn't hear what I heard.

"Why does this song make you sad?" Mom asked.

"I don't get that at all," Todd said after listening to it a second time.

Dad and Katelyn didn't get it either.

Sometimes my feelings were hard to understand. Especially for others. But life had taught me that sad things could be found inside beautiful gifts, just as beauty could be found in sadness. Though the latter was often harder to see.

≈

I turned over onto my stomach and sobbed into my pillow. I was angry with God and scared about my future. And I was scared that I was angry at God.

The bedroom door opened and someone sat on my bed. I felt Mom's hand stroking my hair and Dad as he joined her on the edge of the bed. I rolled over and wiped my eyes.

"Are you okay?" she asked.

"Do you want to talk about it?" Dad asked.

Although I believed God *could* do anything, I had a hard time believing he would in this situation.

I felt abandoned. And helpless.

I didn't want to be mad at God, but I was. I thought God had a plan for my life, for me, but now it seemed he was pulling the rug out from under my dreams.

"I don't want to question God," I said, carefully choosing my words, "but I feel like it's wrong for God to ask me to go through this too." I started crying and buried my face in my hands.

They let me cry until I stopped. Dad handed me a tissue and Mom hugged me tight.

"I just feel like things are so out of control," I said as I pulled away.

"Your life is going to be very different from what you thought," Dad said. "From what we all thought."

He was right. I was going to have to let go of my expectations. They sat on my bed and we talked for nearly an hour. We talked about what we knew, and more importantly, what we didn't know—like the cause of my kidney failure. And as we talked, I began to accept that, like it or not, this was really happening to me. I didn't have a plan, and that part scared me. But scared or not, I was going to have to get through it.

No one could change what I was going through emotionally any more than they could physically. There was nothing my family could do or say to fix me. I was at my lowest point—hurt, disappointed, angry, and afraid.

We finished talking and, with nothing more to say, Mom and Dad got up to leave.

"Come out when you're ready," said Dad.

"If you don't want to join us for Katelyn's birthday dinner, that's okay," said Mom.

The door closed and they were gone.

I knew there was no point staying in bed and feeling sorry for myself. It was still Katelyn's fourteenth birthday. The least I could do was try to enjoy it with her. I got up and washed my face. Though I was close with everyone in my family, Katelyn and I had a special bond because she had been born blind like me. I knew I couldn't miss her special dinner.

I joined the rest of the family in the living room and tried my best to remain interested and engaged as we ate dinner and Katelyn opened her presents. Mom brought out a cake and I caught a glimmer of one of the flames dancing on top of a candle. "Happy birthday to you," Mom sang and the rest of the family joined in.

Next month I would have a birthday.

Will it be my last?

"Happy birthday, dear Katelyn, happy birthday to you!"

The family clapped. Mom cut the cake and served everyone. The chatter increased around the table as everyone commented on how delicious the cake was.

"Happy birthday, Katelyn!" I said. "And many more!"

And then silently, in the midst of my sadness of my circumstances and the beauty of my love for my family, I prayed to God, *Please allow me to be here to celebrate all of them.*

CHAPTER 6

Leap of Faith

A lonely wanderer
Walking on in fear
Fearing fear itself

—FROM "NO FEAR," SCOTT MACINTYRE

Because of my visual impairment, I've learned to trust others in ways few sighted people ever have to. I trust them to guide me around obstacles and lead me safely through public spaces. So far, that trust has been well placed. But there are still honest mistakes anyone can make. Including my own mother.

One day, when Mom was pregnant with Todd, she was walking me into a store. I held on to her hand, and she was slightly ahead of me. I don't know if she was distracted, was in a hurry, or just didn't see it, but I slammed face-first into something metal. And very solid.

I was stunned—until I tasted the blood. Then I knew I was hurt. I cried. Loud. And hard. Through my cries, I heard Mom ask for a cloth to stop the bleeding.

"What happened?" someone asked.

"He walked into that metal bar sticking out from the wall," Mom said, as she tried to console me.

"Didn't he see it?"

"He's blind," Mom said, losing patience with the onlookers. "Look toward me, Scott," she said, turning my head.

"Did he break his tooth?"

"It looks like he broke his two front teeth. One's out but the other's still dangling."

At that point, I cried even harder. I didn't know that teeth could break, and I was terrified of what I thought that meant—that I'd grow up without teeth.

Mom put pressure on my gums to stop the bleeding. Soon the manager came over, and seeing the metal protrusion, he quickly realized the store was at fault.

"We'll be happy to pay for any medical bills," he said.

Mom took me to the dentist to have my dangling tooth pulled, and I spent the afternoon running my tongue over the gap in my teeth and crying a bit because of the pain. But the truth was, the pain wasn't that bad. I was just shocked that teeth could break and fall out—and scared about what that might mean. That is, until I learned they were just baby teeth and I would grow new ones when I was older.

The next morning I woke up with two quarters under my pillow. I was rich! Losing my two front teeth wasn't such a bad thing after all. A few years later I'd learn that weddings paid much better than the tooth fairy—and with a lot less drama. But despite the trauma of the day, the accident was a good lesson for all of us. We became more conscious of how to lead me around safely, and nothing like that happened again.

But that incident also helped me to understand I couldn't always control my environment. It taught me that bad things happened sometimes. Though the pain passed quickly, the fear of it happening again lingered. From a young age, I learned that I had to face the things that scared me most. If I gave into fear, I wouldn't be able to get out of bed in the morning.

~

The Strand is a concrete bike path that begins in the Pacific Palisades area of Los Angeles and runs through several beaches until it ends at Torrance County Beach, twenty-two miles later. The pathway is popular for biking, jogging, rollerblading, and skateboarding, but most of all, for people watching. Volleyball nets scattered along the beaches are frequented by teens looking for a quick pick-up game with friends. Families picnic and sunbathers try to drown them all out with their music. Profiles of surfers and fishermen stand in the foreground of a stunning view of the horizon—where the light sand meets the dark blue of the Pacific Ocean. The Strand is the concrete line in the sand separating the public beaches from cafes, restaurants, exclusive hotels, and some of the world's most expensive beachfront property.

We lived in Redondo Beach until I was ten, and the Strand was within walking distance of our home. Mom would often take us there to play at the beach, sometimes for just an hour but other times for the entire day. Often we had the place to ourselves; it was our private sandbox. But on other days, like the

Fourth of July, the crowds swarmed on the path, pitched tents in the sand, and wandered in the waves.

One day when I was three, Mom asked if I wanted to go run on the beach.

I often ran while holding someone's hand, but she was suggesting something different. "What do you mean?" I asked.

"You can run by yourself."

I had never done that before. There were so many things that could go wrong. What if I tripped and fell? What if I ran into someone or *something*? I ran my tongue over the gap in my teeth and remembered the metal bar.

But the idea of running *alone* was too tantalizing to turn down. "Sure," I said. "But what if I hit something?"

"I'll make sure you don't. In the distance there is a garbage can. Can you see it?"

She lifted my hand and pointed my fingers into the distance. Following the path through the pinhole of my vision, I could make out the small dark object that contrasted with the sand that surrounded it.

"Try to keep your eyes on it and run as fast as you can toward it. When you get there, stop, turn around, and listen for my voice."

So that's what I did. I walked a few steps and then progressed to a slow jog.

"It's okay," Mom said. "There's nothing in your path. You can run as fast as you want."

I started to jog faster. As my courage increased, so did my speed. By the time I neared the garbage can, I was in a full-out sprint. Running with the wind blowing through my hair, and the waves crashing nearby, I felt free. A soft spray of sand kicked into the air as each foot found traction in the shifting sand. By the time I reached the garbage can, I had to stop not so much from exhaustion as from exhilaration. I turned toward the direction I'd come from.

"I'm right here, Scott," Mom called, giving me an auditory cue as to where I could find her. I looked toward the sound of her voice and, after a few seconds, I thought I saw her navy shorts, which contrasted against the white sand.

"Okay, I'm coming!" I said and took off toward her. This time I ran full out from the beginning. I felt like I was flying. As if earth and sky couldn't hold me back. With my eyes fixated on Mom, I couldn't see anything else. I had to trust her word that the path was clear, but it was worth it. Running without abandon was the most freeing experience I'd had, and I couldn't get enough of it. From then on, whenever we'd go to the beach, I'd ask if I could run. Mom would check to make sure it was safe and then she'd say, "Okay, Scott, there's nothing in front of you. Run until you're tired!"

That was all I needed and I ran as fast as I could. Though there were still a lot of unknowns, I didn't let fear of what *might* happen stop me. And yes, occasionally I ran over yesterday's sandcastles, tripped over seaweed, or stepped into a hole that wasn't there the day before. But I didn't let those things stop me from the pleasure of running. Even today, one of my favorite things is to go to the beach with someone I trust, and when they give me the okay, I run.

I run without fear.

And I run free.

~

It was impossible to play in the street where we lived in California. There were too many cars, and drivers weren't used to looking out for kids. So Mom and Dad took Todd and me to a local playground to ride our trikes. The playground had a huge blacktop area with thickly painted white lines that formed a track. The lanes weren't very wide, which was perfect for me. The contrast of the line against the asphalt made it possible for me to track it with my narrow vision, enabling me to ride in a continuous loop without outside help to guide me.

As Todd grew older and it came time for him to learn to ride a regular bike, my parents decided I should learn to ride one too. For Christmas, Santa brought us two new bikes. At three years old, Todd wasn't too excited when he saw his new bike, but I was thrilled. "If he doesn't want it, can I have his too?" I asked. It didn't occur to me that I should be afraid.

Later that day my parents took us to a grassy area in the park. I sat on the bike and felt it wiggle beneath me as I tried to stay balanced. At first, Mom or Dad ran alongside me and encouraged me to pedal. Once I mastered riding a few bike lengths, they would let go, shouting, "Pedal faster!" But it seemed that neither Todd nor I could develop enough speed to keep the bike moving, and we experienced our share of tumbles into the grass.

Understanding that bit of physics, my parents took us to the top of a small grassy hill. The increased speed from the hill would help us keep the bikes upright while we got the hang of balancing. Todd went first, but instead of getting down the hill, all he got was two skinned knees.

My parents ran toward him at the first sounds of his cry. "I can't do it!" he yelled.

I stood at the top of the hill, waiting to mount my bike, slowly realizing what had just happened to Todd. It sounded painful. I could hear Mom saying something about scratches and getting a Band-Aid.

"Okay, Scott, it's your turn," Dad said.

Fear gripped me as I realized that in a few moments I could be crying in pain just like Todd. But what choice did I have? It was either learn to ride the bike or be stuck on my tricycle forever. I climbed on and gripped the handlebars. Dad steadied the bike underneath me. "Okay, I'm going to run with you, and when you get to the hill, I am going to let go."

I started pedaling and eventually felt myself picking up speed. I knew Dad would let go at any moment, so I pedaled faster to keep myself upright. The cool breeze rushed past my face, and I heard the sounds of my parents cheering in the background.

Parents?

That's when I realized Dad must have already let go. I had done it by myself! It was even more exhilarating than running, and now I could go twice as fast! I stopped the bike and got off and waited for my parents to come help me back up the hill. I heard the pride in their voices as they ran toward me. "Great job, Scott!" "You did it!"

Todd quickly learned to ride, and once we mastered riding in the grass, my parents took us to the track at the playground where I rode in endless circles, feeling the freedom of speed as I grew more and more confident.

By the time we moved to Toronto when I was ten, I was a seasoned bike rider. Our house was on a cul-de-sac with lots of kids, and neighborhood parents were vigilant about watching out for us, so we were allowed to ride in the street. A landscaped island with plants and a central tree sat in the middle of the cul-de-sac. Around the perimeter of the island was a small brick path. We rode our bikes up and down the sidewalks, in the street, and on the brick path around the island. As I rode, I memorized the dimensions of each space—how wide the sidewalks were, how far it was from one driveway to the next, and how sharp the curve around the island was. As I became more comfortable sensing distances, I would look to where I thought the curbs and driveways should be and scan the area until my eyes found the contrast between dark pavement and white curb, or between the brick and the green foliage. That enabled me to ride to my heart's content without any supervision.

Sometimes we would ride through the numerous forest trails next to our neighborhood. Todd would ride ahead of me, and I would fix my pin-hole gaze on the back tire of his bike. If he stopped, I stopped. If he sped up, I sped up. It was like tandem bike riding on separate bikes.

There were always new dangers for me on a bicycle because the environment was always changing. Someone could cross my path unexpectedly or park a car in a place I didn't see until it was too late. I had some falls, and a few minor incidents of running into landscaping, bicycles, or people, but after each time, I picked myself up and despite the fear got back on the bike.

∼

Swimming was always a big part of my life. From the beaches of California to backyard pools in Toronto and Arizona, I loved to play in the water. Mom taught me to swim the same way she taught Todd. I started by hanging on to a wall and learning to kick. Then I put my face in the water and learned to blow bubbles. Eventually I learned strokes and how to put it all together and swim across the pool.

I don't remember fearing the water, but I did fear the water slide the *second* time I went down it. The first time I had no idea what was going to happen. But the next time, I anticipated every part of the ride, from sliding down the wet plastic turns to being tossed in the air, hitting the surface of the water, and dropping to the bottom of the pool. The next dozen times down that slide required acts of courage because I knew how scary it was. But each trip down also got easier.

I learned how to jump into the pool from the side, and eventually do cannonballs from the diving board. Each time I jumped, I had to trust that I'd land in the water and not do a cannonball onto the pool deck.

But the scariest jump ever happened on vacation in Northern California. For years my family went to a resort called Trinity Alps. It was very rustic, with dirt grounds and wooden cabins, outdoor barbeques and bingo nights. A favorite of young and old was the swimming hole created by the dam along the river where everyone floated on blow-up rafts. A walking bridge extended across the hole, and guests loved to jump into the water from the high bridge. But there was only one place where the water was deep enough to jump into. If you missed that spot, you risked jumping into shallow water. During several trips I listened as swimmers worked up the courage to make the jump, and then to their squeals of delight as they dropped, landing with a loud splash and a huge spray of water.

One summer I was determined to do the jump, and I asked Dad if he would go with me so I could hold his hand. He agreed. As we walked out onto the bridge, I faintly heard the people swimming below. The laughter and voices that had sounded so close to me when I was in the swimming hole sounded muffled and distant from the bridge. There was no way for me to see how high or low the bridge was, but from the fading sounds, it felt like it had to be ten stories tall. Dad promised me it wasn't nearly that high. My pace slowed and my grip tightened on his hand as we approached the jump spot.

"Are you sure you want to do this?" Dad asked.

I nodded. I was too afraid to speak.

"I need you to just fall straight down," Dad said. "Don't take a running leap or anything. Just step off."

We agreed to jump on three. He began to count.

"Ready? One . . . two—"

"Wait!" I tried to pull my hand out of his strong grip. "What if we miss the hole?"

"If you just step off and jump straight down, you'll be fine," he said. "Okay?"

"Okay."

"Are you ready?"

"I'm ready."

"I want you to be sure, because I don't want to count and then jump without you. Then you could fall and hit the water the wrong way and hurt yourself."

That was a new thought.

Or what if Dad goes without me, and I am stuck on the bridge, holding on for my life?

"I'm ready," I said, tightening my grip on him once again.

"Okay. One, two, three, jump!"

And we did.

The thrill of free-falling through the air was amazing. But I couldn't fully enjoy it, knowing that at any second we would hit the water. And we did. I shot under the surface and cold water rushed up my trunks and my nose. As I shot back toward the surface, I accidently opened my mouth. By the time I emerged I was coughing and sputtering. Jumping was simultaneously the most frightening and exhilarating decision of my life.

"Can we do it again, Dad?"

From learning to kick while hanging on to the wall, to jumping off the bridge at Trinity Alps, each step was successively scarier than the last. Yet I learned to face my fears and overcome them all. I had to if I was going to participate in the fun. Sure there were some missteps, like the time in Toronto when I didn't wait long enough for the person ahead of me to clear the water, and I jumped on top of him. But even then, we both survived and lived to swim another day.

Of course, kidney failure wasn't like riding a bike or jumping into a swimming hole. The consequences were much graver, and no sense of euphoria waited for me on the other side. But perhaps fear was fear. Maybe it could all be handled the same way?

~

People had occasionally asked me if I got nervous when I played in front of large audiences, and some friends and family had asked if I was anxious about giving my graduation speech at Gammage Auditorium. What if I had tripped and fallen on stage? Or what if I had made a huge faux pas during my speech and the audience had laughed?

Fortunately I never focused on that. I believed that the audience wanted the best for me and from me and that I was the one who gave them the cues. If I was tense, they'd be tense. If I was relaxed, they'd be relaxed and pulling for me. People didn't want me to fail. They supported me. Not for a minute did I believe the audience was just sitting there, waiting for me to make a mistake.

During the days following my diagnosis, I thought a lot about that. And I thought a lot about God. If I assumed that people didn't want me to fail, why would I assume that God wanted me to fail? Or for that matter, wanted my kidneys to fail? He loved me more than strangers in an audience did, and his love was perfect. Why couldn't I assume that whatever was happening to my health upset him as much as it upset me?

It was just a thought, but it gave me hope that perhaps God wasn't inflicting this *on* me; perhaps he was going through it *with* me.

If that was the case, then the first step toward overcoming my fear was to take the first step toward the fear itself. As a child, overcoming fear meant finding the courage to increase my speed until I was running on the beach. It meant pedaling faster even when I wanted to slow down, so that I would stay upright. And it meant stepping off into the unknown, trusting that my father would guide me toward the safe spot.

I knew I needed to take a step in the direction of my illness and trust my heavenly Father the same way. And I knew my first step was to learn more about what was happening to me and why. Only by facing my fears would I have a chance of conquering them. As a blind person, I had done a lot of walking in the dark. Now I would have to walk through my darkest fears. It wouldn't be easy. But life had taught me it was the only way to get to the other side.

CHAPTER 7

The Search Begins

It's time to get over this
Faced with the truth
What would you do
Swim or go down?
—FROM "KEEP THE LINES OPEN," SCOTT MACINTYRE

Over the weekend I pushed my way through the fear and hopelessness, and by Monday I was determined to figure out what was causing the kidney failure so I could fix it and move to Cambridge in September. But I had less than a month to figure it out. We planned to travel to England on June 11 to scout out a place for me to live in September. If I wasn't healthy enough to go for a year, there would be no point going in June.

My parents had spent the weekend thinking about the news, and like me, they knew the kidney disease wasn't going away by itself. So far, a transplant was the only solution anyone had offered, and none of us wanted that—it seemed like such an extreme thing for a nineteen-year-old to do. So we started investigating other options. More than anyone, Mom believed we'd find a solution. Her words from the other day still echoed in my ears: "You're not going to have to get a transplant." I hoped she was right.

The first step was to get a second opinion. We talked with a representative from our health insurance provider, and they recommended a doctor about an hour away in Phoenix. We made an appointment.

After examining me and looking at my test results, the second doctor basically said the same thing as the first. "You're going to need a transplant." Though he didn't think I'd need it within three months, he felt sure I'd need it within the year, which meant I wouldn't be going to England. This time, we were ready for his prognosis and were prepared with the big question: "What caused this?"

During the weekend we had done our research and learned that sometimes kidney failure could be reversed or slowed depending on what had caused it. Perhaps knowing why my kidneys were failing would help me do the same.

But the doctor didn't seem to have any answers or even suggestions of what to test for next. He recommended weekly blood tests to track my creatinine level and confirmed that the medication the first doctor prescribed for my anemia was the right one. Beyond that, all he could offer was to wait and watch for things to get worse.

~

Creatinine is a by-product of muscle metabolism. As our bodies convert food into energy, creatine phosphate in muscle produces the creatinine, which enters the bloodstream, and then is filtered and removed from the body through the kidneys. Testing creatinine levels in blood and urine tells us how well the kidneys are functioning. In a healthy adult, normal creatinine levels range from 0.5 to 1.5 milligrams per deciliter. But as the kidneys deteriorate, more creatinine remains in the bloodstream, resulting in a higher creatinine level. Simultaneously, the creatinine levels in the urine will decrease because more remains in the bloodstream.

Creatinine levels are logarithmic, meaning the higher the number goes, the more significant the increase is. So an increase from three to four is much more worrisome than from two to three. It's like a curve on a graph that gets steeper as the numbers get higher. That's why it was so important to keep watching the numbers.

Although I understood the need for constant monitoring, weekly lab work in Phoenix meant spending two hours a week driving from our home in Scottsdale. Fortunately the Mayo Clinic was only twenty minutes away, and our insurance company agreed to let us see someone there. So later that week we saw our third nephrologist (a doctor who specializes in treating kidney disease).

Maybe we were just immune to doctors tossing out bad news like candy at a parade, but we agreed that of all the doctors we had talked to, Dr. Grant had the best bedside manner. Since he was also the closest, it made sense to have him take the lead in my treatment. But, unfortunately, he didn't seem to have any answers either.

"I can't tell you why this is happening," he said. "I wish I could."

"Is it related to his blindness?" Dad asked.

"We can look into that, although I'm not aware of anything linking the two. But you're right—by finding the cause we can figure out the best treatment."

Sunlight streamed through his office window, crossed his desk, and landed on my knee. I stared at the contrast of light against my denim jeans as my mind began to wander. Beethoven's Second Concerto played in my head and my fingers began to mindlessly play through the notes. I only had a few weeks before I had to make a decision about Cambridge. I wondered how long it would take to get any answers about the cause of my illness.

"Here's the thing," the doctor continued. "A transplant will be your best solution, but if we don't know the cause, the same thing that's killing your kidneys now could kill a new kidney, or cause your body to reject it."

The music in my mind stopped playing and I focused on the conversation.

"So what should we do?" Mom asked. "We keep hearing he needs a transplant, but now you're saying it might not even work?"

I could hear the concern in her voice, but the doctor's voice remained unchanged. "I'd like to do a biopsy."

"A biopsy?" I asked. I didn't like the sound of that.

"It's a simple procedure," explained Dr. Grant. "You're awake the whole time. We numb an area on your back. Then, using an ultrasound to guide us, we insert a needle three or four times into your kidneys to withdraw tissue samples. When we're done, we send the samples out to a pathologist who will check for unusual deposits—scarring, infections, and other abnormalities."

"What are the risks involved?" Mom asked.

"The procedure is generally safe. But I have to warn you that sometimes taking a biopsy can inadvertently cause further damage to the kidneys."

"If his kidneys are already failing, why would we want to take that chance?" Dad asked.

"Because it's really the only thing that could tell us what's going on," the doctor said.

"*Could?*" I asked.

"There's a chance the biopsy will tell us what's going on with your kidneys. However, there's also a chance the results will come back inconclusive."

That was all Mom needed to hear. "Let's wait on the biopsy. We can start with the shots for anemia and then go from there."

∼

In the car we were all quiet. As I sank into the back seat, I replayed the conversation and tried to wrap my mind around everything the doctor had said. Finally Mom broke the silence. "I don't think Scott should have the biopsy.

The doctor admitted it could make his kidneys worse, and it might not even tell us what's wrong."

I thought about all the testing the doctors had done to try to find the cause of my blindness when I was young. Some of the tests had been painful, and some, like the metal contact lens on my cornea, seemed downright cruel. In the end they hadn't proved anything. But now the thought of undergoing a kidney transplant without knowing why scared me as much as the thought of the transplant itself. What if the doctor was right and the same thing happened to a new kidney after a transplant? What if there was no way out?

"We shouldn't make any hasty decisions," Dad said. "I like this doctor. He understands we need to find the cause, and he thinks the biopsy is the best way to do that."

"I like him, too, but we're just hearing more of the same," Mom said. "There must be other things we can do before jumping to do a biopsy."

I understood Mom's position, as well as Dad's, and was just thankful their diverse opinions would give me more options to consider.

And they did.

A friend suggested we contact Al Chen, a biochemist and naturopath who consulted with doctors nationally on nutritional supplements and alternative forms of healing. When our friend's relative had been sick, and traditional doctors couldn't find a cause, Al had been helpful not only in finding the cause but in suggesting treatments that eventually helped him get well. Perhaps he could help us too. We set up a conference call to talk with him.

At the appointed time, Mom, Dad, and I sat on the floor of my bedroom, huddled together around the phone. Before calling, we prayed together— for God to be in the midst of our conversation and for a ray of hope in Al. Then Dad dialed the number and put the phone on speaker so we could all hear.

By his voice, I could tell Al was a middle-aged Asian man. He was sincere when he spoke, and there was a comforting quality in his voice, as if he really cared about me—a sharp contrast to the mood in any of the three doctors' offices.

"Why don't you tell me what's going on," Al said.

We filled him in on everything we knew. Al listened patiently, only interrupting occasionally to ask for more details. When we finished explaining our situation, Al said, "Scott, tell me how you're feeling."

"That's what's so crazy," I said. "I feel fine. If we didn't have the tests to prove my kidneys were failing, I'd never even know there was a problem."

"So you're not tired?"

"No."

"Have you lost your appetite?"

Everybody laughed. "No. I ate half of a chicken by myself yesterday."

I could hear Al typing notes into his computer.

"There's a bit of a time crunch to get this resolved," Dad said. He told Al about our plans to visit England. "We've already bought the airline tickets, but we're not sure Scott's okay to go."

"I see," Al said. "The problem is that his latest creatinine level is 3.9 and that's astronomically high. It's also higher than it was last week. Someone with his levels should be feeling horrible. I'm guessing the only reason he's not is because he's so young. I want to do more tests, but it will probably be okay for him to go in June. The question is whether or not he should go in the fall."

"The doctors keep saying I have to have a transplant," I said. "But we want to avoid that if at all possible."

"A transplant isn't going to solve whatever's causing this. But I'd rather you have a transplant and never have to see a dialysis machine."

It was the first time anyone had mentioned the word *dialysis*. I didn't know what that meant, and I wasn't sure I wanted to find out.

"But a transplant should be a last resort. We can try other things first," Al said confidently.

I think we all let out a big sigh at that point. Finally, someone was willing to work with us to explore all options, not just the most invasive ones.

Al continued. "But as you said, Doug, time is running out. We've got to get moving."

"One doctor is saying we should do a biopsy," Mom said, "but he's not even sure it'll help find the cause. Plus he says it *could* cause more damage."

"Don't do the biopsy!" It was the most animated Al had been. "I'm determined to figure out what caused this, and there are a number of things we can do that aren't nearly as invasive."

For the first time I was hopeful. "Like what?" I asked.

"We can test for harmful viruses and test your autoimmune system to see if that's a factor. And there's a dentist I want you to see. Since some teeth lie on the kidney meridian, the bioenergy channel related to the kidney, it's worth exploring. Something as simple as a dead tooth or gum infection could be affecting your kidney function. I also want you to see a chiropractor to make sure your spine is aligned."

As Al spoke, I could hear Dad trying to scribble down everything he said. It was the most information we'd received from anyone about possible causes. Each suggestion Al made put distance between me and the kidney transplant the doctors were advocating. The longer he spoke, the better I felt.

"I'm going to e-mail you a list of doctors that I work with. I'll tell you which tests I want them to run. That way we can begin eliminating things until we find the cause. In the meantime, I'd like you to start on a regime of enhanced supplements and detox formulas to boost your immune system." He paused for a moment and then spoke slowly and carefully. "I've had patients who've completely turned their kidney problems around, and I'm cautiously optimistic that I can help Scott."

"Thank you so much," Mom said. "You're the first real hope we've had."

The mood in the room had gotten a little brighter, and hope buoyed our spirits.

~

I had many appointments during the next few weeks—sometimes more than one a day. I saw homeopaths, naturopaths, and chiropractors. Each one did extensive testing—much of it not covered by insurance. Once again, Mom and Dad spent thousands of dollars visiting those professionals; they were willing to do whatever was required to help me find a cause and a cure.

Some answers came back immediately. I didn't test positive for any of the viruses they tested me for, and my autoimmune system seemed to be working fine. Neither did I have a dead tooth pressing on my kidney meridian. But other tests and exams gave us hope that we might be close to finding a cause. The chiropractor found that I did have a spine that was misaligned—probably from playing the piano while hunched over the keyboard. The location of the misalignment was in the exact place where my kidney nerves connected with my spine. Al believed that getting my spine in alignment had the potential to reverse the kidney disease, so I began intensive appointments with the chiropractor.

Al also suggested some dietary changes to make it easier on my kidneys. Our family had always been very health-conscious when it came to food, but now my life was on the line. I began to eat more raw foods and cut out dairy products, though I still ate organic sheep and goat cheeses. Instead of making burgers with ground beef, Mom started making turkey burgers. When we made homemade pizza, we used whole-wheat flour for the crust and chicken instead of sausage. I even drank freshly juiced wheat grass every day. We were excited to have a course of action that we could control, and we jumped in wholeheartedly.

Unfortunately, my creatinine levels continued to inch upward. In mid-May it was 4.0, and by June 1 it was 4.2. But we were okay with that. We didn't expect changes immediately, and I still felt good. So we stuck with the plan and prayed that we would see results soon.

CHAPTER 8

Say a Little Prayer for Me

And when we feel
Incredible fear
Let us recall
That He's always near
Did you ever think to say a word in prayer?
You know that He will hear

—FROM "NO FEAR," SCOTT MACINTYRE

Our family had always been a praying family. Both together and individually, we believed spending time in prayer brought us closer to God in a way nothing else could. But ever since I'd received the news about my kidney disease, both the frequency and the urgency of our family prayers had increased. *Which doctor should we see next? Should we do the biopsy? Is there anything we can do to reverse this?* Each day presented us with new opportunities to run from, or toward, God. For the most part, we ran toward him.

Although we were seeking help from outside the mainstream medical community by working with Al Chen and others, we continued to meet with my nephrologist, Dr. Grant, since the Marshall Commission needed his approval if I was to move to England in the fall. Dr. Grant agreed with Al that I should be okay to at least travel to London for a brief visit. I felt good, and we were planning to be gone for only two weeks. But he wasn't yet willing to clear me to travel for a whole year. He wanted to watch my creatinine levels through the summer before he made a decision.

That left me in a difficult spot. We'd already informed the Marshall staff about what was going on and promised to update them as soon as we knew more. Now we were planning to take the June trip to prepare me for a year of study that might not happen. Of course I wanted to study at Cambridge, and my parents wanted me to live out my dreams, but would this preliminary trip just waste everyone's time? There was no easy answer. All we could do was pray.

~

I was five when I first understood that I had a choice about how to live my life. One day, at Vacation Bible School, a speaker told us we could choose to live for ourselves or we could choose to live our lives for Jesus. I knew I wanted to live for him. When I got home that night, I told my parents what I'd decided and together we prayed—asking God to forgive me of my sins, telling him how much I loved him, and promising to try to live like him. After that, I knew that Jesus was my Savior and that one day I would spend eternity with him in heaven.

But as I got older and learned more about what God wanted from his people—to live holy lives separate from the ways of this world—I realized it would be much harder than I thought. I realized I needed his saving grace as much as anyone. I rarely got into trouble, so it probably looked like I had it all together. But sometimes, even the smallest things I thought I had done wrong weighed on my conscience.

Once when I was twelve years old, the pastor was preparing the congregation for communion. "It's important that your heart be right with God and with others before you partake of the Lord's table. If you need to ask for forgiveness, or if you need to extend forgiveness, do that before you receive communion." He reminded us that the bread and wine symbolized Jesus' broken body and the blood he shed for us, so it was important to have a clean heart before consuming them.

I listened intently as he spoke, and although I couldn't think of anything specific I'd done, just to be sure I turned to Dad and whispered, "I'm sorry for anything that I said to you that I shouldn't have, or if I hurt you or anything." I could tell Dad appreciated my words, and that made me feel at peace inside. Because I was so young, he probably thought it was sweet, but I was extremely serious. I wanted to make sure my heart was right with God.

~

We had a bedtime routine while we lived in Toronto—after Mom read us a story, Dad would come into our rooms and pray with us before we went to sleep. I would hear him in Katelyn's room, first giving her pillow rides, and then kneeling by her bedside to pray. He'd then go to Todd's room, and though Todd was too old for pillow rides, he'd play or wrestle with him. I'd hear them laughing a little and then they would pray. When they were done, Dad would say, "Good night, Todd," and then I knew it was my time.

The floorboard would squeak when he walked across the hall and into my room. He would kneel beside my bed and we would talk about our day or what was happening the next morning. Then before he left he'd say, "Let's pray together. I'll start, then you can finish." Sometimes he would ask for things on my behalf. "Lord, help Scott with his schoolwork tomorrow." Or, "Please help Scott to get a good night's sleep tonight." If there were an upcoming piano competition, he might pray for me to retain the music of the piece I was working on. But after I was done praying, he always finished the same way: "In Jesus' name, Amen."

That was my cue to snuggle deep down into my bed, and he'd tuck my covers around me and whisper, "Good night, Scott," before turning off the lights and closing the door.

~

Growing up, piano was my sport. And just as a baseball player might play in a tournament or a match, I played in competitions—first locally and then nationally. Dad and Mom came with me to each one, and right before I was supposed to go backstage, we would all pray for my performance together. Dad would ask God to help me have great recall of the music and to be relaxed and comfortable on stage. Mom often thanked God for giving me the talent and ability to play. Though I won many of the competitions I entered, one thing they never asked God for was to help me win. Instead, they prayed that I would do my best or that I would have fun. But when we closed in prayer, one of them always added, "Please let Scott be a blessing to all those who hear him."

When I was fifteen years old, I entered a competition and won the opportunity to perform with an orchestra for the first time. I was to be the guest piano soloist with the Phoenix Symphony for a sold-out crowd at Phoenix Symphony Hall. Although much of the time the conductor's job was to keep the other musicians playing in time with me, occasionally there were times in the score when I was supposed to follow him. But when there was a pause in the music, there was no way I could see his arms cuing everyone to start playing again.

Since I had never performed with an orchestra before, I was nervous about what would happen if I started to play when I wasn't supposed to, or if I waited too long to join back in. Then I would be out of sync with the orchestra. So,

I did what I often did when I worried; I turned it over to God. *God, I have no idea how to solve this problem but I know you already have an answer. Please show me what I can do to make this work.*

A few days later in rehearsal I realized that if the conductor were to breathe in time with the music, and if I did the same, I would know exactly when to come in again. I told the conductor my idea and he agreed to try it out.

It worked.

The night of the performance, whenever there was a critical moment in the music, he would breathe in time with the beat and I hit every cue exactly as I was supposed to. Whether God answered the prayer directly, or whether praying stopped me from worrying and helped me find a creative solution, didn't matter. In my mind the credit all went to God.

Even though I was now older, my parents continued to pray for me before each performance, and I often joined in. Although the content of their prayers varied depending on the situation, their most heartfelt request remained the same.

"Please let Scott be a blessing to those who hear his music."

That petition has always stayed with me. Even now, before a performance, I pray, *Let my music be a blessing to those who hear me play.*

After much prayer and conversation about whether I should travel to England, it occurred to me that it wasn't really a medical question—it was a faith question. The doctors had already cleared me to take the preliminary trip. My only lingering concern was what would happen in the fall. But I wouldn't have a definitive answer on that for several more months. By the time the doctors made that decision, it would be too late to secure a place for me to live. I had to make the trip now if I wanted to go in the fall.

I truly believed that God wanted me to go, at least for the preliminary trip, and realizing that, I changed my prayers. Rather than praying about the decision, I chose to have faith in God's plan for me and I prayed for protection during the trip. While there was still a very good chance the kidney disease might prevent me from going in the fall, I was committed to doing what I believed God wanted me to do right now. And if I was meant to go in the fall, I believed God would make it possible. My family began to prepare for the trip. Todd had to stay behind because he was performing in a musical, but Mom, Dad, and Katelyn would be going with me.

I began making a list of things I needed to arrange for the coming academic year. It was exciting to allow myself to think about the next few years again. Assuming I got the medical clearance, I would leave for Cambridge in September. The master's degree in musicology that I would be working toward would primarily be a research-based degree. The next year I would attend Royal Holloway University of London, where I would do research on the psychology and history of performance practice, while simultaneously studying at the world-renowned Royal College of Music. There I would take piano and vocal lessons, and at the end of the course, give solo recitals. By the time I finished both years, I would have earned two master's degrees—one in musicology and one in performance studies.

I had had several conversations with Cambridge, and the university had given me a verbal acceptance over the phone. I was just waiting for the official acceptance letter. The plan for our preliminary trip was to explore the Cambridge campus so I would be familiar with it and could assess the living situation before I moved in. After that, we planned to meet with the people in the Marshall office in London to coordinate any last-minute details.

With only two days before our trip, things were moving along nicely. Mom was making and freezing a few meals for Todd to eat while we were gone, and Katelyn and I were practicing our British accents while we packed. I'd been taking the nutritional supplements recommended by Al for almost three weeks, and it seemed that they had stabilized my creatinine levels. I'd had two more creatinine tests done and they'd both come back at 4.2. Things were starting to look up.

I took a break from packing to check my e-mail. I moved the mouse to the top left corner of the screen so I could find it with my eyes, then I slowly followed it down until it hovered over the Inbox listings. The digitized GPS-like voice of my screen reader said, "Cambridge University." I had finally received the information I was expecting.

"Mom!" I yelled. "I just got the acceptance from Cambridge. Wanna read it?"

While I could read the e-mail myself using the screen reader, I wanted to wait so she could share in the excitement too. I clicked open the e-mail as Mom entered the room. She leaned over my shoulder and started reading.

"Dear Scott," she read. But then she abruptly stopped.

"What's wrong?" I asked.

"Oh no . . ."

"What?"

She started reading again. "Dear Scott, we regret to inform you that we will not be able to accept you to Cambridge University at this time. We do not feel that your qualifications from a US university are a sufficient prerequisite to serve as a reasonable foundation for the course work of this program. Thank you so much." It was signed by someone in admissions.

"How's that possible?" I was so confused. "They already accepted me! The woman from the music department told me that I was admitted! She said, 'We're so happy to accept you into Cambridge.'"

"From what I can tell," Mom said, "it seems they don't think your under-graduate degree from a United States university is enough to get you in."

"That doesn't make sense. Lots of students from here go on to study at Cambridge."

"I don't understand," Mom said. "It's as if they retracted your offer."

"But I graduated summa cum laude. I can't understand why they'd turn down a Marshall Scholar."

For a moment I wondered if Cambridge's sudden reluctance was rooted in a lack of understanding about my blindness and the things I had done to over-come it. I had only talked to them over the phone, so they obviously hadn't observed my independent spirit firsthand. They had no way of knowing what I could or couldn't do. Were they concerned about my ability to complete the course work because of my blindness?

Throughout my life, I had rarely been discriminated against because of my disability. But the few times I had, I remembered. Once I was denied a part in a national youth orchestra though I had all the qualifications. Instead of giv-ing me a chance to prove myself, they just assumed that without sight it would be too difficult for me to learn the music. The few times something like this had happened, it hurt. But I couldn't truly know the reasons behind the e-mail from Cambridge, so I pulled myself together and decided to do my best to find another way.

"Is there anyone you can call?" Mom asked.

"I can call the Marshall office in London and see if they can help. But if they can't, what do I do?" I felt tears start to well up in my eyes. Not only was my kidney failure a huge unanswered question, but now I had nowhere to go even if I was cleared to move to England. If Cambridge didn't let me in, it might already be too late to get into another school.

I had told my family and friends that I would be studying at Cambridge, and they were so proud and excited for me to be studying at such a prestigious university. Now I had to tell them I wouldn't be going there. I would technically be a Marshall Scholar, but the scholarship would go to waste. What would I have to show for it?

I rubbed my eyes and tried to blink back the tears. Whenever I hurt, I turned to God, believing that even though I couldn't see why this was happening, he had a reason. So I prayed, pouring out my emotions to him. *God, I don't understand why this is happening. This seems to be going against everything I thought you were calling me to do. If this is a mistake, please show me how I can fix it. If it is not a mistake, please lead me on the path you have for me. Lord, it feels like there is just one obstacle after another keeping me from studying in England, and I feel lost and helpless. Please show me the way.*

I wanted to call the Marshall office in London immediately, but with the time difference, it was too late. Their offices were closed, and I would have to wait until the next morning.

~

That night my family got together and prayed for me. Ever since that day outside of the doctor's office when I'd received the diagnosis, we had been praying regularly praying as a family. For the previous few weeks, the focus of our prayers had been for guidance and direction regarding my health. And knowing that God was bigger than anything we faced, we were never shy to ask, "God, if it be your will, please heal Scott."

Once again we were praying for guidance and direction—only this time it was not about my health, but about my educational plan in England. We asked God to work through the Marshall office in London to resolve this, and we asked for his will to be done for the upcoming school year. I don't remember how the prayer ended; my mind was distracted by my circumstances. But later as I fell asleep, I realized that there were prayers in my life that were worth repeating.

"In Jesus' name, Amen."

"Please let Scott be a blessing to those who hear him."

"Please, God, just heal Scott."

"Show me your will, Lord."

Once again, the path was not clear and I couldn't see where he was leading me. But despite my questions, I chose to follow him.

By faith.

Not by sight.

It was the theme of my life.

CHAPTER 9

The Marshall Plan

Feels like I'm running in circles
Inside my mind
Something is driving me deeply
To keep on this time
—FROM "VIEW FROM ABOVE," SCOTT MACINTYRE

The coordinator in London was a woman named Charlotte. She and I had been in regular contact since I found out I'd won the Marshall Scholarship. Our first conversations were about my blindness and whether I would need any special accommodations. She was excited and gracious about helping me make a smooth transition. The week after graduation, I called to tell her about my kidney failure. Though she was sorry to hear the news, she remained optimistic that everything would be fine and I would still be in London that fall. Since then, I had regularly communicated with her as we learned more about my condition. Through it all, Charlotte continued to be confident that everything would work out.

But the next day, as I dialed her number, my heart was heavy. *What if telling her that Cambridge had retracted my offer was the final straw? What if she wasn't willing to work through this too?*

But I shouldn't have worried. Though Charlotte sounded surprised when I gave her the news, there was an edge to her voice that made me think this kind of thing had happened before. "Let me make some calls and see what I can do. By the time you get here later in the week, I hope I'll have some answers for you."

~

Our first stop in London was to visit Charlotte's office. And true to her word, she was already working on a plan. "How would you feel about reversing your two years?" she asked me in her sprightly British accent.

"What do you mean?"

"Instead of doing Royal Holloway and Royal College of Music your second year, I was thinking perhaps you could start with that program this year."

I had already tried to talk to my contacts at Cambridge and they weren't budging. I needed to do something else, and Charlotte's suggestion sounded like a great idea. I was already familiar with the program—this would be the first year the two institutions would jointly award a degree. The plan was to combine the best of the university's academic course work with the conservatory's world-class performance training to give performing musicians a well-rounded education at the highest level.

"But haven't the application deadlines all passed?" I asked. I knew the Michaelmas term—the first academic term of the school year in the United Kingdom, which coincided with the fall semester in the United States, was only a few months away.

But once again, Charlotte wasn't worried. "One of our past Marshall Scholars, Peter Malink, is heading up the program at Royal Holloway. I'll give him a call. He's originally from the United States, but he came here as a Marshall, fell in love with a girl, married her, and never went back."

Mom chuckled. "We keep saying that's going to happen to Scott."

"I'll call Peter and see what we need to do to make this happen," Charlotte said. "In the meantime, you'll need a place to live. I think you should consider Goodenough College. It's the hardest college in London to get admitted to, but a lot of Marshall Scholars end up there."

"Colleges" in England aren't exactly the same as they are in the United States. In the States, a college is an academic division of a university, so there might be a College of Business and a College of Medicine under one university umbrella. But in England, colleges are a combination of fraternity, dorm, and student services center. Students live in a college, sometimes along with faculty or tutors, but colleges are more than just residence halls—they form the basis of a student's educational support system and social life. Some colleges have their own sports teams or put on concerts, so it was important to find a college that was a good fit for me both socially and academically.

"Goodenough College is well known for accepting a diverse group of post-graduate students from around the world," Charlotte continued, "so they restrict the number of students they will accept from each country. I don't know yet how many they've taken from the United States for the upcoming year, so we'll have to keep our fingers crossed. I'll see what I can find out, but you should go and take a visit as long as you're here. And be sure to pick up an application."

Charlotte told me that Goodenough College had an extensive admittance process, so it wouldn't hurt to start filling out the paperwork immediately. She also told me they'd be looking for me to demonstrate not only intellectual ability but cultural value as well, and to keep that in mind as I wrote the required essay.

"I'll ring your mobile if I hear anything," Charlotte said.

~

The next morning my family and I took the rapid transit system, the London Underground (or, as it's affectionately called, "the Tube"), from our hotel to Russell Square. The station was only two blocks from the college, which was located between Guilford Street and Mecklenburgh Square. Founded in 1930 by Frederick Goodenough, Goodenough College had served as home to notable writers, artists, physicians, and politicians.

The location was perfect, with restaurants, shops, a post office, a bank, and a library nearby. It was about an hour's walk from the Royal College of Music, which was in south Kensington. And the main campus of the Royal Holloway University was about a forty-minute train ride outside London. But most of my academic lectures would be held on Royal Holloway's London campus, which was much closer. The Russell Square Tube stop was just a couple of blocks away, and from there I could get anywhere in London.

Architecturally, Goodenough College was modeled after some of the famous colleges at Cambridge and Oxford. The stately structure had four wings that enclosed a huge courtyard in the center of the building. Though the college was in one of the world's largest urban areas, it would be like having a huge park—with grass, flowers, and trees—right outside my door.

Our visit among the old brick walls was brief, but I could tell the college housed a vibrant community. There was a large dining room with long tables that resembled the dining room at Hogwarts in the Harry Potter movies. Meals were served buffet style, so I wouldn't have to cook unless I wanted to. Benches in pathways around the courtyard created space for people to gather in small groups for conversation. Though everyone had a private room, there were common living areas where students gathered to socialize or debate the news of the day. I knew I would find the environment stimulating and would enjoy living among such cultural diversity.

While in London my parents helped familiarize me with the neighborhood around Goodenough College and the Russell Square Tube station. We spent time traveling to tour the campuses of both universities and we also did some sightseeing as a family. By the time we left London, I felt comfortable with everything I had seen.

Now all I had to do was be accepted.

～

It was the summer of waiting.

Back home in Scottsdale, I waited for news—about whether I was admitted into the program, whether I had been accepted into Goodenough College, and of course the biggest looming question, the cause of my kidney failure.

We had arrived home at the end of June and the doctors' appointments continued. Before the trip, my creatinine level had been a 4.2, and three weeks after it was a 4.3. Since it wasn't rising very fast, my doctor said we could drop back to testing it every two weeks instead of once a week. By July the number had dropped back to a 4.2, giving us hope that perhaps it had stabilized and was now possibly reversing.

I'd been through a lot of testing both before I left and after I came back from our trip to England, but as the summer wore on and no cause for the kidney failure appeared, we realized the doctors were giving up the search. To my mom, it was reminiscent of the time and money spent looking for the cause of my blindness.

Tens of thousands of dollars in tests.

Countless hours in doctors' offices.

And nothing to show for it.

I continued taking the nutritional supplements. Although they didn't taste good, I was hopeful they were playing a part in keeping the creatinine levels at bay. I would do whatever it took.

～

After we'd been home a week, Charlotte called from the Marshall office. "I talked with Peter and asked if there was anything he could do to get you into the Royal Holloway and Royal College program," Charlotte said. "The biggest problem is you don't have time to audition for the school."

She was right. The deadlines for fall had long passed. The Royal College of Music also required potential students to audition in person so they could assess their skill level. I had done that when I applied for Arizona State, and I knew the bar had to be much higher for the Royal College of Music.

"I wasn't planning on being in London again until just before the Michaelmas term." I racked my brain for ways I could make it happen before then.

"I know," Charlotte said, with sympathy in her voice. "Even if you could fly back here, most of the faculty is off for the rest of the summer, so it wouldn't matter anyway." Just when I thought my chances were over, Charlotte continued. "But Peter says if you can get a recording made immediately, he thinks they can bypass the traditional procedures and admit you on the basis of the recording. Is there any way you can make that happen?"

"A recording? Absolutely!" I had been making my own recordings since I was five and had already produced five CDs. "I have a recording studio in my house, as well as recordings of some of my recent performances. I can get something out right away."

And I did.

Later that week, I spoke to Peter on the phone, and he gave me more details about the program and where we stood with the expedited acceptance.

"Thank you," I told him. "I know you had to pull some strings to make this happen, and I appreciate it so much."

"You're certainly welcome. But it was made easier because of the power and connections that come with you being a Marshall Scholar."

Before I knew it, both the university and the conservatory had accepted me. I was the first student of the joint program. A few weeks later, an envelope arrived from Goodenough College. They had accepted me as a resident for the upcoming year, along with fifteen other Marshall Scholars who were all studying at various universities in London. I would be living with graduate students from Australia, Pakistan, Brazil, Ireland, India, China, Luxemburg, Germany, Canada, and more. Some were from countries I'd barely even heard of. The Marshall Scholars took up most of the quota for American students.

Now that my new Marshall plan was in place, I could clearly imagine myself living in London. But I was getting ahead of myself. I still needed medical clearance, and without knowing the cause of my kidney failure, the prognosis was that my condition would continue to decline until my kidneys failed completely. It appeared the only way I would get clearance—really, the only way I would live—was to have a transplant. But it had all happened so fast, and that still seemed like such a dramatic step that we wanted to avoid. Plus, having a transplant and the time spent in recovery would prevent me from going to London at all. To us a transplant was still out of the question.

~

On July 7, Mom turned on the television and found that programming had been interrupted for breaking news from London. Video footage showed bodies lying on the sidewalk covered in sheets, a double decker bus with its top blown off, and wounded commuters streaming from underground stations.

Stunned witnesses with soot on their faces described being on the Tube when the bombs went off. The lights had gone out and it was pitch black before emergency power was restored. They smelled something burning and heard screams. Fearing for their lives, they tried to break the windows with their bare hands. The microphones of the first reporters on the scene picked up the sounds of women crying and people praying. Within hours it became apparent that terrorists were responsible. Suicide bombers had planned a coordinated attack aboard the Tube. Fifty-two people died and more than seven hundred were injured.

One of the bombs detonated on the Piccadilly line, just five hundred yards from the Russell Square stop—only a few blocks from Goodenough College.

The first call came from a family friend who'd traveled to London many times and knew how close the college was to one of the bombing sites. Mom left the room to take the call, but I could hear her side of it from the kitchen.

"Of course we're going to let him go . . . Yes, I understand it was terrorists, but there are terrorists in New York and we didn't stop going there . . . No, he doesn't need to stay home . . . This is a once-in-a-lifetime opportunity for him. He has to take it. He'll be fine . . . No, I'm not worried about him. He's quite capable of handling things for himself . . ."

During the next few days there were more calls just like that one. Relatives wanted to talk about it over coffee, and friends from church wanted to discuss it in hallway conversations. Many of those well-meaning friends and relatives were already surprised to learn that I'd traveled to England once with my kidney condition. They couldn't believe my parents would even consider letting me go for a year. Now they saw the terrorist bombings as just one more compelling reason why Mom and Dad shouldn't let their blind and sick son go to London.

It was hard enough for me to fight against the overwhelming obstacles that had come up, but it was even harder when those who should have supported me were trying to turn me away from my dreams. Mom did her best to shield me from the calls. During the next few weeks she handled countless conversations from people who said they were "only trying to help." Though I know Mom shared their concerns, she didn't back down from her position that I should be able to go, regardless of the obstacles. Her resolve gave me hope. But even so, I knew she didn't have the final say—the doctors did.

~

My parents had believed in me from the very beginning, but Todd and Katelyn had always supported my dreams too. They knew how important it was for me to go to London, and they did their best to encourage me through each setback.

Todd was born not long before I was three, and I don't remember life without him. He has a servant's heart and a protective-big-brother mentality. Although he was the middle child, in many ways he was also our leader. As the only sighted child in the family, he sometimes assumed the role of sighted guide for Katelyn and me. Mom and Dad never placed expectations on him as far as being responsible for us, but because he was always so willing to serve, they had to make sure he had time for himself and his own activities.

Katelyn was born when I was six. She was a little dough ball, and I used to kiss her on the cheek and play with her hands and feet. Because we were home-schooled, the three of us bonded at a very young age and are still best friends today.

We all shared a common interest in music, and when we moved to Canada, we started making music together. Todd and I recorded a CD called *Brothers for All Seasons*. It was a mixture of classical and folk music that also included a few of my original compositions. During that time, Mom joined the three of us kids to form a family quartet called the MacIntyre Family Singers. We started performing together for churches and charitable events in Toronto, and continued after relocating to Arizona. Before I graduated from ASU, we'd released a self-titled CD of four-part classical, jazz, gospel, and Broadway music.

From the time I'd won the Marshall Scholarship, I knew the hardest thing about that amazing opportunity would be living away from my brother and sister. Though I had traveled a fair amount, and even traveled internationally for my music, we'd mostly traveled together as a family. The longest we had been separated was when one of us was gone for a few weeks to a music camp. If I spent the next year in London, I would miss them both terribly. So I planned to spend extra time with them over the summer.

But now I had to ask what would happen if I didn't go to London. They each had big things planned for next year, plans that didn't involve me. I'd be the one at home while they were off pursuing their dreams. Katelyn had loved riding horses since she was little, and recently she'd picked up an interest in clogging and was spending more time doing both activities. Todd seemed to move from one musical theater role to the next as directors discovered his quadruple threats—singing, dancing, acting, and good looks. Up until then, I had been the busy one. Now I realized if I didn't get to go to London, I would still miss spending time with them—only I'd be the one at home.

~

In August Todd and Katelyn went back to school. Todd attended ASU, and Katelyn supplemented her homeschooling with classes at a local community college. The start of their classes signaled the time to make a decision about mine. My parents and I were in agreement that I should be allowed to go. I felt great, with no loss of energy or appetite. But my creatinine levels had started to creep up. By the third week of August, they were at 4.7, the highest they'd been.

It seemed that our prayers weren't being answered. I didn't know what was causing my kidneys to fail and I had experienced no sudden healing—but we kept praying. My next doctor appointment was scheduled for September 7, and though I hoped for the best, things weren't looking good. Life had taught me there were some things that I couldn't control, and it was becoming increasingly obvious my kidney failure might be one of them.

CHAPTER 10

Music Education

Suddenly the world around feels like it's wrong
'Cause you will never get to hear this song

—FROM "THIS SONG," SCOTT MACINTYRE

Her name was Laurie Z. I don't know if she was born with that last name, married into it, or at some point changed it, but for as long as I knew her, her last name was just "Z." The first time we met I was five and she was working at Nordstrom department store. At that time, none of us could have predicted the impact that she would have on my musical career.

Mom had finished shopping, and we were taking the escalator down to the ground floor to head home when I heard piano music. As the silver stairs glided down another floor, the sound got louder. "Where is that coming from?" I asked Mom.

"There's a pianist on the next floor near the escalator. It's a woman dressed in white and she's sitting at a grand piano."

We continued on down and past the woman. But even as we got off on the ground floor, I couldn't stop thinking about the music. I wanted to hear more. "Mom, can we go back and listen?"

Mom and I stood next to the pianist and listened as she finished her song.

"What's your name?" the woman asked between pieces.

"Scott."

"Hi, Scott. I'm Laurie Z."

She played another piece and then asked, "How old are you?"

"Five and a half."

"Well, Scott, I don't normally do this, but I'm going to play you something that no one else has ever heard. Usually, I wait until a song is recorded before I play it in public, but today I'm going to play one for you that hasn't been recorded yet."

That's cool, I thought. The song she played was similar in style to Jim

Brickman's music, and it was beautiful. Mom and I both complimented her when she finished.

Laurie got up from the piano and talked with us for a few minutes. Mom told her that I played. No doubt noticing that I was blind, she said, "I don't read sheet music. I don't even know how. When I play and when I compose, I do it all by ear." That was encouraging news to us. I'd tried reading sheet music with my limited vision, but it had to be placed in direct lighting and even then I could only see one note at a time. I had also tried learning braille music, but it was clear I learned music much faster by listening. We bought the CD she had for sale, and Laurie handed us her card. "Call me anytime if I can be of help."

~

Growing up I had many different piano teachers, but the one thing they had in common was that they each taught me at least one thing no one else had. Some taught me about the piano and music. Some taught me about myself.

The good ones did both.

My first piano teacher was a woman from our neighborhood. Though she was worried about teaching a three-year-old blind boy, she did her best, and as a result helped to uncover some hidden talents we didn't know I had. Initially, she and Mom agreed that I should start by learning the notes on the piano, but after a few lessons I had memorized them all, so she quickly moved on to teaching me how different combinations of notes could make intervals and chords.

A few weeks later, while at the Los Angeles Science Museum, I picked up a seashell and put it to my ear. Then I handed it to Mom. "Do you hear it?" I asked.

"Yes, I can hear the ocean."

I quickly corrected her. "No, it's an F-sharp." I picked up another one. "This is a B-flat."

A few days later, we were at Price Club in Long Beach when I heard the whistle of a train passing nearby. I matter-of-factly told Mom, "That's an F-sharp minor 7 chord."

Realizing there might be more going on than she thought, Mom tested me when we got home. She played notes on the piano. "What's this, Scott."

I listened for a moment then answered, "That's a B."

"How about this one?"

"A-flat."

Once that first piano teacher learned I had perfect pitch, she told Mom

I needed a more qualified instructor. Next came Lynn, who taught me the Suzuki method, a form of study that emphasized playing by ear. Because of Lynn's focus on rhythm, I started to recognize rhythmic patterns in the music I listened to at home and at church. As songs progressed, I noticed how each rhythm was repeated, changed, or combined with other rhythms. This helped me understand how songs were put together, and I began applying what I learned when writing my own music. As a result, my compositions became more rhythmically complex.

Lynn also encouraged my parents to buy a grand piano for me to use at home. "He really needs to be playing on a proper instrument if he's going to continue to move forward," she told Mom.

Up until that point, I had been playing that same old upright piano. Some of the ivory keys were chipped, and the pedals creaked when I pressed them. Over a hundred years old, the keyboard was also several inches higher than it would've been on a modern piano. When I played it, my elbows bent at a forty-five-degree angle and my wrists stuck out toward the ceiling. Lynn explained to my parents that it was important for my arms to be parallel with the floor and my wrists straight so I would have the most leverage possible while playing.

It was a big expense for a young family with three children and only one working parent, but they decided they could live with a black-and-white TV for a little longer and saved up and bought a used, six-foot Schimmel grand piano.

The first time I played the magnificent instrument I couldn't believe the difference. The sound was beautiful to my ears and so much more crisp and clear than the upright. Because the keys were heavier, it also gave me more control over how loud or soft I played each note and having that kind of control allowed me to more fully express the music as I heard it in my head.

It was while taking lessons with Lynn that I began playing in the praise band for the college and career ministry at my church. One day Lynn came to church to see me perform. Mom was excited for her to hear all that I was doing.

"What did you think?" she said to Lynn afterward.

"Well, you know," said Lynn with disappointment, "what he's playing isn't classical music. It's *ear candy*."

It was the first time a line had been drawn in my musical sandbox. From then on, classical music was on one side and pop music was on the other. And though I didn't know it then, a day was coming when I would have to choose between the two.

When Lynn felt she had taught me all she could, I moved on to Diane, a well-respected Los Angeles–area teacher who taught some of the top piano students in the area. Most of Diane's students had taken lessons for years, and many of them practiced up to four hours a day. For most of Diane's students, playing the piano wasn't a part of their lives—it *was* their lives. And those lives had strict parameters—they could only learn classical music and only through note reading, never by ear. Needless to say, Diane wasn't a fan of the Suzuki method. But like a great librarian, she opened my mind, and repertoire, to books of music I might not have otherwise discovered. While I benefited greatly from that, I also struggled with her rigid attitude. She pushed her students hard and made no apologies about doing so. That aggressive learning environment was new to me. I never had to be pushed to achieve and wasn't used to an antagonistic relationship between teacher and student. All of my prior teachers had been nurturing and loving.

Mom came to my lessons with me and sat in an adjoining space to listen. Many times she had Todd and Katelyn with her, and they would play quietly during the lesson. Since I was only six years old, being present for lessons helped Mom see what was going on. One day, after I had been taking lessons for a few months, Diane said to Mom, "Scott is going to go the farthest of any of my students."

But several lessons later, she was frustrated with me. I hadn't learned as much during that week as she expected me to. "You need to work harder. I'm disappointed in you, Scott. I expect that next week you will have practiced until you have mastered this section and the next."

Perhaps it was her confidence in my ability that made her push me so hard, but she kept the pressure up. A few months later, I missed several notes while playing a piece for her. She sighed. "Some of the notes you played are wrong. Try it again." So I played it again. Unfortunately, the second time was the same as the first.

I was sitting at a second piano next to hers, and I knew I was in trouble as soon as I heard her get up.

When I had studied with Lynn, it was easy to learn new songs by ear and I was used to doing it. As soon as I learned a new song, I played it confidently, and never worried if all the notes were exactly right. If I got a note or two out of place—and not reading sheet music meant that I often would—Lynn would just explain what I missed or what I was doing wrong. Then I could quickly and easily fix it right there in the lesson.

But Diane didn't seem to understand how I learned music and demanded things of me that I couldn't do. Though I couldn't see it, the music was open in front of me. Diane leaned over and stabbed the sheet music with her finger. "Look at this page! What note is that?"

"I don't know."

I was helpless. There was no way I could scan the sheet and find the note in time to respond to her impatient question. But even if I could, I wouldn't have been able to identify it through the tears that blurred my eyes. Perhaps I had fooled Diane into believing my visual impairment wasn't that bad. Or maybe she was so used to working with sighted students, she forgot that sheet music was worthless to me in a situation like that. Either way it was too much for me. Mom watched it all happen and she agreed. Though Diane was a good instructor, it was clear we were not a good fit. After a year and a half of lessons, several of which ended in tears, I left her studio to find a more compatible teacher.

My time with Diane taught me the importance of technical piano proficiency, but it also taught me a few things about myself. Although I couldn't exactly put it into words at that age, at some level I realized I had a delicate emotional spirit. If I cared about a person, I could be very sensitive to their tone. Perhaps because I took in so much information through hearing rather than seeing, a harsh word did more emotional damage to me than actions.

My next teacher, Sarah, was a kindly grandmother who baked cookies for her students and held recitals that were actually fun—not competitions. But once again, it wasn't long before Sarah felt she had taught me all she could and urged Mom to find a teacher who could take me to the next level. I didn't want to leave Sarah, not only because she was so kind, but because I loved her cookies. But it was a good thing we eventually did move on, as my next piano teacher taught me an incredible life lesson.

~

Gregg was my first male piano teacher, and while he thought I had a lot of potential, he also noticed I had some bad habits. One day he told me, "You need to stop feeling for the keys. You need to *know* where each key is and have faith that you'll hit it."

Like many blind piano players, I was used to feeling my way up the keyboard. If there was a jump of an octave or more, my hand crawled across the keys like a sand crab. But Gregg wanted me to lift my fingers from the keyboard and move them through an invisible arc in the air until they landed in the right place.

The first time he asked me to do it I was hesitant. "What if I hit the wrong key?"

"You can do this. Play the first note, then lift your hand off the keyboard and come down on the next note."

He was asking me to take a leap of faith musically and do something I had never done before. I wasn't comfortable with what he was asking, mostly because I knew I could do it my way, and I was unsure if it would work like he described. But I trusted Gregg and so I tried it. When I got to the place in the music with the big jump, I pressed down the first key and then lifted my hand through the air, and as I landed, I hoped for the best.

I completely missed my target.

I wasn't even close.

I tried again. And missed it again. "Good!" said Gregg.

"But I still didn't get it," I said a little frustrated.

"No, but you were closer that time. Try again."

So I kept trying until eventually I found the note I was looking for.

"Great job! Now you just need to have faith that the note is going to be in the same place every time."

Gregg created exercises to help break the patterns that were already so ingrained. If I landed on the wrong key, I repeated the exercise until I got it right. And the more I practiced, the more often I got it right. I made those arcs over and over until I could get them right every time without even thinking about them. And he was right; the key was always in the same place, I just needed faith to believe it would always be there and that faith came through practice.

Gregg taught me to be a more confident piano player, but I carried that confidence with me for the rest of my life. I learned many lessons from that experience—like not being afraid to step out of my comfort zone, how it was okay to make a mistake, and how through dedicated practice I could overcome even my most ingrained habits. But more importantly, I learned that I could do whatever I set my mind to. Though I only studied with Gregg for a few months before we moved to Toronto, his lessons have stayed with me for life.

∼

After meeting Laurie Z. at Nordstrom, Mom called her the next week and asked if I could come in for a lesson. I was already taking lessons with another teacher at the time, but Mom thought since Laurie only played by ear, she would have a different perspective—one that might be helpful to me as a blind piano player. During my first session I played her a few of the classical pieces I'd been working on in my lessons, then I played two pieces I'd written myself.

"Wow, he is so much more expressive when he plays his own music," said Laurie. "And he has a real gift for improvisation."

I took lessons from Laurie for only a year, overlapping with my more traditional teachers, but Laurie offered me something they didn't—she saw me as more than just a piano player; she saw me as an artist. As a result, Laurie probably had a bigger effect on me, and my future career, than any other teacher, because she taught me to take my dreams seriously.

"Of all the kids I've worked with, you're the best I've seen at picking things up by ear. What do you want to do with music when you grow up?"

"I want to make an album and go on tour someday."

"Well, why don't you do that now?"

Laurie believed that you didn't have to wait on someone else to make your dreams come true. You could take those dreams into your own hands and make them happen. She told me how I could record my own music and then use software to clean up the tracks until they sounded like I wanted them to. And she expanded my vision for composing when she showed me the Musical Instrument Digital Interface (or MIDI) system on her computer. Using MIDI I could play something on my keyboard and then use a computer to make it sound like a flute or saxophone. Soon, I was using MIDI to record a variety of instrumental accompaniments for my compositions.

A traditional record label never represented Laurie; she recorded, mixed, produced, and sold her own CDs independently. She encouraged me to do the same.

When Laurie found out I had an upcoming performance attended by several hundred people, she said, "Why don't you make an album? You can sell it at your concert."

"Can he do that?" Mom asked.

"Why not? Just go for it!"

"But the concert's in six weeks," she said.

"With a little bit of help, you can do it in a month."

I wasn't able to make it happen that quickly, but a couple of years later after the move to Toronto I did. *Seeing Through Sound* was my first independently released CD. With Laurie's encouragement and Mom and Dad's help—Dad read the software instruction manuals to me; Mom took the cover photos and researched CD packaging companies—I had a professional-looking CD by the time I was eleven. Selling those CDs at performances provided the seed money to create my next CD a couple of years later. Since then, I have released one CD about every two years.

Laurie never saw me as a little kid, but as the accomplished artist and composer she believed I could someday be. She taught me everything she knew about the music business. Though other piano teachers would come and go, my relationship with Laurie grew. She may have started out as a piano teacher, but she quickly became one of my most important mentors.

~

I never planned to go to college at fourteen; it just happened.

We had moved from Toronto to Arizona, and for a variety of reasons, Mom thought that perhaps it was time for me to enroll in public school. I had been homeschooled for many years and had never taken a standardized test before, but the local school system required me to take one so they knew where to place me.

To everyone's surprise, I tested in the 99th percentile. While looking into possible programs for me—like the International Baccalaureate program—Mom found that I had already been taught much of the curriculum they were covering in the local school. The local high school counselor suggested a different plan.

"Why don't you just have him take his SATs, and if he scores high enough, just enroll him at ASU?"

Academically, that made sense. The college curriculum would be more challenging and engaging for me than what was offered by the local high school, but there was another more important reason to consider ASU. In Toronto I had excellent and accomplished piano teachers who strongly recommended ASU's music department for furthering my music education. It seemed that ASU might be the best solution for both music and academics.

I took the SATs and scored high enough to get into ASU and the Honors

College. So in January 2000, at the age of fourteen, I enrolled at ASU. I started with some piano classes with Walter Cosand, and then over the next four years added more music and academic classes. Walter was an amazing piano professor, and he deepened my understanding of music and brought my playing to a whole new level. I had enrolled at ASU expecting to receive an education in music, but what I didn't expect was that I would also get another type of musical education on the drive to and from school.

Though Mom was my primary driver, Dad often took me or picked me up from ASU. While driving, he would have the radio tuned to a local pop station. Other than the few songs the babysitter had introduced me to, I had grown up listening only to classical music and had never spent a lot of time listening to the radio. So each time I rode with Dad, I was exposed to a whole new form of music.

"That song has a lot of piano in it," Dad said one day while we were driving. "You could write something like that."

The song was "Drops of Jupiter" by a band called Train, and it was different than anything I had ever heard. I thought about it the rest of the way to school. By the time we got there, I said, "Yeah, I could do something like that."

I began spending more time listening to pop music, and eventually began to try my hand at writing it. My writing was influenced by what I heard. For example, Vertical Horizon's songs were so catchy. I would hear "You're a God" and "Everything You Want" on the way home from school, and when I went to bed that night, they'd still be playing in my head. And there were other artists. I loved Vanessa Carlton's "A Thousand Miles." It was a song that begged to be sung. And when the band Creed asked, "Can you take me higher?" the heavens seemed to open up. I wanted to grab my air guitar and play along.

So during the day I studied Bach, Beethoven, Prokofiev, and Chopin with Walter Cosand. But on the way to and from school, I studied Our Lady Peace, Third Eye Blind, Three Doors Down, and Blink-182 with Dad. I especially loved the songs with the distorted guitar sound. Something about those songs lit a fire inside of me because the sound was unlike anything I could produce on the piano.

I paid attention to the patterns in pop music: verse, chorus, verse, chorus, bridge, and final chorus. I tried to predict what would happen next—even in songs I'd never heard before. "I bet there's gonna be a guitar solo before the bridge," I'd tell Dad. Often I was right. But when I was wrong, I was even more intrigued. The artist broke the pattern and surprised me by doing something unexpected. That just made me more curious as to how they did it.

As my studies at ASU got more intense, pop music became a release for me. I lived and breathed classical music, and there was a lot of pressure in the piano performance program. I had to memorize many new pieces each semester, and some were almost an hour long. Playing and singing pop music allowed me to decompress. If I had time between classes, instead of practicing my classical music, I'd sing while playing the upright piano in one of the practice rooms. I also wrote a lot of music in those practice rooms for my first Christian CD, *My Guarantee*, as well as songs that appeared on later CDs, like "Silver," "Somewhere Else," and "Dream World."

Just thinking about it made my creative juices flow. Though it's impossible to play the piano exactly like you would play the electric guitar, I still tried to play power chords on the piano to imitate the sounds I heard in my head. I also wrote pop and rock songs using some new techniques on the piano that simulated guitar riffs from my favorite bands. My new compositions had more energy and forward momentum than my previous work. Pop songs made music come alive in me in ways that I had never experienced. Sometimes they even became an emotional release for me, and as CNN had predicted so many years earlier, I began writing ballads to profess my love to girls I liked. They responded to my pop music much better than my performance of Rachmaninoff's piano concerto.

Because I expressed so many of my feelings through music, songwriting was a very personal process for me. When I wrote songs, my mind was completely focused on the music. I got lost inside my own thoughts as each new piece of melody or lyric found its place inside the context of a song. Because I was so focused, I could write anywhere. Sometimes I wrote at home where it was often quiet and I could be completely alone. Other times I wrote in a practice room at ASU, drawing energy from the nearby sounds of violins, clarinets, trumpets, and vocalists as other musicians practiced their individual repertoires. Though the practice halls could sound like a chaotic symphony of mismatched melodies, it didn't distract me. In fact, it could have the opposite effect, sometimes stimulating creative urges I didn't know I had in me. There was something about making music in community, even if we weren't making it together, that took composing to another level for me.

As I had told Laurie Z. so many years before, my dream as a musician was to do an arena tour. I could picture myself on stage with a band, lights, and ten thousand cheering fans. I imagined the blaring guitars and rhythm-pounding drums all around me. I would be center stage, seated behind the grand piano, and singing with all my heart. Then, just as the music built into a crescendo, I would jump up from the piano, grab a microphone, and dance in time with the pulsating music as I finished my song.

But as real as all that was in my mind, I knew that wouldn't happen with Chopin Ballade No. 2. Classical music was my reality, but pop music was rapidly becoming my fantasy. Listening to pop music with my dad, I finally realized this was the kind of music that could help me live out my dream.

Unfortunately, the people who came to my classical concerts didn't know me as a singer-songwriter. They knew me as an accomplished pianist. *Was it even plausible to think that I could take on a new musical identity and be successful at it?*

~

During the summer of 2005, I waited on answers from doctors. And I waited on answers from schools in England. Basically, I waited on my future.

But as I waited, I worked on honing my skills as a songwriter. It was a happy distraction from all the negative things happening to me and I was anxious to finish some tracks so I could share them with Laurie before I went to London. *If* I went to London.

Pop music wasn't as respected by my professors and classical piano peers at ASU, and I wondered if the same would be true in London. Most academics believed there was a clear fork in the musical road and you had to choose which path you were going to take. I believed I could do *both*. Why not? I had already performed many times as a guest artist with the Phoenix Symphony and expected to do more of that in the future. Pop music started out as my guilty pleasure, but more and more, I wondered if it was the path to my dreams.

So unless someone forced me to choose, I planned to pursue both.

CHAPTER 11

Decision Time

I've been in places where I thought the world was over
Until somebody came along and lit the spark
—FROM "THE GOOD, THE BAD, THE UGLY," SCOTT MACINTYRE

It was a tense drive to Dr. Grant's office. We knew this was the make-or-break appointment. If Dr. Grant cleared me, I would head off to London to pursue a future that had been on hold since graduation day. But if he thought it was too dangerous and refused to sign the medical release, no matter how much I wanted to, I wouldn't be going.

Dr. Grant came in and sat down on the rolling stool. I could hear him flipping through the pages of my chart, and the occasional clicking of his pen as he made notes. The ticking from the clock on the wall seemed much too loud. So did the sound of my heartbeat. My stomach felt like it was tied in knots. I was teetering on the edge of hope and despair, feeling the same fear as when I jumped off the bridge at Trinity Alps. Everything depended on where I landed.

We'd said everything there was to say. We had prayed everything there was to pray. Now it was his decision, and his decision alone. Waiting for him to speak, I could tell he was considering it with the gravity it deserved. He knew how important this was to me, yet no one believed it was worth risking my life.

"I know how much you want to go to London," he said. "The problem is, you're still in renal failure and you are still going to need a transplant. The creatinine levels are slightly higher than they've been before, but they're still mostly stable." I held my breath as he paused. "Since this is such a huge opportunity, I'm going to sign the medical release, but we'll still need to monitor your levels at least monthly while you're gone."

I'm going to London! Relief and exhilaration washed over me.

"Thank you so much," I said. "You have no idea how much this means to me."

I couldn't believe he was letting me go! During the previous few weeks, I'd gone from the shock of hearing I had to have a transplant immediately, to now being stable enough to live overseas for a year. I knew I wasn't cured—there was still a medical cloud hovering over me. But perhaps they had overreacted? It didn't matter. I had a temporary reprieve. And while I had it, I wanted to do as much living as I could.

∽

The very first time I went to school by myself, I was three and a half years old. Mom had a brand-new baby and her hands were full, so she investigated local preschools that would be right for me.

She found a private preschool that allowed me to be a part of their regular classroom, and I enrolled for two mornings a week (that's all we could afford). The preschool directors, Miss Sandy and Miss Ramona, were amazing women and progressive educators who used a teaching style similar to the Montessori method. They recognized my musical talent and allowed me to play the piano in the classroom. Like my parents, they believed I could do anything I set my mind to, and they never coddled me. They only encouraged my development. The Braille Institute in Los Angeles was a great resource for my parents. At no charge, they provided an aide who went to preschool with me. She was a young woman who had an undergraduate degree in special education and hoped to eventually teach blind children.

As you can imagine, a blind child in a sighted preschool can be a dangerous thing. Blind people depend on objects remaining in the same place so they can learn to safely navigate familiar environments. But in a preschool, everything changed constantly. One day, finger paintings would hang from an easel in the middle of the room; the next day Legos would be scattered across the story rug. The aide helped me get around the potential pitfalls. But even an aide couldn't protect me from everything.

One day I came home with a bump on the side of my head. "What happened?" Mom asked me. I had no idea.

She called the aide and asked her about it. The aide told Mom that a boy had wanted to help me, and before she could stop him, he grabbed my hand and walked me right into the side of the playhouse.

On a different day I came home complaining that my stomach hurt. Mom made another call to the aide. Apparently another boy had punched me in the stomach during story time. I couldn't see it coming and so I didn't do anything to protect myself. By the time the aide stopped him, he had gotten in two good jabs.

Once Mom understood the context of the injuries, she would make suggestions for the aide to prevent future occurrences of the same incident. But she was never tempted to pull me out of the school. Accidents and occasional unwanted contacts were bound to happen when sighted and visually impaired kids were in the same classroom. Still, Mom believed it was better for me to get out and experience the world—bumps and all—than to stay at home encased in bubble wrap. She wanted me to function in a sighted world, not a blind world. Regardless of whether I was three and a half, or nineteen and heading to London, she was willing to do whatever it took to make that happen, even if it meant a few bruises.

~

I had a week to pack my stuff and have it shipped to London. Katelyn and my parents would be traveling with me to Washington, DC, where I would meet the other Marshall Scholars and together we'd have several days of orientation. After that, we would travel to London so I could get settled at Goodenough College by September 23 before classes started.

Once again Todd stayed home since his classes at ASU had already started. Saying good-bye to him was hard. He was my best friend, and we spent so much time together. We were often in the same activities, and shared many of the same friends. But from everything I learned about the Marshall program, I knew I was going to have the opportunity to meet some of the most interesting people in the world. So though I was sad to leave Todd, I was also very excited. I couldn't wait for this new adventure to start.

~

Some environments were more accessible to me than others. For example, I understood how airports were supposed to be laid out—security, long hallways with many gates, and arrival areas separate from departure lobbies—but successfully navigating an airport without being able to read signs was impossible. I could be standing right next to my gate and never know it. That's why I always traveled with a sighted guide.

When it came to meeting people, small environments where people generally stayed in the same place—like a sit-down dinner—were easiest for me to navigate. I could put the sound of someone's voice with a location and it helped me to know who I was talking to. Crowded cocktail parties were just the opposite.

Walking around in an open space I had to be mindful not only of furniture placement, but where people were standing. Since Todd and I shared a lot of friends growing up, he was my sighted guide at my earliest social events. He'd lead me in and help me get oriented with the space and then we'd each do our own thing with him occasionally checking on me throughout the night. If I needed something and he wasn't around, I wasn't shy about asking the person next to me to help me refill a glass, or point me in the direction of food or a restroom.

Though I had learned ways to safely navigate the environment at a party, it was still difficult to engage others in conversation unless they were next to me. Usually, I had no idea how close or far apart the other people were. I was completely dependent on auditory cues. With lots of conversations and usually some background music, I had to listen really carefully to identify voices and place them spatially in the room.

The ambient chatter at a party could lead me to think someone was talking with me, when they were actually speaking to someone else. And when I was included in a discussion with several people, it was occasionally hard to make my words connect. I'd jump in and direct my comments to the last location I'd heard the voice I wanted to respond to. Sometimes I got it right, but sometimes I didn't. Occasionally, I would learn that the person I thought I was talking to had already walked away.

I couldn't survey a room to see who was there. I remained oblivious to the presence of friends or even a cute girl smiling at me. At parties, people turn their heads as they talk. They move around the room as conversation partners change or when they want something to eat or drink. But it was impossible for me to track a person in a huge room full of strangers.

Social events sometimes presented other awkward moments, like when someone held out his hand for me to shake. Since I couldn't see his hand, I didn't offer mine, or I would reciprocate just a little too late. Or perhaps someone might try to hug me, but because I didn't see them coming, I would go for the handshake. I wasn't overly self-conscious about these things, but I did worry about people misinterpreting my actions. The more parties and social gatherings I went to, the more comfortable I became with my limitations and how to best fit in despite them. But then because I didn't necessarily look blind, sometimes people didn't even realize I was.

If I had any jitters about the social gatherings in Washington, DC, it was that. The orientation in Washington would include several cocktail parties and networking events with high-level government officials from both the US and the UK. I never wanted to make anyone feel awkward because I was visually impaired, but there was a limit to how much I could control.

~

During one of the last car rides Todd and I took together before I left for London, I was thinking about the other Marshall Scholars that I would soon meet. I remembered the grueling interview process that I'd been through to earn this scholarship. Everything I had experienced during the Marshall application process led me to believe that the other scholars might be über-intellectuals who were in love with academia. I wondered how much I would have in common with them, and whether I would have a hard time relating. We were in the old minivan that Todd always drove and listening to some of the rock bands we enjoyed when one of our favorite songs came on.

"I bet I'm the only Marshall Scholar who listens to Linkin Park," I said. We both laughed.

Once in Washington, DC, I considered what else might separate me from my fellow Marshalls and what I could do to bridge the gap. I especially wanted to do whatever I could to help them overlook my blindness and get to know me as a person. But as soon as I exited the car and Dad walked me up the steps of the British ambassador's residence, I knew I wouldn't have to give it a second thought.

A woman greeted me as we entered. "You must be Mr. MacIntyre," said the elegant voice of an older lady.

"Yes, I am," I said. I could smell her expensive perfume as I held out my hand.

Instead of shaking it, she slipped it under her arm and said, "Come with me, Scott. I'll take you into the party."

And with that kind gesture, I instantly felt at home. She introduced herself as the hostess, but I didn't catch her name. We entered a larger room, and I was temporarily distracted by the acoustics—music from a string quartet and the sounds of laughter and conversation bounced off walls and a high ceiling. The floor was hard and slightly slippery, perhaps a polished hardwood or maybe even a marble. The hostess took me to a group of other Marshall students and introduced me. "This is Scott MacIntyre. He is also a Marshall Scholar. I'll let you each introduce yourself to him." And then she was gone to welcome more guests.

The names and introductions happened quickly. There were the expected biology, computer science, engineering, and physics scholars, but there were some unexpected finds as well. Ankur had graduated with two degrees in journalism and was interested in migrant populations. Mary studied music composition at Oberlin, and in addition to being an accomplished violin player, she planned to study vocal performance while in England. I liked Jay Choi from the moment I met him. He had graduated from the United States Military Academy and had been a helicopter pilot who'd spent two months working in a West African hospital.

I found myself so fascinated by the people I met and the stories they told that the night just flew by. By the time the party ended, I had made a whole host of new friends. More importantly, I'd discovered that many of the Marshall Scholars were like the students I knew at ASU. They also listened to Green Day and Linkin Park. And if the party was any indication, like college students everywhere, they sometimes drank too much. The only difference was they managed to be absolutely brilliant at whatever they did after they woke up the next morning.

At our first meeting in Washington, the people in charge of the Marshall program told us the next three days would be a whirlwind, and they were right. It was cocktail reception after cocktail reception. The most casual ones required a suit, while the formal ones required a tux. Each party came with its own set of dignitaries. I met barons and baronesses, senators, and various government officials. Some parties were in posh halls with chandeliers and champagne, while others were held in stately old mansions.

It was like a montage in a movie, where each clip was more exciting than the last. As Marshall Scholars, I think we were all honored to have such incredible people throw lavish parties for us. But for me, the best part was meeting those other scholars, or as I now thought of them, *friends*. As my new friends got to know me, each one did his or her best to make me feel comfortable and accepted. Before I left Arizona, everyone told me what a great academic opportunity I'd have as a Marshall Scholar, but after just a few days, I could see the social connections were just as valuable. Most important, I was having the time of my life.

After three days, the party didn't end; it just moved on to London. I flew with my fellow Marshall Scholars, and Mom, Dad, and Katelyn followed on another flight. There the orientation continued with more parties that included

British royalty, the American ambassador, and a representative from the prime minister's office. Soon I began to feel like royalty too.

Until the orientation ended, at least. That's when they gave each of us our stipend check and sent us on our way. Fortunately, my parents were staying around for a few days to help me get settled in and learn my way around.

~

Goodenough College was a series of multi-story, compound-like buildings that took up several entire city blocks. My room was on the third floor in London House, one of the two "houses" that made up the college, and it was larger than a typical American dorm room. The bed had a very thin mattress—almost like a cot—and was along the same wall as the door. On the left wall was a set of shelves where I kept my stereo and speakers, as well as my books and other personal items. There was also a comfortable chair for reading or listening to music.

Straight ahead was a desk where I arranged my computer and adaptive technology. The desk was under a big window that overlooked the courtyard. I loved having my desk there because as I worked, I could feel the breeze and hear lively chatter from the courtyard below. On the right side was a closet where I hung my suits and tux, as well as my "London" apparel—rain jackets and overcoats. Though they had practice rooms in the basement and a grand piano in the large common room, I'd also brought my keyboard just in case I needed it. If I plugged in my headphones, I could play in my room without anyone hearing me. My parents and Katelyn helped me unpack everything and get the room all set up.

Once I got settled in and had a moment to think, I realized just how happy I was. Everything about the Marshall experience so far had been exciting and stimulating, and I knew I'd only had a taste of what was to come. It had been a roller-coaster ride of a summer, but now that I was in London, I decided to let the past be the past. I planned to make up for lost time by taking advantage of every minute in my new city with my new friends and enjoying it as fully as I possibly could.

CHAPTER 12

Crossing the Road to a Dream

Sweet dreams take flight
Sweet dreams tonight
Wherever you are
I know you're not far
You're only a dream away

—FROM "SWEET DREAMS," SCOTT MACINTYRE

"You're going to be living *by yourself*? In *London*?"

I was always surprised when people asked me that. But I understood their concern. To many people, the thought of living in a foreign country was scary enough, and to them, the idea of a blind person living there by himself was unfathomable. Although I had the doctor's permission, some friends and family still thought it was wrong for me to move to London. Because of my blindness, the bombings, and of course my kidney failure, they felt I was taking too many risks. They meant well, but it was hard not to be hurt by their reactions. It felt as though they didn't believe in me.

Some people expressed their skepticism and some just sighed in disbelief, but most asked, "How are you going to do that?"

It was a good question, but the truth was, I planned to live in London the same way I lived in the United States or in Canada. What the questioner didn't always understand was that a blind person is always chasing a dream. Often the dream is something others would consider ordinary—like being able to walk across the street or purchase something from a drugstore. But I also had extraordinary dreams—like sharing my music with the world—and I knew the process of making big dreams happen was the same process I used to make ordinary things happen.

Cross the street, live in London, go on tour—I couldn't pursue one while running in fear from the others. Each goal was accomplished in the same way—by focusing on what I wanted and then taking that first step of faith.

~

Orientation and Mobility, or O&M, is the term used for the training given to visually impaired people to help them understand the space they're in and where they want to go (orientation), then how to move safely and confidently to that destination (mobility). My first O&M training began when I was three. My instructor, Jon Reed, would come to my house, and although I was very young at the time, I vividly remember many of my sessions with Jon. What he taught me made a profound impact; it opened up a whole new world of mobility for me.

One day he guided me around my Redondo Beach neighborhood and taught me how to position my cane diagonally across my body, from my right hand to the sidewalk in front of my left foot. "This is called the diagonal technique. Your cane is like a superhero shield. It's your defense. If anything hip level or lower gets in your way, the cane will deflect it before it hits your hand, or it'll alert you to move out of the way." I liked the idea of having a superhero shield.

Jon taught me other techniques with my cane, like sliding, tapping, or dragging it in various directions so I could identify obstacles, find curbs, and track with walls and fences. Once I mastered one skill, he helped me build on it until I could walk around my neighborhood by myself, guided by sidewalks, fences, and curbs.

When I was four, Jon taught me about traffic patterns by playing with Matchbox cars on a relief map. Then we'd go out to a street to test what I'd learned. Although no street was easy for a visually impaired person to cross, streets without crossing lines were especially dangerous. If I wandered off course, I could walk into oncoming traffic, never reach the other side, or get hit by a car.

At intersections he taught me not to get distracted by the sounds of trucks beeping, radios playing, or the exhaust fumes. Instead he taught me how to listen until I could hear each lane of cars and determine whether those cars were stopped, driving across the intersection, or making a left turn. "When you hear the parallel traffic next to you start moving, just step off and walk across in a straight line," said Jon. "Use your cane as a feeler until you find the curb on the other side. Stay focused on your goal and don't get distracted."

By the time I was four and a half, I was crossing busy six-lane intersections while Jon stood back and watched. But Jon also told me what to do if I started to feel lost. "If you ever get to a place where you feel uncomfortable, or you don't know where you're going, you should go back to your starting place and try again." That advice might seem mundane to the average sighted person. But to a little kid, knowing I could always make it back to where I'd started gave me the courage to take the first step.

As a preschooler, I naturally reached up to hold the hand of the person walking with me. But as I grew older and got taller, I learned that wasn't the safest way to be led. Instead I learned to hold on to my guide's elbow. Since the elbow was located closer to the guide's body, I was less likely to run into something. Hanging on that way also left the guide's hands free for holding a purse or opening a door.

I would rest my fingertips lightly on my guide's elbow and follow his or her movements. Through my fingertips, I could feel when my guide stopped, started, turned, or pivoted. My years of classical piano training had helped me develop extremely sensitive fingers. New guides were often surprised that I didn't keep a death grip on them or that they didn't have to hold their arms in some stiff, awkward position.

Most sighted people aren't used to taking up twice their normal width when walking, so if my guide wasn't careful, they could run me off the sidewalk or inadvertently walk me into low-hanging tree branches or other protrusions. Jon taught me that even with a guide, I also needed to use my cane to protect myself.

~

My parents took it upon themselves to learn as much as they could about O&M training techniques, and by the time I was at ASU, my parents handled all my O&M training. After the schedule came out each semester, Mom or Dad would take me to campus and orient me on how to get to each building. Learning to navigate a large campus with multiple buildings and more than sixty thousand students was no small task.

I always started by understanding the lay of the land. For me, it was a matter of memorizing how far to walk in one direction, or how to use my cane to track a border until I ran into a physical landmark such as a curb, a fountain, or a set of stairs. Then I'd have to memorize what came next. For one class, I might walk down the sidewalk from the parking lot until I came to the second intersecting sidewalk where I took a right. I then would walk a little further until my cane hit the steps of the building. At the top of five steps, I would enter through the door and turn right. I'd track the left wall, and when it opened into another hallway, I'd take a left. My classroom was the third door on the left.

If I continued down the hall, there would be a men's room and water fountain on the right.

Once I mastered the basics, I learned the details of how many floors were in a building, what the seating arrangement was like in an auditorium, and other specifics, like where the trash cans were located. It usually only took my parents guiding me through each area two or three times before I had it memorized.

But living alone in London would present challenges on a whole new level. Even the simplest things, like reading a bill, knowing how much to pay, and where to send the check would be difficult. Most of my living expenses—food, housing, and utilities—would be streamlined through Goodenough College. But there would still be other things I'd have to learn how to pay for. The obvious things, like books, involved trips to campus. But the less obvious, like new electronics, train cards, or tickets to concerts, meant navigating to unfamiliar places and figuring it out as I went.

In addition, there were also everyday things most people took for granted, like having a barber, knowing what hours banks were open, where to find a library, and what was located in each aisle of the grocery store. I would have to learn to navigate those places on my own.

~

After helping me move in, my family went to a nearby hotel. Alone in my room at Goodenough College, I could faintly hear the sounds of London through my open window. The sounds of the city were a reminder that my dreams were coming true. From inside the college, I heard the unfamiliar noises of people in the hall, doors opening and closing, and creaky floors. The noises didn't bother me, rather, the cacophony seemed like a musical accompaniment to my dreams—not only my dreams as I slept, but also my dreams for my future.

I slept well, and the next morning I woke with a sense of expectation. I jumped out of bed and threw on my clothes. I was full of energy and couldn't wait to get started. But I couldn't just take off and run down the streets of London like I used to run down the beach in California. First I had to get some help.

The plan was to meet my family at nine o'clock in the reception area of the college. But I was so energized I couldn't wait. Using my cane to guide me, I took the elevator down from the third story and exited on the main floor where I walked past the security desk and out the large doors onto Mecklenburgh

Square. Because the square was sheltered from the busy streets nearby, I didn't hear cars or pedestrians—only birds and insects as they greeted the new morning. The moist smell of the morning dew still lingered, but the warmth of the sun told me it wouldn't be there long. Somewhere a bell chimed nine o'clock and, right on schedule, I heard the voices of my family as they turned the corner.

The first order of business was to open a bank account so I could cash my stipend check, but when we tried, I was told I couldn't open a bank account until I had a cell phone. So we went to the cell phone store only to be told that I had to have a bank account to get a cell phone. We were literally caught between a rock and a hard place—or in this case, a bank and a cell phone company. Finally, after bringing in a copy of my university acceptance letter, my passport, and proof of residence, I was allowed to open a bank account and purchase a cell phone. During our outing, Mom and Dad taught me marketplace skills, such as how to tell the difference between various denominations of British coins and bills by feeling the texture and size of each.

Then, using my class and lesson schedule as a guide, Mom and Dad helped me get oriented on each campus I would need to visit as well as how to make my way between them. It was great having my parents as my guides because they would point out helpful things that an O&M instructor wouldn't know, such as the locations of my favorite kinds of restaurants. But we also needed to use the services of a professional O&M instructor who was familiar with some of the distinctive features of London.

～

The Marshall program recommended a woman named Esther as my O&M instructor. The first thing Esther taught me was that London had an ingenious way of helping blind people cross the street. When I walked around other cities, in addition to listening to traffic patterns, certain intersections were equipped with a beeping sound. These sounds were used to help a blind person know that the light had turned. But not all street crossings had the beeping noise, and when they did, the sound wasn't standard between cities. In London, Esther showed me that when I pushed the button for the light to change, I could reach under the box and feel a screw that rotated. No one would ever know it was there unless they were told. After the light turned, the screw would spin, and that's how I knew it was safe to cross. It was especially helpful at noisy and crowded crosswalks.

Esther spent a lot of time teaching me how to navigate the five subway stations I'd use the most. Tube stations posed unique challenges. It was always difficult for me to walk through a crowded room that didn't have square walls or angles to track with my cane. When that room was the size of a Tube station, it was nearly impossible. Some of the Tube stops had odd-shaped walls, and when the room got crowded, I could easily become disoriented. Esther taught me how to use auditory cues where physical markers weren't as accessible. She showed me how to enter a station and listen for the sounds of other people going in and out of the turnstiles. Once I identified the sound of the turnstiles, I could move toward the entrance.

Locating the right train required a different navigational process at each of the stations. Esther taught me how to find my way to the train I needed by memorizing each step along the way. In one station, I had to walk along a curved wall that opened into a hallway. But that wasn't the hallway I needed, so I had to walk past it and find the wall on the other side. Then, using that wall, I could track it to another corridor that branched to the right. From there, I took a hallway on the left and went down three escalators to the train, which would arrive on my left.

Once I had several routes completely memorized, I could build upon what I already knew. Within the first few weeks of school, I became comfortable going to new stations on my own. As my music research picked up during the year, I often needed to travel to other schools or libraries across the city to get books. And of course, taking advantage of the cultural opportunities London offered meant expanding my geographical boundaries to include museums, concert halls, theaters, and restaurants.

When my bills came, I studied them hard the first time, running my adaptive magnifying glass across the paper trying to find the important information. Then I'd remember how they were laid out for next time. That way I could quickly locate the amount owed without having to scan the entire bill each month. If I needed a phone number, there was a main desk downstairs and I could call them and they would look it up for me.

I could go where I needed to go and complete any necessary transactions. I had learned the ins and outs of my new city, how the Tube system worked, and the layout of the campus and neighborhoods where I'd spend most of my time. Within weeks I was completely self-sufficient and able to handle everything on my own. Although I made lots of friends, I never had to ask one of them to take me somewhere. If I needed to go, I did it by myself.

~

Before my parents left London, there was one more important thing to do—find a doctor so I could have regular testing. My creatinine level had been an all-time high of 4.7 on the day we visited Dr. Grant, but I'd had one more test done before I left the States, and the level had dropped down to 4.4. The lower number seemed to confirm the decision to go. Though I would head back to the States for Christmas and Easter breaks, I would still need at least monthly testing. We found a hospital with lab services where I could get that done, and before my parents left, we set up an appointment to schedule my testing visits.

The hospital was a study in contrasts. The halls were a crisp white, and the bright tile floor gleamed as though lit from beneath. The place seemed so shiny and freshly cleaned that it should have been a happy place. But I knew there was pain and suffering hidden behind each patient's door. It was a metaphor for my own life. I was so happy and excited to think of the endless possibility London held for me on the outside, but somewhere inside of me darkness still loomed in my kidneys.

We met the doctor and his staff. One of the nurses was a kind woman who would be assisting me when I came back to take blood and urine tests. When she found out I was a Marshall Scholar and a musician, she asked a lot of questions. She was very chatty. As we finished the appointment and she led us to the door, she said, "I hope it doesn't happen, but if you have to go on dialysis, or if you need anything else major done, don't do it here in London. Go back to the United States and have it done there."

It was a scary thought. And advice I prayed I would never have to heed.

~

Saying good-bye to my parents and Katelyn the night before they left was hard. I'd never been separated from them for such a long period, and I was going to miss them terribly. My parents and my siblings were the first people I wanted to talk to when something good or bad happened. They were the ones I wanted to share the details of my life with, and I knew that living an ocean away, things would be different. Though we would still be close, we wouldn't have the level of intimacy we'd all been used to. But I also knew this was exactly what they had raised me to do—to go out into the world, pursue my dreams, and not let anything stop me.

People who live the life they dream about are people who aren't afraid to take chances, regardless of what obstacles stand in their way. Although I still made mistakes and had moments of confusion, living on my own in London gave me proof of what I'd always believed. With enough support and preparation, and with God's blessing, I was capable of doing anything I dreamed.

CHAPTER 13

The Rich Life

I've seen the good, the bad, the ugly
Every horizon changes, people come and go
One day the sun shines down upon me
The very next I see my shadow start to grow
—FROM "THE GOOD, THE BAD, THE UGLY," SCOTT MACINTYRE

Yonty Solomon, a professor at the Royal College of Music in London, was nearly seventy years old when I began piano lessons with him. His student-teacher lineage traced back to Chopin and Liszt, which was one reason I had hoped to study with him. But Yonty's connection to fame wasn't purely classical. He had consulted on two high-profile films, one starring Shirley MacLaine, and the other, Hugh Grant. He was also a childhood friend of Elton John's. Yonty was born and raised in South Africa, the youngest of seven children born to Lithuanian immigrants. By the time we worked together, he had been living in London for many years and his British accent was strong.

Yonty demanded from his students a total commitment to learning. At the same time, he seemed open to musical and artistic expressions other than those indicative of classical music. Perhaps it was because he knew so much about the arts in general, or perhaps it was because he had played boogie-woogie and jazz since the age of sixteen, but Yonty was very different from my other classical piano professors. Unlike the formal musical terms used by Dr. Cosand during a lesson at ASU, Yonty preferred colorful metaphors. Instead of saying "Try to soften the peripheral notes so the melody can stand out more clearly," he would say, "Scott, we need to play this section like a boat rocking on the water. Yes, and now we hear a church bell in the distance."

After studying with him for only a few weeks, I wanted to play him some of my pop music, but I was concerned about how he would receive it. There could be consequences if Yonty didn't like it. None of my piano teachers so far had been truly supportive of my pop music interests; their reactions had ranged from disinterested to miffed that I'd waste my time with such "ear candy." Even the teachers who pretended to like it seemed disappointed—as though I betrayed them by playing something other than classical. I had to wait for the right moment with Yonty and hope for the best.

About a month into my lessons, I came in and sat down at the piano like I always did. But on that day, Yonty seemed to be in an especially good mood. Instead of getting right down to business, he said, "Play me something I haven't heard yet. Something you're working on."

This is my chance, I thought.

"This probably isn't what you were thinking," I said, "but it's one of my originals." I played and sang one of my newest pop pieces. I'd never sung for Yonty before. Though he didn't try to stop me, he also didn't give me any encouragement while I played. When I finished I decided to go for broke and segued into another piece. After that, I folded my hands and waited for what would come next.

I didn't have to wait long.

"I love it!" Yonty said, drawing out the word *love* to emphasize his reaction.

And I could tell he sincerely did. I was so relieved. At every lesson from then on, in addition to my classical pieces, Yonty asked me to play more "jazz"; that's what he called all my pop music. Some days he'd just listen, and other days he'd offer suggestions. One day I played him a couple of new songs I was working on, and he stopped me and said, "Wait here. I'll be right back."

I could hear him pick up his phone and dial a number.

"Kay? I have a student in my studio right now, and you really must hear his jazz!" There was a pause and then, "Good! His name is Scott MacIntyre. I'll tell him you'll be in touch."

When Yonty got off the phone, he explained that he'd called Kay Burley, one of the most popular talk show hosts on Sky News Europe, the European equivalent of CNN or FOX. She called me, and a few weeks later, I appeared as a guest on her show.

Yonty was the first classical piano professor who was supportive of my pop interests. He seemed to think I could have it all musically—that my "jazz" wasn't a hindrance from my classical studies. His support and encouragement were priceless, and I learned so much from him while I was in London.

∽

Goodenough College turned out to be the rich experience I had hoped for. My days were filled with deep conversations that not only stimulated my thinking but made me more culturally sensitive to those around me. It was a new experience for me to have close friends from countries whose governments weren't necessarily on good terms with mine. But my peers at Goodenough were brilliant and informed people, and I respected them all. Our conversations changed the way I looked at the world.

I loved the meals at Goodenough, and through the mealtime conversations, I met dozens of new friends. We would hang out together in London, see West End shows, attend concerts, and try out new restaurants. One of our favorites was a thriving restaurant called Ciao Bella. The place was packed with people until well after eleven o'clock at night. It was run by an Italian family, and their pastas were the best I had ever tasted in my life. I loved the *penne alla arrabiata*, which they brought to the table on a large plate with the spicy sauce still steaming. I became a regular at Ciao Bella, and when the owners found out I was a musician, they started to give me free meals if I played their old upright piano and sang.

Some nights I practiced at an upright piano in the basement, working on a classical piece all by myself. But other times I wanted to hear the grand piano echo in the large common room and I didn't care who heard me practice. The common room was also one of my favorite places to sing. That's where I was practicing a concerto one fall night when I heard someone in heels walk across the wood floor and stop near the piano. When I finished the final glissando, my friend Celine said, "Bravo!" We talked for a few minutes and then she asked, "So, are you working on any new songs?"

Celine was one of my dearest friends in London, and the reverberant sound of my voice and the grand piano echoing through the halls always seemed to draw her away from her studies. "Have you heard this one?" I might ask before I played and sang the chorus of my latest song.

When my friends learned I was writing pop music, they encouraged me to share it with them. I loved it when they gave me feedback. It was always so interesting to get an international perspective on the words and music as I was writing. Despite so much cultural diversity among my friends, it was amazing how we could find a common language in pop music. Our shared love of song and its ability to express emotion affirmed something I'd thought about and experienced for many years—music had the ability to transform people, and to engage them on a deeper level than almost anything else. Had I been studying economics or biology I doubt that I would have made friends as fast as I did, or that we would have grown as close as we did. Those friends certainly wouldn't have stood around my pile of textbooks and said, "Did you come up with any new ideas today?"

One day I played my song "Stranger Things" for Celine, and then I asked her how she liked it.

"I like the music, but I don't think I get the lyrics. Shouldn't it be 'sadder things,' not 'stranger things'?"

"It's an expression that people use . . . 'stranger things have happened.'"

"What does it mean?"

Celine spoke excellent English, but her native language was French, so she wasn't familiar with all of the idioms, metaphors, and clichés.

"Well, take us for example. Although it's unlikely you and I would ever become more than friends, stranger things than that have happened, so it's possible."

"Oh, I see now. I like it!"

There was a vibrant music community at Goodenough. Students got together and formed orchestras, ensembles, and bands. We would gather in one of the college's many common areas and give concerts for the whole college. My friends influenced me and helped me develop not just musically but also as an artist. I experimented with the way I played the piano. Sometimes I played it to sound like pop rock and other times I gave it more of a jazz feel. Something about being in London had energized my creativity. During the day I studied the classics and did research on dead composers, but at night I came alive writing pop songs and sharing them.

And the more I wrote, the more easily new songs came to me. In many ways, I got writing songs down to a science. If I heard something in conversation that caught my attention and it made a great hook line, I would instantly hear a melody in my head. That was the moment of inspiration. From that point, I could systematically figure out what the song should be about, how to say it, and what it should sound like. I would be riding on the Tube in London and come up with a great hook, and by the time I made it back home, I had the song completely written in my mind. The hook line for one of the songs on my

Heartstrings album, "The Good, the Bad, the Ugly," came to me in the back of a London taxicab. I kept singing the one line over and over, and when I got home later that day, I planted myself at one of the basement practice room pianos until I finished the song.

One day I heard someone walk by my room. He was talking on the phone and said, "Yeah, we'll just keep the lines open." It dawned on me that the phrase could be a perfect song title, and almost immediately I started singing, "We'll keep the lines open . . . ," and as the melody developed, I filled in sounds for the words I hadn't yet written. "We'll keep the lines open, da da da da da da." I continued to hum the melody as I thought about the lyrics.

I knew the song should be about the importance of communication—it could have been one of my theme songs. It seemed that before I ever got into a relationship with a girl, we'd have a problem communicating. I would like her from a distance but say nothing. By the time I worked up enough courage to share my feelings with her, she would just want to be friends. Then because I had shared so freely, she'd feel awkward and embarrassed and it wasn't even possible to be friends. If getting into a relationship was that difficult, I could only imagine how important it was that both parties clearly communicated their feelings *within* a relationship. In fact, if one or both parties felt that they couldn't share their feelings in a way that was open, honest, and safe, what was the point of the relationship?

Within a few minutes I had the chorus:

> *We'll keep the lines open*
> *So both of us know when*
> *It's time to move on with our lives*
> *We're better off knowing*
> *Where romance is going*
> *We'll keep the lines open tonight*

During the next couple of hours, I went on to write the verses of "Keep the Lines Open" which would later appear on my *Somewhere Else* CD.

Living in Arizona, certain aspects of each day were similar, and so were most of my conversations. If I wasn't talking to my family, I was hanging out with many of the same friends I'd had since I was fourteen, or getting lunch with the same classmates at ASU. Each semester at ASU was scheduled class by class, hour by hour, and I knew what to expect each day. But in London, no two days were the same. For the first time in my life, I had the freedom to come and go as I pleased without having to rely on a driver. I was meeting new people every day. And the academic environment was largely one of self-guided research. The novelty of being in a new place and not having a highly structured routine sparked my creativity and caused me to write and compose so much faster than I ever had.

~

There were so many churches in London that were on fire for Christ. They were growing numerically and spiritually as they reached out in love to the communities around them. I was pleased to discover that Hillsong, the large Australian church, had a ministry in London, and I attended several other churches that reminded me of Scottsdale Bible Church, my home church since I'd moved to Arizona.

Even Goodenough College had a small, but very active, Christian community. Morrie Brown, the college's chaplain, held services in a small chapel off the London House courtyard every Sunday. Several of us also attended a men's Bible study he led. I liked Morrie. He was committed to Christ and to sharing God's love with everyone he met. He exposed me to new ideas about baptism and challenged my thinking in ways that deepened my faith.

Morrie lived in a chaplain's house near Mecklenberg Square. It was a two-story house, and we would meet for Bible study on the second floor. Morrie took us through several books of the Bible, passage by passage. But instead of teaching us everything he knew, or sharing information from one of the many commentaries he possessed, he left it up to us to learn on our own and then share what we discovered. We were responsible for figuring out what a passage meant, and how it related to the rest of the chapter, to the Bible as a whole, and to our lives.

Eight to ten guys attended on any given night. During the year, we all grew very close. They were humble men doing their best to seek the Lord and to care for each other. I became especially close to Jay Choi, the helicopter pilot and Marshall Scholar I first met in Washington. Early on I confided in Jay about my kidney failure. Each time I made a trip back to the States to have some tests done, I asked him to pray for me. Even if I didn't talk about it, he would bring it up. He always wanted to know how I was doing. Sometimes the two of us prayed together, and sometimes Morrie would invite the whole group to pray for me.

Although I was still under a medical cloud, I didn't spend much time dwelling on it. But during the times I did, it was great to have friends who helped me deal with the unknown.

Some of the most intimate relationships of my life were formed with those godly Christian men. Spiritually, I grew more while I was in London than I ever had. I even found myself talking about my faith with friends of other religions and discussing our similarities and differences over dinner. Those who weren't believers could tell there was something different about me, and they often asked me questions about my faith and what I believed. Alone in my room at night, I found myself praying for them and for other friends who didn't know Jesus. The more I prayed for the faith of others, the more mine grew. While I was in London, I saw four of my closest friends become Christians. They were the last people I would have expected to follow Christ, but by then, I'd learned that London was a very spiritual place where both Christ and Christianity were very much alive.

And so was I.

I'd never had so much freedom, creative stimulation, and spiritual growth. It was a rich life indeed. And despite my kidney failure, I was committed to living every moment to its fullest while I could.

CHAPTER 14

Unexpected Loss

This song is a memory of you
How long will I miss one I thought I'd never lose?
Suddenly the world around feels like it's wrong
Cause you will never get to hear this song
—FROM "THIS SONG," SCOTT MACINTYRE

As fall turned to winter, the sounds and smells of London changed. Christmas music spilled onto the streets as retailers tried to attract holiday shoppers. Restaurants served thick, hearty-smelling soups that encouraged passersby to come in from the cold. Pubs seemed noisier, as if everyone who entered had brought a group of friends with them. While walking through the city at night, I got a pinhole view of Harrod's Christmas lights, and during the day, I took in the smell of cider and roasted nuts from the Christmas market in Hyde Park. Church bells marked time with their usual regularity, but now they seemed to have a prominent part in a seasonal chorus of bells.

I loved the atmosphere of London at Christmastime, but I was also looking forward to going home on break. I had been writing my friends at home and telling them what I was experiencing and how much I was looking forward to seeing them. One of those friends was Christina. I'd had a crush on her since we first met, when we were both performing in the musical *The Music Man*. We had spent a lot of time together talking backstage during rehearsals and performances and we became close friends. I had been interested in taking it further, but she wasn't.

At least that's what she told *me*.

I knew she had some feelings for me, but it often felt like she was denying her true feelings. So I did what I always did when I was trying to sort out relationship issues—I wrote a song about it. The summer after graduation, I recorded a song called "How Long Will You Deny." While in London, I e-mailed it to a couple of her girlfriends I knew and mentioned that Christina had inspired the song in hopes that they would tease her about it. Maybe that would get things started between us again.

~

I had stayed in contact with my mentor, Laurie Z., and I thought now might be a good time to ask for some of her insightful and helpful feedback. The last song she had heard was "No Fear" from my contemporary Christian CD *My Guarantee*, and I felt I had made a lot of progress since then. So I e-mailed her and brought her up to date on all that had happened since I last saw her, including graduation, the Marshall Scholarship, and my performance studies in London.

Laurie was one of the few people who understood my interest in both classical and pop music, so I told her how I continued to write music in lots of genres including pop, rock, adult contemporary, and even punk. She had encouraged me to join Taxi Music, a service that sent out listings on behalf of publishers and labels that were searching for new music. Musicians like me subscribed to it, and if we had a song that was a fit for one of the listings, we could submit it for a small fee. If the label or publisher were interested, they would negotiate a contract directly with the composer.

"I have finally joined Taxi," I wrote. "I've been getting some great feedback. Ironically, the first 'forward' I got was for some punk rock tracks I recently produced." I knew she'd like hearing that; she always celebrated my successes. I told about the MacIntyre Family Singers CD and asked her if I could send her a copy and perhaps a current recording of one of the pop songs I had written.

A few days later she responded. She said she'd been traveling and was sorry to have been out of touch. She told me how proud she was of everything I had accomplished and that she would love to hear anything I had recorded. "I'm sure it's wonderful," she wrote. "Will try to write more when I'm home. Please give my very best to your family, and wishing you all a wonderful Christmas and New Year."

She ended it as she ended all her notes. "Best always, Laurie."

I e-mailed her a copy of "How Long Will You Deny," the song about Christina. I knew it would take her at least a couple of days before she could listen to it, and perhaps as much as a month if she was on the road. But I could always count on Laurie Z. If she said she'd listen to it, she would.

∼

The night of my ASU graduation party, I had spent some time talking with my uncle Matt. He worked as a director of photography in Los Angeles, and he knew a lot of interesting people. During the party, he asked about my London plans and about my hopes for after that.

I told him about my academic ambitions but also told him how I dreamed about making it as a recording artist in the pop music industry. Thinking Matt might know someone who could help me, I asked if he knew anyone in the music business.

"I can introduce you to Parker. He's a friend of mine and works in post-production. Really cool guy. And he knows a ton of people, so I'm sure he could help."

A few weeks before I left for London, Parker called. He told me a little bit about his job and the kinds of people he worked with. I learned that he had a hand in many different aspects of film music, from placing popular songs in films to working with orchestral composers. "That's really interesting," I said. "But that's not where I see myself. I see myself as more of a touring performer. Do you know anyone who works with that side of the industry?"

"In that case, you've got to meet Jerry Lindahl. He's with Bill Silva Management and works with artists such as Jason Mraz. Send me your bio and your best song and I'll pass it on to him."

I sent him "Lost in a Meadow."

After I arrived in London, Parker e-mailed to say he'd passed on my info and song to Jerry and that Jerry would be contacting me. But weeks, then months, went by and I didn't hear anything. Since he was my best music industry contact, I didn't want to let the opportunity to speak with him slip by. I found Jerry's number at Bill Silva Management and tried to call him several times. But with the time difference, I never could connect with him. The best I could do was leave a message.

So after e-mailing Laurie Z., I also e-mailed Jerry and reminded him that a few months earlier Parker had sent my bio and a song. I also let him know that I had several new songs I could send if he was interested.

But unlike Laurie, there was no reply from Jerry.

∼

Christmas was my first trip back home since moving to London, and it was great to spend time with my family. Katelyn wanted me to play every song I'd written in London, and Todd and I enjoyed hanging out and comparing notes about ASU. One day I went to campus with Todd and I stopped by the music building. I saw Walter Cosand, my piano professor, and told him about the research I was doing and my lessons with Yonty. "That's great," he said, in his usual understated way. I could tell he was pleased.

I also saw a few friends and spent some time hanging out with Christina. I found out she had heard "How Long Will You Deny," and she seemed to be flattered. But that's as far as it went.

The time passed quickly, and soon I had to fly back to London to start my second trimester.

~

I wasn't in London long before I was headed back to the States, however. In February, Learning Ally (formerly known as Recording for the Blind & Dyslexic) had awarded me a generous scholarship. Each year they chose three college students from a national applicant pool who demonstrated academic excellence in spite of learning challenges. I felt so honored to be chosen. Unfortunately, with the start of classes, I couldn't attend the awards ceremony. So in my absence, Mom and Dad flew to Washington, DC, and accepted for me. That night they e-mailed me a picture of them accepting my award while holding a picture of me.

A few weeks after the ceremony, the winners were invited to the White House to meet First Lady Laura Bush. I was able to work a break into my schedule so I could make a quick trip there and back. Mom flew to DC and met me at the airport and then went to the White House with me. I wore my good suit and even had my curly hair slicked back.

We were ushered into the China Room, a small rectangular room used to display the growing collection of White House china. Almost every past president was represented. As we entered, we were greeted by polite waiters dressed in dark suits with white gloves. They carried silver platters of tea sandwiches and drinks. I thought back to all the times Mom had encouraged me with my table manners joking, "You can't eat like that if you're going to eat in the White House someday." As we waited for Mrs. Bush, my pulse quickened as the reality of where I was and who I was about to meet slowly sunk in. Mom read the descriptions by each set of china and described all the colors and patterns of each set to me.

Then we were lead into the Diplomatic Reception Room, an oval room used to greet visitors and the place of Roosevelt's famous fireside chats.

Then Mrs. Bush entered. She was soft spoken—with the same familiar and genteel Texas drawl I recognized from TV—and extremely gracious. She told us that as a former librarian, she knew how important the work of Learning Ally was to people with visual and processing disabilities. I couldn't have agreed more. Learning Ally had provided me with most of my classroom materials over the years, including many of my college textbooks. Before we left, the First Lady posed with my mom and me in front of the famous fireplace underneath the iconic portrait of George Washington, the one that inspired his likeness on the dollar bill. It was a surreal moment. I never thought I would be handing the First Lady a copy of my latest CD!

Afterward my mom and I were treated to dinner, and the next morning, I was on a flight back to London. It was a quick trip but worth every moment.

～

My next trip home was during the trimester break for Easter. English schools were on a trimester system, with the first one starting in fall, the second one in January, and the third just after Easter. During my year in London, I made a dozen transatlantic trips, more than half of them by myself. Flying alone was becoming just one more step in my journey of independence.

～

I did my best to not think about the kidney failure when I was in London, but I couldn't help but be reminded about it when I was back in the States. We used my return trips as opportunities to visit my doctor and see how I was doing. Though my family and I continued to pray that the disease would just go away, we also investigated anything that might help restore function to my kidneys. In addition to praying for healing, we also prayed for wisdom for the doctors who continued to seek answers on my behalf.

My creatinine levels seemed to move around a bit. In October my level had risen to 5.1, but by December 7, it had dropped back down to 4.0—the lowest it had been in a long time. By Christmas it had risen to 5.3. The doctors suggested eating less protein and more raw foods, and when they tested me a week later, it had dropped back to 4.9. I was still holding there in mid-January before I returned to London. Though I had tested high a few times, I was reassured that the numbers always seemed to drop back to the fours.

I hadn't experienced a miraculous healing, but neither did I sit around and think the worst. During the third trimester in London, I did what I'd done all year; I just enjoyed being in the moment, and I hung on to hope wherever I found it—in my music, in my new friends, in decreasing creatinine levels, and in my faith.

~

I woke up one morning in May and knew it was going to be a beautiful day. Lying in bed, I could smell the fresh air and hear birds singing in the court-yard. I'd opened the window in my room the night before to cool it down from the encroaching warmth of spring. Now I could detect the brilliant rays of sunshine bursting through the window and filling the room with light.

But that bright and shiny morning stood in huge contrast to my mood. I felt heaviness in my chest and an emotion that could only be described as grief. It was an intense sadness that I couldn't seem to shake.

And I knew what caused it.

A bad dream about Laurie Z. had woken me during the middle of the night. I'd dreamed that she had died. Of course, I knew it wasn't real; Laurie Z. wasn't that old, and she was in good health the last time I saw her. But the feeling of loss stayed with me through the night. I woke feeling tired rather than refreshed.

As I got up and got dressed, I thought about the last time I had heard from Laurie Z. It had been at least four months since I'd sent her a copy of "How Long Will You Deny." It wasn't like her to take so long to reply. I made a mental note to e-mail her soon.

After my classes and lesson, I took a walk through Bloomsbury and decided to stop at Ciao Bella. I wasn't hungry enough for my usual dinner portion, so I just ordered a salad and sat at one of the outside tables to enjoy the day. I had just finished eating when my cell phone rang. It was Mom. "I have to tell you something," she said. "I got an e-mail from Taxi Music today." Mom often got excited when she read something that she thought was a fit for one of my songs, but by the tone of her voice, I could tell that wasn't why she was calling me now.

"The e-mail included some news about independent artists. There was something in it about Laurie Z., and I thought you should know."

"About Laurie Z.? What did it say?"

"It said that she passed away."

I tried to silently process what she'd just told me, but it didn't make sense. Slowly I replied, "What? How?"

"Apparently she's had cancer for the past two years and it finally took her."

"Wait . . ." I did a quick calculation in my head. "If she had it for two years, that means she had cancer when she was at our house for dinner."

"I know, Scott. It's really sad."

"But . . . she didn't say anything about it . . . and neither did her husband . . ."

"That's the thing, Scott. Apparently, her husband died too. From a heart attack, *six months ago.*"

It was too much to take in. Laurie and I had exchanged e-mails just four months ago. She didn't even mention her husband's death. Maybe she didn't want me to worry—Laurie Z. was one of the most positive people I'd ever met in my life—but still, she could have said something.

It was hard to imagine all that Laurie must have gone through. But in a small way, I felt a certain bond with her memory, as I now treaded in my own sea of uncertainty. I had never told Laurie about my kidney failure. I didn't have any answers yet, and so it was the kind of thing I didn't tell many of my industry contacts—I didn't want them to see me as incapable in any way. Maybe Laurie felt the same way. I thought about my dream from the night before. It wasn't the kind of dream I'd thought would come true, but now I realized God used it to prepare me for this devastating news.

I paid my bill, and left Ciao Bella to walk back to Goodenough. Though I was shocked by the news of both Laurie and her husband, I didn't cry. Being in London, I felt so removed from it all—like her death hadn't really happened. But still, I couldn't stop thinking about Laurie Z. Without her influence, I might never have released my first independent CD, or any of the ones that followed. It was Laurie's do-it-yourself attitude that helped inspire my independent spirit for music.

Back at Goodenough I headed into the old wood chapel that was a part of the quad. The chapel was very secluded, and it was my favorite place to go when I needed a quiet place to pray, think, or just be alone. The thick wood door creaked when I opened it and again when it closed slowly behind me. The sound of my cane sweeping across the uneven floorboards punctuated the silence. I inhaled the familiar smell of antiques and furniture polish as I made my way to the old upright piano in the back of the chapel. Some days when I was alone in the chapel, I softly played the piano but the dry acoustics in the room made each note much louder than seemed possible from such an old instrument.

On other days, I just kneeled in silent supplication, praying for whatever was on my heart. Sometimes it was a prayer for a friend or for those I knew who were sick or hurting. Other times it was a prayer for my exam, for my career, and even that I would somehow connect with Jerry Lindahl. I often prayed for my family, and occasionally, I prayed for my kidneys to be healed. The chapel was littered with my prayers like a street after a ticker-tape parade.

But on that day, I didn't pray.

I just sat quietly. I could have sat in any of the pews, but I chose a chair in the back of the room. I felt a stillness, almost a reverential silence, as if the room itself understood the sacredness of the burdens that were brought inside.

The next morning I woke up and went straight to the grand piano in the large common room. The news about Laurie was still heavy on my heart. I couldn't believe after so many years of knowing her—just like that—she was gone. I didn't know what to think or say, but I knew I had to try. As my fingers touched the keys, I instantly began to express my heart through music. I sat there for an hour, and when I got up, I had written a new song just for Laurie.

This Song

I just heard the news of late
Seems I lost a friend today
That's when it hit me
She had been with me from the start
Is it real? I forgot
Came to me as quite a shock
She was the reason
I started singin' from my heart
This song is a memory of you
How long will I miss one I thought I'd never lose?
Suddenly the world around feels like it's wrong
Cause you will never get to hear this song
You taught me how to live my life
To stand for what I know is right

Even when others
Are trying to cover up my eyes
I can't let it end this way
So much more I wanna say
Isn't it strange I knew you so well
But not at all
This song is a memory of you
How long will I miss one I thought I'd never lose?
Suddenly the world around feels like it's wrong
Cause you will never get to hear this song
Maybe if angels take the time to stop
And hear the church bells throng
Then if you listen you can hear
This song

I realized Laurie Z. would never hear "This Song." And she wouldn't be around to see me working out my dreams of a music career. But though she had died, she would always be with me. Laurie Z. would live on in the example and inspiration she'd given to me and to so many other independent musicians. In many ways, our music would always be a tribute to her life.

CHAPTER 15

California Dreaming

A day spent in paradise walking on a cloud
We were so high we were never coming down

—from "Never Tired," Scott MacIntyre

The school year was coming to an end, and I still hadn't connected with Jerry Lindahl from Bill Silva Management. With less than two months before I was scheduled to return to Arizona for the summer, I tried to call him one last time. Typically I tried to catch him in the morning, but this time I called late in the day, hoping I might still catch him in the office. Even so, I was still caught off guard when he answered.

"Hello?"

"Is Jerry Lindahl in?"

"This is Jerry. Who's calling?"

"Jerry? Hi! This is Scott MacIntyre. Parker Kann sent you my bio and a song I'd written."

"I'm on my way out. But I really want to talk to you. Can we try it another time?"

"Yeah, I can call back whenever it's good for you, or I can give you my number. I'm in London right now—"

"Are you going to be in Tuscany next week by chance?"

It was an odd question, but maybe that's the way they did things in high-powered music circles? "No, I'm sorry I won't be. But I will be in California later this summer. Maybe we could meet then?"

"Great! Let's do it. Call me when you're in town." *Click.* He was gone.

It was my first glimmer of hope that Jerry might actually be interested in me and my music. It wasn't much, but I was an optimist. All I needed were just the fumes of hopes to keep my dreams alive—and that's what Jerry had just given me.

~

As the school year drew to a close, everything went well academically. My stud-ies were wrapping up, I was giving lectures, and I was on target to get my master's degree—all I needed to do was finish my dissertation on Chopin. But I also needed to make a plan for next year's studies.

The Marshall Scholarship allowed me to study for two years (possibly three if I petitioned) in England, and I wanted to take advantage of all that it offered. But when Cambridge had rescinded their offer, I had switched my planned second year of studies to my first year. Now I didn't have a plan for my second year. It was time to look into what options were available.

I'd never felt right about the way things ended at Cambridge. Since I was now living in London, I thought that if I could meet with the Cambridge people in person, I could talk my way back in. I had a hunch they'd be willing to meet with me, and I believed I could change their mind about my abilities and qualifications. I also knew that some of the music department professors would be interested in my thesis research, so I contacted them.

To my surprise, they agreed to a meeting.

We met in a boardroom at the Faculty of Music building on the Cambridge campus. From what I could tell, it felt more like a classroom. The room was square and very stark with white walls and vertical shutters covering the win-dows. A long table with metal legs sat in the middle of the carpeted room. I had visited the campus before as a tourist, so the room stood out in its contrast to the ornate polished wood found in other parts of the university. We spent a little less than an hour together. I told them about my research on Chopin's Ballade No. 2 and how different performers interpreted it through their playing styles. They asked me questions about how I had learned to navigate London on my own and they wanted more information about my current class load and grades. By the end of the meeting, they simply said they would discuss the possibility of my joining them for the next school year. They promised to be in touch before I left for the States in a few weeks. The meeting concluded without an indication of what they were thinking.

I felt good about the meeting, but I tried not to get my hopes up. If noth-ing else, I believed I had done my best to convince them I was a good candidate for their university, but the decision was in their hands.

I needed to have another plan in case Cambridge didn't work out, so I also interviewed at Oxford. Leaving the Oxford interview was a completely differ-ent experience. I knew I had done well in the interview, and I could tell they were excited about my joining them. I was sure that I was in, but I wanted to wait for the letter so it would be official. I didn't want any surprises like the rescission letter I'd received last summer. But still, I had the strong sense that at least one of the schools would come through, and I felt relieved to have some options for the next year.

~

It was a busy spring. For my course work, I read through piles of literature about the psychology of performance and historical performance analysis. As the trimester drew to a close, I was also preparing for my final recital with Yonty, delivering some lectures, and finishing the research on my dissertation, which meant borrowing books from libraries located all over London. I was worn out.

One night I decided to take a break from all the work and head to Ciao Bella with a few friends. I ordered my usual—*penne alla arrabiata*. Though I enjoyed the food, I only ate half of it. I didn't notice that I hadn't eaten that much until the owner came over. "What's wrong?" he said. "You can't eat the whole pasta?"

"No, it was excellent, as usual. I'm just full for some reason," I replied.

I tried to think back. *Had I eaten a big lunch?* I didn't remember doing so, but I could have. I had a lot on my mind; I wasn't paying attention to the inconsequential.

Several times during the next few weeks, I ordered food that sounded good initially, but I was always too full to finish. It was as if I didn't have the capacity to eat as much as I once did. It was probably the stress.

~

As spring turned into summer and classes ended, I was also weighing a difficult decision. A few weeks earlier, an envelope had arrived from the Board of Graduate Studies at Cambridge University. It was a business-sized envelope, and as far as college acceptances go, that usually meant bad news. I slowly opened the envelope and pulled out the sheet that was on top. I anxiously scanned the letter with my magnifying glass until I found the opening line. One letter at a time I read: "We are pleased to inform you that you have been unconditionally accepted . . ."

Cambridge had finally accepted me! A few weeks earlier, I had received a similar letter from Oxford. I felt so honored to have received written offers from both Cambridge and Oxford, but that also left me with a dilemma. *Which one should I choose?* It wasn't a bad choice to have to make.

A year earlier, when Cambridge rescinded their offer, I had been so disappointed. But because of that decision, so many good things had happened. I had been able to study at Royal Holloway and the Royal Conservatory of Music. I'd studied with Yonty and been profiled on Sky News. I had made so many new friends and experienced so many new things, and they had all helped to feed my musical creativity as well as my social, emotional, and spiritual growth. Had I gone to Cambridge first, I likely would have spent that first year with my head buried in books rather than in performance.

I was so grateful for the year I'd spent living in London, and now I could say that I'd been admitted to *two* of the most prestigious universities in the world—Cambridge and Oxford. That wouldn't have happened had I gone to Cambridge the first year. I was proud of myself for having the tenacity to request that follow-up meeting. Had I not believed in myself, my last experience with Cambridge would have been that awful e-mail telling me I couldn't come.

After much thought and prayer, I decided to accept the Cambridge offer. Cambridge, with its castle-like buildings and rolling green hills, would be like living and working in a Renaissance painting. The beautiful River Cam ran through the town, and the area was lush with vegetation. Oxford also had a river, but the area had much more of an industrial feel than did the nature-rich Cambridge. I could now go home for the summer with the confidence that next year would be as meaningful and exciting as the past year had been.

With classes over, the pace of things slowed down. I had chosen to stay a few weeks longer to work on my research. My thesis wasn't due for a couple more months, and what I didn't finish in London, I planned to take home and finish over the summer. So during the day I worked extra hard, and at night, I hung out with friends before bidding them each farewell as they returned home to their country or headed off to new careers.

Saying good-bye was sad. We shared such close bonds, and I knew it was likely that we'd lose touch. Even if they would be returning for the next school year, I would be at Cambridge and wouldn't see them on a daily basis. I would miss them. My London friendships were some of the most intimate and creatively stimulating I'd ever had, and I prayed that our paths would cross again.

While in London I had studied voice in addition to piano. And I was writing and composing more than ever—but all in the pop genre. Not only was Yonty supportive, but my friends at Goodenough appreciated my voice and encouraged me to write more songs. For the first time in my musical career, I was surrounded by knowledgeable musicians who embraced my pop music interests.

In addition to the music on my computer, I'd brought four CDs with me to London: two by Jason Mraz, *Waiting for My Rocket to Come* and *Mr. A-Z*, Steven Curtis Chapman's *All Things New*, and Mark Schultz's *Stories & Songs*. I often fell asleep listening to one of those CDs. As a result, I was listening to more pop music than classical music, even though I studied classical piano every day.

For months I had considered moving away from classical and toward pop music as a career choice. Someday I wanted to get married and raise a family, and I couldn't help thinking that pop music would be more lucrative. I had witnessed a select few of America's well-known pianists play in major concert halls to very full crowds. But in many cases, I'd heard some of the best classical musicians in the United States, Canada, Austria, Prague, and England perform before an audience of twenty people or less who each paid only a few dollars to be there. There wasn't a lot of money in classical music, but there was huge competition. For every big name out there, there were dozens of lesser names who all played flawlessly while waiting to take their turn in the upper echelons of music royalty. Pianists knew that if they skipped practicing for a few days and their skills slipped even the slightest, the critics could be harsh.

When the hours a pianist spent practicing were divided by their income, I suspected most fast-food restaurant workers were paid more per hour. It took an incredible amount of practice to maintain proficient technique at the professional level, and even more passion to do it for little money or respect. There was constant pressure to always perform at the highest levels technically and emotionally. I couldn't imagine spending my life under that kind of pressure.

Music was how I expressed myself, but it seemed that classical piano was a bit like modern dance—people had to interpret the story of the piece—its message wasn't clear on its own. I didn't want to have to explain and defend my art; I wanted my music to speak for me and tell a story without explanation. Words and music together did that for me. Pop music could equally be understood by the educated and uneducated, and it could be transformational to all who heard it.

In London I witnessed the ability of pop music to tell a story and emotionally move my friends, patrons of the Italian restaurant, and audiences at my performances. The marriage of words and melody was very powerful. I felt a deep sense of pride when I could say, "That was my song. I wrote it." To me, it was much more gratifying than playing someone else's music.

When I played and sang, I felt that people instantly connected with me in ways that would otherwise take weeks of getting to know one another. Sharing my music was a relationship accelerant for anyone listening, but for me it was even more profound. My blindness had often created a distance between other people and me. Over the years I had worked hard to minimize that distance, by doing simple things like turning to look at the person who was speaking or holding my head up when I walked. But now I had found that pop music could do much of the work for me. My music allowed people to approach and connect with me in ways they otherwise might not have.

Pop music made me feel alive. In London I spent a lot of time thinking about where my heart was, and it wasn't with classical music. The dual track of pop and classical music had reached the fork in the road that many advisors said it would. It was time to commit all my efforts in one direction. And that was to be the best singer-songwriter I could be. I wasn't finished with academia just yet, but in my heart I had decided what kind of music I wanted to make—for the first time, pop music would take priority over classical. With that decision, I was one step closer to my dream of touring arenas and inspiring people with my songs.

~

A few weeks before I was scheduled to go home, my family came for one last visit. Todd hadn't been able to make it on the previous trips, so it was great to see him. He stayed in my dorm with me while everyone else stayed in the hotel. It was good to spend some time with my family—a reminder of the fun we'd have when I was home for the summer.

After they left, I made a few more visits to various libraries and got the materials I would need to take home with me. I only packed what I needed for the summer and left the rest of it behind in my room. My plan was to return a week before classes started and move it all to Cambridge.

It seemed fitting that I was leaving London alone. A year earlier I believed I could make it on my own. Now I had proved I could. But it was also a very sentimental time. I had never expected to make such close friends, grow so much

1. My first birthday—June 22, 1986.
2. Pool party! I loved the water.
3. My favorite place to be...in mom's arms, 6 months old.
4. I would lift each pumpkin to see how heavy it was.
5. Exhausted from running on the beach with mom.
6. Listening for hours to my cassettes and boom box, 1 year old.
7. My tactile world—feeling dirt.

1. Todd and I were ring bearers and mom was a bridesmaid in my aunt's wedding.

2. Christmas in Southern California.

3. The king and his court! We loved wearing costumes.

4. Baby Katelyn is born May 13, 1991. We all jumped on mom's bed in the delivery room.

5. Getting ready to dive in the pool with Todd, 4 years old.

6. I loved playing with my little sister Katelyn.

1. Playing songs with chords, 4 years old.

2. I was grateful to be on any stage, let alone the *American Idol* stage.

3. Writing songs again after my kidney transplant, before my catheter was removed in 2007.

4. First prize in songwriting competition, Toronto, Canada, with my music festival medals.

5. Lost in my music on the old ivory keyed upright piano.

6. Practicing for my first wedding performance in Redondo Beach, CA, at 6 years old.
   My two front teeth are still missing!

1, 2. Boogie board wars with Todd.

3. Traveling with my family, 11 years old: Arc de Triomphe—Paris, France.

4. Singing on the forest trails behind our house in Toronto.

5. Beautiful Redondo Beach sunsets.

6. Cast as Mayor Shinn in the *Music Man*.

7. First symphony performance at 15 years old.

1. So excited to be accepted to Oxford...

2. ...and Cambridge University for further graduate study.

3. Living in London, England, 20 years old.

4. Graduating from Arizona State University summa cum laude at 19 years old, minutes before I found out I had stage 4 kidney failure.

5. As the "outstanding graduate" I delivered the commencement speech.

6. Meeting First Lady Laura Bush at the White House in 2006.

To Scott MacIntyre With best wishes, Laura Bush

1. Skiing at Lake Tahoe with my family after my transplant.

2. MacIntyre Family Singers perform at the Kennedy Center in Washington, DC in 2008.

3. MacIntyre family, October 1991.

4. Thanksgiving in Scottsdale, AZ, after both of our transplants. We had a lot to be thankful for.

1. On tour bantering with the audience mid-way through my set.

2. Setting up in one of the fifty-two arenas on the *American Idol* tour.

3. Press and interviews in NYC following the tour.

4. Putting on my "in-ears" backstage with Todd.

5. Times Square as the *American Idol* tour rolled through NYC.

6. Getting dressed and just before going on stage.

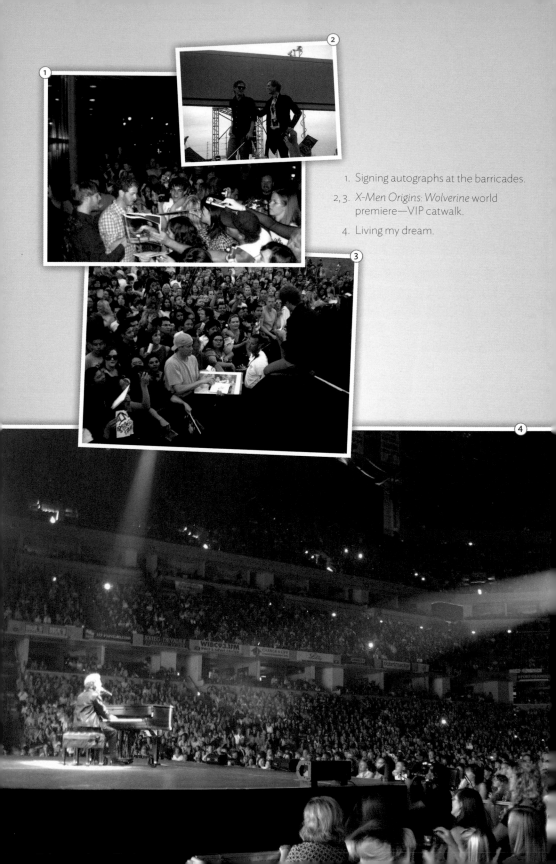

1. Signing autographs at the barricades.

2, 3. *X-Men Origins: Wolverine* world premiere—VIP catwalk.

4. Living my dream.

spiritually, or have such rich creative experiences. I wondered if those things could ever happen again. I was sad to leave, but I still left with the same sense of hope I had possessed when I arrived. In addition to a London Tube T-shirt, I took home a few other things I'd picked up in London—independence, validation, and a sense that I could overcome anything.

~

From London I flew straight to California for a family reunion. While there, I planned to perform a couple of concerts and, if everything went according to plan, finally meet with Jerry Lindahl.

My mom's grandmother was one of twelve children, and every four years her side of the family got together in a different location for a weekend-long celebration of family. The California reunion was crazy, noisy, and full of delicious food—everything you would expect when two hundred people who haven't seen each other for years spent time together.

After the reunion my family and I drove to central California for the Kingsbury Community Festival. We had hoped to have all of the MacIntyre Family Singers there to perform, but Todd was studying at the same summer music program I had attended several years earlier at Boston University Tanglewood Institute, so he couldn't join us. Still, Katelyn, Mom, and I had a great time performing before a crowd of thousands in the large park. On the way back to Los Angeles, I also performed at a couple of churches I had scheduled before I left London.

Our last days in California were spent back in Redondo Beach at my grandpa's house. While there we took a trip to Disneyland, which brought back a lot of homeschooling memories. Walking through the amusement park, I was reminded of all the times Mom had brought us there when we lived in California. We would come when everyone else was in school and Mom, always the teacher, would use the environment as teaching illustrations.

"Look at the architecture of the Indiana Jones ride," she'd say to Todd. "Now tell me what architectural features you see in the design."

We had gone on the Indiana Jones ride the day it opened. It was during the week, and there weren't a lot of people in line, so the Disneyland cast members spent time telling us how the ride was designed. Depending on the different routes and variables used in each ride sequence, they could create up to five thousand unique rides. One ride could simulate bad brakes and the next might have a bad engine. The cast members were enthusiastic about all the possible iterations. Mom was enthusiastic about all the possible math equations. "If each ride takes five minutes and you had a different ride every time, how long would it take to ride all five thousand versions?"

Now, standing in line for the Indiana Jones ride, I wasn't wondering about math equations. I was wondering about Jerry Lindahl and hoping he wasn't taking me for a ride. We were scheduled to meet the next morning before I headed back to Arizona, but he'd already cancelled two meetings since I'd been in California. If he cancelled again, it was likely we wouldn't be able to meet again for months, or until after I got back from England again a year later. Or it might not happen at all. Now that I had decided to pursue pop music, I needed to make the same kinds of connections in that field that I had already established in the classical world, and I was hoping and praying that Jerry would be one of them.

Around nine thirty that night, after a family dinner, my cell phone rang. It was Jerry. I nervously answered the phone, anticipating yet another cancellation.

"I know we talked about getting together tomorrow, but . . ." I held my breath. "I'd really have a lot more time if you could come over to my house right now."

He was in West Hollywood; we were in South Redondo Beach. It was at least a twenty-mile drive, and with traffic could easily take over an hour. I didn't care.

"Yeah! Let me check on it, but I think that would work. I'll call you right back."

I hung up the phone to make sure someone was available to drive me. When Mom offered, I called Jerry and told him we were on our way. My hair was a mess, and I hadn't shaved in a couple days, but I threw on a fresh shirt and we started driving.

We arrived at his house around ten thirty.

"I'm Jerry, c'mon in," he said, shaking my hand and guiding me inside the door. "The piano's over here." He made small talk as I walked with Mom to the piano and sat down. I ran my fingers over the keys to make sure I was squared off with middle C.

The first thing I noticed was that it was the *worst* piano I had ever played in my life. I had dealt with keys that stuck before, but this piano had entire notes that were missing! "Wow, this is some piano," I said as my fingers tripped over the holes where there should have been keys.

"Isn't it great?" said Jerry. "I actually watched my neighbor push this thing down the stairs of his house and into the front yard. He planned to leave it for the trash men to haul away, but I rescued it."

The missing keys were the self-respecting ones. The keys that were left didn't even sound like notes; they made ticking noises when I played them.

"Go ahead. You can play whenever you're ready."

I started by playing one of my new songs, "Keep the Lines Open," but instead of the accompaniment, all I heard was *bum, tick, tick, bum, tick, tick, bum.*

It had to be my worst performance ever. But for some reason, my playing fascinated Jerry. When I finished, he said, "You know, I'm trying to concentrate on your lyrics, but I keep getting distracted watching your fingers."

We moved to some couches in an adjoining room and Jerry continued talking. He told me a little about himself and his experience in the music business. Eventually the conversation turned to Jason Mraz.

"Actually, I've been listening to a lot of his music in London," I said.

"Well, Jason and I go way back. We used to be roommates," Jerry said. "I was around him when he was just starting out. We used to ship his CDs from the house when people ordered them from the website. That was before things really took off."

"Really? I knew that he was represented by Bill Silva management, but I didn't know Jason and you knew each other personally."

I admired Jason Mraz because he wrote all his own music and lyrics, and he was unique. When I heard Jason's song "The Remedy" on the radio for the first time, it helped me to see how one day my songs could fit onto a radio play list. Over the past few years several people had mentioned that there was something in my voice that reminded them of Jason Mraz—they described it as a similar warmth and flair when I sang. I took that as a huge compliment. It was hard to believe that I was now discussing his music in the living room of one of his best friends.

Too soon, it was time to leave. There were no promises about representation or management, but I think both Jerry and I felt a connection.

～

During the next few months, Jerry and I talked on the phone and e-mailed. In one of our conversations he admitted that before our first meeting, he hadn't taken time to look at my website and he had no idea I was blind until I stepped out of the car with my cane that night. To my surprise, he apologized for acting like a "typical Hollywood producer" and not giving me the time of day in the beginning. Though I hadn't noticed his attitude, his words meant a lot. He told me he was trying to change.

As our friendship grew, it seemed our relationship was having some kind of effect on him. One day he called and said he wanted to give up swearing. "You just make me want to be a better person," he said.

Meeting Jerry seemed to once again validate my hopes and dreams. If my songs could inspire pop music insiders like Jerry, I knew I could inspire large numbers of fans.

Everything was falling into place. I had the summer off to enjoy my family and soon I would return to another creative and stimulating year at Cambridge. And now, for the first time, I felt like I knew someone in the music industry who could actually help me achieve my dreams of becoming a recording artist and sharing my music on a larger level.

Life couldn't have been better. Once again, I was on the highest of highs.

CHAPTER 16

Running out of Time

Today I may say this is too much
But tomorrow I'll wish I had tried
—FROM "NEVER TIRED," SCOTT MACINTYRE

It wasn't just my emotions that were running high; apparently so was my creatinine level. As soon as we got back to Scottsdale, Mom took me to have it tested. My creatinine level had risen to 6.6. Though it was a surprise to me, Mom had suspected something wrong while we were in California.

The morning after I saw Jerry, we headed home to Arizona. Once we were in the car, I fell asleep and didn't wake up until we stopped for gas. When I got up to use the restroom, Mom asked how I was feeling.

"I feel fine. I think it's just been a busy couple of weeks and I'm tired."

"You look a little pale. We should get a creatinine level done when we get home. It's been awhile."

She was right; I hadn't done a single test during my third trimester. I was busy, and to be honest, I'd become complacent. I felt good, and despite some ups and downs, my numbers earlier that year had held relatively steady. That's why I had been so surprised when the tests came back and my levels had risen to a 6.6. My last test in January had only been 4.9.

The doctor wanted me tested a month later. When that second test came back a 7.1, we were stunned.

I was in serious trouble.

～

Coming home to Scottsdale was everything I'd hoped it would be, and I quickly fell into a routine. Each day I would wake up and work at the piano for a couple of hours, then I'd spend a few hours working on my dissertation. Katelyn and I enjoyed a lot of time hanging out with friends in the pool, and Todd joined us after he got home from Tanglewood. At night, more friends would come over to play board games or we'd go to their house to hang out.

Though I hadn't lived at home for nearly a year, I still knew the layout of every room like the back of my hand and I quickly resumed old routines. For example, there was a specific path I always took from my bedroom to my recording studio in our home. I exited my room and walked down the hall, through the kitchen, up two steps into the family room, around the sofa, and down a second hall. The grand piano was to my right and my studio with my keyboards and recording equipment was to my left. When I finished working or playing, I'd take the same route back to the kitchen or my bedroom. Even when I was walking at full speed, I didn't have to use my cane. I could do it without thinking. Being on autopilot was a reminder of how different things had been in London where I constantly faced unfamiliar settings.

I also loved to lie down and stretch out on the living room floor, right next to the steps up from the kitchen. Although it was one of the main pathways through the house, it was a fairly open space and very conducive to stretching my arms and legs as far as they could reach. I'd stare at the air conditioning vent while I thought about my music or the dissertation. Maybe it was all of those months hunched over the piano while I practiced, but now that I was home, lying on the living room floor was one of the things I enjoyed most.

But the comfortable setting of my home couldn't make up for the disorienting feeling of having my body fall apart on me. I still didn't know what was causing my illness—it was a complete mystery—and I didn't know what was going to happen to me. With my creatinine level climbing, I was moving further into unfamiliar territory.

Al Chen continued to run tests to check for viruses as well as other possible causes, but their results came back negative. Meanwhile, the doctor also asked me a lot of questions, some of which really bothered me.

"Do you drink?"

"No, I don't like alcohol."

"Are you sure? Would you tell us if you did?"

"Yes, I'm sure, and yes, I would tell you if I did. I want to find the cause even more than you do."

"Do you use drugs?"

"Only the ones you've prescribed for me."

"I'm asking about illegal drugs. Have you ever tried marijuana, cocaine, heroin, or anything else?"

"No."

"Have you ever taken a friend's prescription?"

"No."

"Have you taken any painkillers—even Tylenol or aspirin—and taken more than what is directed on the box?"

"I've rarely taken anything. I'm healthy, and I don't get headaches."

"Would you like me to ask your parents to leave so you can tell me more in private?"

"There's nothing to tell. I don't drink, I don't use drugs, and I've only taken a Tylenol a couple of times in my life!"

Catastrophic kidney failure didn't usually happen to nineteen-year-olds unless there was some kind of substance abuse, so I knew that was why he was asking. When I told him I didn't drink at all, not even casually, and not even after turning twenty-one, he seemed to find it hard to believe.

When later test results showed no alcohol or drug use, the doctor was at a loss as to what to look for next. Eventually, he said there was nothing left to do—my only option was to choose between dialysis and a transplant. They gave us materials to read about both.

~

As the realization hit that my kidneys were failing at a fast rate, we went into overdrive to find a cure—or at least something to slow the kidney failure. I still wasn't convinced that a transplant or dialysis were my only two options, and we intensified our search for solutions.

A friend with a medical background recommended some Chinese herbs, and we added those to my diet as prescribed. I continued seeing the chiropractor in case my kidneys were failing due to the misalignment in my spine.

Al Chen wouldn't give up trying to find the cause of my illness, and he continued to give us hope. He referred us to another naturopath who recommended that I get an IV of colloidal silver. Silver had long been known to have an anti-viral effect and was often used to treat external wounds. Popular among practitioners of alternative medicine as a treatment for cancer, diabetes, HIV, and other diseases, there was anecdotal (but not scientific) evidence that it could be effective. Besides, the risks were thought to be minimal. It was a last-ditch effort to aggressively kill anything in my body that was causing the kidney disease.

On the day of the IV treatment, I sat in a chair as a nurse inserted the needle into my arm and connected the IV bag. As the silver pumped through my body,

I began to feel sick. By the time it was finished, I felt like I had pneumonia. A doctor had warned me there could be side effects, but that didn't make them any easier to tolerate. I felt awful, but I was willing to do whatever it took. Desperate people do desperate things, and my desperation rose with my creatinine levels.

The previous summer, before I left for London, I had started on a raw and whole food diet. I tried to eat food in as natural a state as possible—unprocessed, without added chemicals or preservatives. Even organic foods weren't good enough because, as I learned, pesticides could remain in the ground for many years even if they weren't used on the current crops. So I eliminated things like peanuts. I also cut back on sugar and salt. After a few weeks my body had felt noticeably cleaner and I felt healthier. And when I occasionally ate something that wasn't on the diet like pizza, I could immediately feel changes in my body.

We believed my diet may have been one of the factors that had helped to hold my creatinine levels steady during that time. But it was hard to continue the diet while I was living and eating at Goodenough College, so I gave up on it. But now that I was back home, we decided to try it again, and do it more aggressively. This time, my whole family made a commitment to try it with me. Mom began growing and juicing wheat grass again, and we all started taking expensive nutritional supplements. The entire family began to lose weight, but I was the only one who continued to grow weaker. As I got thinner, I also got paler. Friends and family noticed and said, "Are you sure you're okay? You don't look good."

My September 5 blood test showed why—my creatinine levels had continued to climb, now reaching an all-time high of 7.3. If I was going to Cambridge, I was scheduled to start on October 1, but I had to return to Goodenough before September 23 to clean out my room. If my numbers kept rising, there was no way I could go back. For the second summer in a row, my studies in England were in serious jeopardy.

~

Friends I hadn't seen in ten months stopped by once they heard I was home. It was good to catch up and hear about what they'd been up to. One afternoon, Todd's friend Jimmy Bradley came over with his brothers. We sat cross-legged on the floor and played cards. Around two o'clock, we decided to go out for lunch. When we got up to go, my muscles had painfully stiffened up. I'd recently noticed that it was getting harder to transition from standing to sitting, or from sitting to standing, but nothing dramatic had happened before. I couldn't walk. Fortunately, I was near the sofa and was able to lean into it. After a few seconds, things seemed to loosen up and I could move again. No one noticed, and I didn't say anything.

Outside we all loaded into Jimmy's car. I don't remember what he drove, but I remember that it was low to the ground. I was concerned about what had just happened, and worried that it might happen again, but I didn't want to tell anyone. I climbed into the backseat and hoped for the best. On the way to the restaurant, I smiled and laughed as the brothers teased each other, and I pretended to have a good time without a care in the world.

When we arrived, I got out and the same thing happened again. My muscles hardened up. This time I was expecting it. But I also felt dizzy. I leaned against the car to keep my balance. By the time everyone got out, I felt better. I gripped Todd's elbow, though tighter than usual, and followed him into the restaurant.

During the next several weeks, the muscle stiffening continued to increase in both intensity and frequency. If I sat in one position for longer than a minute, I felt as if rigor mortis had set in—like what happens to a dead animal alongside the road. It seemed that the toxins and impurities my kidneys could no longer filter were building up in my skin and muscle tissue. I actually felt as if I was fossilizing. It didn't hurt as long as I stayed in the same position—sometimes I didn't even notice it until I tried to move. But the longer I stayed in the same position, the harder it would be to move when I had to.

My family could see things were getting worse.

One day Mom was rubbing my feet and she noted how thin my ankles were.

Later that night, when I got up to get a drink, I heard her and Dad talking. With her voice cracking, she said to Dad, "It's like literally watching my own child disappear before my eyes."

I knew they were scared.

So was I.

～

All summer I continued to hope that my numbers would reverse, or at least stabilize, so I could return to England and study at Cambridge. I prayed for a reversal of fortune, like the previous summer when the doctor decided to let me go at the last minute. I was so grateful for the opportunity. I'd enjoyed the best year of my life in London, and it was an experience I'd never forget. I imagined the same thing would happen during my time in Cambridge should I be healthy enough to go.

With my numbers continuing to increase, however, I had to face the likelihood that it wasn't going to happen. When we spoke with the doctors, they were surprised that I continued to function so well despite the fact that my creatinine level was so high. Despite that, they were unanimous in their opinion: "You can't go to England. You need to stay here in the States and monitor this." My parents agreed. And so did I. There was no reason to be stupid and risk my life just to go back for another year. When it came down to it, the decision was easy, but it was still bitter medicine to swallow.

I wrote letters to both Cambridge and the Marshall Commission explaining my situation and informing them that I was not able to return to England until further notice. To my surprise, they both offered to hold my place for a year while I dealt with my health situation. I was humbled and thankful; I knew they didn't have to do that.

In the middle of September, Dad flew to London and packed up my room at Goodenough College. I was grateful for his help, but sad too. It hurt to close the door on the life I had lived in London. I had e-mailed and called most of my friends to let them know I wouldn't be coming back. It was doubly hard sharing the news. Not only did I have to tell them I wouldn't be going to Cambridge, but I also had to tell them I was getting sicker.

When Dad got back, he told me stories of what it took for him and a couple of my friends to pack up my room since I was notoriously messy. I had to laugh. I always preferred to think of it as organized chaos. The funniest part was listening to him describe how he had to return my borrowed books to libraries all over London. He took the Tube, buses, and cabs, and sometimes he walked—occasionally getting lost along the way. I felt proud I'd been able to do all that blind. And I knew he was proud of me too.

～

Many well-meaning people gave us lots of unsolicited advice about my health. I knew Mom and Dad protected me from it—especially when I overheard people talking to them at church and they didn't mention it to me later.

"You really should take Scott to see Dr. Porter," someone said. "I hear she can cure anything."

"I know you're going to a chiropractor already," another said. "But I just wanted to give you my brother-in-law's card. He's really good and not all chiropractors are, you know."

Their advice ranged from the medical to the spiritual. "Have you thought about having one of the church elders pray for you? Last year, one of them prayed for three people with cancer, and they're all doing better now."

Ever since the diagnosis, we had been praying together as a family, and although we hadn't seen answers to all of our prayers, we'd been grateful for the ones we had seen. We did want others to pray for us, but we didn't want our prayer time to become an opportunity for unsolicited advice. Slowly and carefully, we invited a few close friends from church to pray with us.

Every Sunday, several members of our fellowship group would join us in our living room to petition God for healing and for wisdom from the doctors. They prayed for me and for my parents. They prayed for medical progress and for comfort from the symptoms. Sometimes their prayers felt cumbersome and somber. But on other nights, their prayers felt light and uplifting. The nights we found laughter in spite of the tears were the nights we treasured.

The frenetic activity of seeking a cure, or at least a way to stabilize the disease, made time pass quickly. We kept busy with medical appointments, chiropractic treatments, and lab visits. But the harder we pushed to find a cure, the more frustrating things got. We were spending several days a week in medical offices and spending thousands of dollars only to learn weeks later that nothing had worked. It defeated our spirits.

But even during the most depressing days, we didn't place our trust in our emotions. We truly believed that God had a trick up his sleeve, and at the right moment, he would pull out his cure card and I'd be better. It wasn't that we were naïve; we knew the bleakness of my situation. But at the same time, we knew God was the great physician, and that he had the power to heal me at any time. I questioned my circumstances. *Why shouldn't that time be now? What is God waiting for?*

At the time, I couldn't imagine a more powerful demonstration of his power or a more inspirational story of what he could do than to say that God had miraculously healed me from my illness.

But on October 10, my creatinine level reached 8.4.

If God was going to act, he was going to have to do it quickly. Time was running out.

CHAPTER 17

The Day the Music Died

Music had filled our home since before I was born. At eighteen months, when I started plunking out notes on the piano, I was only adding to the melodies already coming from our stereo and tape player, melodies that formed the soundtrack of my young life. As our family grew, Todd and Katelyn each added to the music in their own ways. They both took piano lessons and sang, and after we moved to Toronto, the three of us studied voice together. Before long we were all singing together—Todd's rich baritone, Katelyn's young soprano, Mom's mature alto, and me filling in whatever part was left. We had fun singing around the house, and then in public, as the MacIntyre Family Singers. Our house was filled with instruments—the old upright piano, a new grand piano, several keyboards, guitars, and a drum set. If I wasn't practicing or composing at one of the pianos, I was mixing something in my recording studio. I blended voices and instruments until the sounds in the recording matched the sounds I heard in my head. There was always music in our house.

But as I got sicker, the music faded.

I was deteriorating from the inside out. I would sit at the piano and try to sing, willing my lungs to push enough air to stir my vocal chords, but the sound that came out was so frail and weak, I didn't recognize it. Playing the piano wasn't much easier. I got tired quickly and just wanted to lie down.

For a while I spent time in my studio just listening to music. But eventually even that was too hard. As I stopped doing other fun things, like swimming in the pool, playing board games, or having friends over, the whole family stopped doing those things. And when I stopped playing and listening to music, the whole family suddenly got very quiet. Todd had started another semester at university, and Katelyn had resumed her homeschooling and several community college classes. But for some reason, neither of them practiced at home. It seemed that if I couldn't make music, they weren't going to either.

I spent a lot of time in my favorite spot in the living room—lying on the carpet, staring at the vent, not thinking about anything at all. I could feel my family moving around. No one was tempted to tickle me or pretend that they were going to stand on my stomach. My parents tried to get me to go out in the sunshine and Todd and Katelyn tried to engage me in conversation, but despite their best attempts, I often didn't feel like moving or talking. It seemed that my presence was heavy and weighed everything down. The joviality was gone, and the house was serious.

On October 24 Dad received a fax with my latest creatinine results, and when he called home with the somber news, it matched the mood at the house.

"It's gone up again. It's now 8.9. The doctor wants to see us next week."

We set up an appointment for October 31—Halloween.

~

Although I knew I was sick, I was still surprised at how it affected me. I was exhausted. Everything took more energy than I possessed. Occasionally my brain felt foggy, as if I had to try harder to think. But there was no pain, other than the occasional stiffening. The real symptoms were much more subtle. The motivation, ambition, and energy to do the things I once loved, like music, were completely gone, and there was no sign they'd ever return. By now I didn't even walk over to the piano. Playing it made me tired, but more significantly, it no longer gave me joy. The piano felt like a discarded toy from my youth—I had fond memories of playing it, but it was too much effort to even think of doing that now. It was easier to just avoid it. I no longer even listened to music in my studio.

I know my behavior alarmed my family. They were used to seeing me at the piano for hours. They had seen how much joy it brought me. For years, when acquaintances and the media asked me about my blindness, I said that my music had more than compensated for my lack of vision. "If I had to choose between my musical gifts and the ability to see, I would choose to be blind forever."

My parents understood. They said things like that too. "Scott can't play baseball, but he can play music." Or, "Scott can't drive, but he can take people on a ride with his songs."

My piano playing, my voice, and my ability to write music were tremendous gifts that brought me great joy—joy that I could share with others.

But now the gifts were disappearing, and the joy had left with them.

It didn't make sense. I knew God had given me those gifts, and without a doubt I knew his plan was for me to share them with others, share them for his glory. But I couldn't do it anymore.

I was so confused. The world I had always lived in suddenly seemed to be turned upside down. *Why would God want this? Why would he leave me helpless, unable to use the very gifts he gave me?* But as I lay on the floor and stared at the vent, I even ran out of the strength to question God. I was just too tired. I had to trust him—even if I couldn't understand his will or what was happening to me. Nothing made sense, but what else was there to cling to?

It was God or nothing.

~

The Halloween doctor's appointment was no treat. The doctor plainly said I would need a transplant *before* Christmas. Though I had been listed on the national transplant waiting list for months, the average wait time on the list was at least four years, and some people died before a donor could be found. With my condition worsening, the doctor strongly suggested we look into finding a live donor.

Mom and Dad were both willing to donate a kidney, but the doctor said they might not be the best matches. Ideally, a perfect match meant the donor would have the same six protein antigens I had. Since I inherited three antigens from each parent, the best they could do was match me three antigens each. We hoped to find a stronger match. Plus, if Dad donated a kidney, he would miss a lot of work. If Mom donated a kidney, we'd still need Dad to stay home and take care of us while we recovered. If two of us had surgery, the third would have to be our caretaker, as well as take care of Todd and Katelyn. That would be extremely stressful, and the doctor impressed upon us the need for a strong family system during recovery.

There were also other issues to consider, like the age, health, and blood type of my parents. I wasn't willing to allow either of them to go through the surgery unless we truly had no other option.

At lunch over soup and Caesar salads, we tried to decompress from the disturbing news. "Do we even know anyone who'd be willing to donate a kidney?" I asked.

"I don't know," Dad said.

"How do you even ask for something like that?" Mom said, more to herself than to us.

That was a good question. How exactly do you ask a friend to donate a kidney? Not only was it an awkward thing to ask for, but there were many laws and regulations involved. You can't offer to pay for one, and you can't make any promises that could be construed as manipulation.

"Can we atleast pay for a donor's medical expenses?" I asked.

"Thankfully our insurance will cover the cost of the donor's medical expenses," Dad said. "I already looked into that."

But there was more to it than that. If the donor was an adult, they'd have to take time off of work for the surgery and the recovery. So it had to be someone who could afford to do that, or who had benefits that would pay them while off work.

"It's a lot to ask of someone," I said, wondering if the situation were reversed, would I be willing to donate my kidney to a friend?

Even if a volunteer came forward, they would still have to be tested to see if they were a match, and the testing process could take up to eight weeks. Since Mayo only tested one potential donor at a time, the whole process could take many months. They'd also have to go through a counseling process. The counselors would present the donors with every possible scenario, potentially scaring them away, but it had to be done. It was a decision that couldn't be made without a lot of thought. Though the surgery on the donor had improved during the past twenty-five years—it was now being done with laparoscopy and the complications and recovery time had been reduced—there were still risks for the donor.

And for me.

Whoever agreed to donate a kidney had to really want to.

Our conversation that day was the first time we seriously talked about finding a live kidney donor. As long as a transplant wasn't imminent, I had been able to hold on to hope that there might be another way. But one by one, my options had been eliminated. The things we tried left us with more questions than answers. Until the doctor said I would need a transplant before Christmas, I hadn't faced the reality that I might actually have to go through with it. Now I had to face it.

Later that night, I thought back to the first conversation my parents and I had with Al Chen on the phone. He had said then that he would rather have me undergo a transplant than dialysis. Perhaps he was right. I had tried to run from a transplant, but I was quickly running out of places to hide. I realized that perhaps it was time for me to stop searching for a cause and instead have a transplant before things got worse. But, it turns out, I didn't have much time to dwell on thoughts of the surgery. During the next few days, I got so sick that I spent more time lying on the floor than I did sitting upright. It became harder to think, and I spoke less than usual. One day in November, I had been lying in one place for so long that, as Dad walked by, he said, "Are you okay, Scott?"

"I don't know."

"What do you mean?"

I could sense that my answer alarmed him. I'd never been a complainer, and I could tolerate a lot of discomfort, so usually, I just said, "I'm fine." But this time, I knew that wasn't true. "I don't feel very good," I said. I wasn't making a lot of sense, but I didn't know how else to describe what I was feeling. It was as if life itself had drained out of me. I realized I couldn't stand up, but even if I could, I had no will to do so. Every desire I had, even for the simplest things like eating and sleeping, had been stripped away. I needed help, and I no longer had the ability to ask for it. Not only was my body giving up, but I was also giving up the hope that this would all reverse itself and go away.

Dad didn't waste any time. "I'm gonna call the doctor right now. We need to let him know what's going on," he said. The sound of fear in his voice should have scared me, but I was too weak to care.

Later someone helped me to the sofa, and I just lay there, too tired to even think. I closed my eyes and listened to the TV, which had been left on. When a commercial came on, it didn't make any sense. Logically, the components of the advertisement didn't line up. The ideas didn't flow from one to the next like every other commercial I'd heard in my life. It was as if the writers of the commercial were completely irrational and expected the TV-watching public to be the same way.

Then I realized it wasn't the TV, the commercial, or the writers. In a moment of clarity, I understood what was happening. The toxins had entered my brain and were affecting my ability to think clearly. My mental faculties were coming and going like a satellite TV signal during a thunderstorm. One moment everything was clear; the next things were pixelated and confusing.

Losing my kidney was one thing, but losing my mind was in a whole other category. I was a Marshall and a Fulbright Scholar; I graduated at the top of my class in college. My intelligence had helped me overcome obstacles I had faced as a blind person. And as a musician, I relied entirely on my mind. Every song that I had written but not yet recorded was in my head. Every note from every classical piece I had ever memorized was there too. *What if I start forgetting my music? What if my memory is gone and I can no longer play the songs I've memorized? If my ability to think clearly has left me once, what will prevent it from happening again?*

I was terrified that I was losing my mind and there wasn't anything I could do about it.

～

The next day, the doctor asked me a lot of questions. "Have you experienced any loss of appetite?"

"I haven't been able to eat much for the past week."

"How about before that?"

"No, I always ate. Just not as much as I once had."

"What do you mean?"

I told the doctor about the time at Ciao Bella in the spring when I couldn't finish my usual order of pasta, and how for months after, I would order something that sounded good but not be able to eat it all.

"That's a loss of appetite," said the doctor.

"Okay," I said, conceding the point. I couldn't sugarcoat my situation any longer.

"Tell me how your muscles feel," said the doctor.

I told him about the stiffening and the cramp-like pain I'd started experiencing earlier in the fall.

"Has that gotten worse?"

"Yeah, it has."

"How about your energy level?"

"Well, I haven't had enough energy to play the piano or sing for a couple weeks."

Dad interrupted. "He doesn't even have the energy to sit up anymore. He's been lying on the floor or on the sofa for the past week."

The doctor took a deep breath and then let out a long sigh.

"Scott, you need emergency dialysis. You need to start on it tomorrow."

"Can we wait one more week and see if my numbers get any better?" I asked. My numbers had only gone up, and at a faster rate. But if there was a chance—

"No," the doctor replied curtly. "Time has run out."

"Even just a few days to see if anything changes?"

"If you don't start dialysis tomorrow, you won't be alive in a week."

His words made the room spin. I felt like I was going to lose my balance, and I tightened my grip on the edges of the examination table.

It was official. I was dying.

Emergency surgery was scheduled for the next morning to insert a catheter into my chest for the dialysis.

During the car ride home, we didn't talk much. For the first time, there weren't options to consider or decisions to make. We had to do this. My choices were dialysis or death. Dialysis would keep my body alive, but what would happen to my music?

I felt like it had already died.

CHAPTER 18

Going Under

Showing severe dehydration
My body's fried
Thought I was on a vacation
Not in a fight

—FROM "THE VIEW FROM ABOVE," SCOTT MACINTYRE

I was wearing a worn hospital gown as I lay back against the raised bed and tried to think positive thoughts.

"I'm going to give you something to help you relax," the nurse said. I felt the prick as she stuck a needle in the back of my hand and then the stretching of my skin under the tape as she secured it in place. As she adjusted the IV bag, I wondered if she caught the irony of sticking me with a needle while telling me it would help me relax.

"The doctor should be here in a few minutes, and he'll explain what's going to happen," she said, patting me on the arm. She turned to leave, and I heard the metal grommets of the curtain pulled aside and then closed again, and then her shoes squeaked down the hall.

I sighed.

"Are you okay, Scott?" Mom asked.

"Yes." And I was.

Though the doctor's news the day before was unexpected, it had also given me a bit of hope. Perhaps dialysis would help me feel better? I wasn't looking forward to dialysis—I still wasn't even sure what it would involve or how I would feel—but I hoped it would provide the relief that our intense searching during the past eighteen months hadn't. Maybe I was just worn out, but I felt that I'd fought a valiant fight to prevent this from happening and I'd lost. Now it was someone else's fight, and I was willing to surrender to what came next. The strategy had to change, and I was no longer in charge of the battle plan. It was now up to my doctors to save my life. There were no more decisions for me to make.

Several nurses entered and started readying me for surgery. Mom and Dad prayed over me and then kissed me. The brake released on the bed, and I was rolled into a fluorescent-lit hallway. I leaned my head to the side and said, "I love you."

Eventually they wheeled my bed into the center of a large room with bright lights coming from the ceiling. My mind was already foggy, and with the medicine kicking in, I started to get sleepy. When the doctor came in and asked me a few questions, I answered, but I had trouble focusing. I just wanted to sleep.

~

In the doctor's office the day before, we learned that there were three types of vascular access, meaning three different ways to access the blood for dialysis and return it to the body. The first was an arteriovenous (AV) fistula, the second an AV graft, and the third, a central venous catheter.

Of those, the AV fistula was the preferred method for long-term dialysis. In that method, the surgeon joined an artery and vein that were separate, causing the blood to flow more quickly. For that to work, the fistula had to be created four to six weeks before dialysis began, and we didn't have that much time.

The second option, the AV graft, was similar except it used an artificial vessel to join the artery and vein. It was faster than the AV fistula, but it still took a couple of weeks to mature, so it wasn't an option either. So the plan was to insert a central venous catheter.

The doctor had explained that they would insert a catheter into the vena cava, one of the largest veins in my neck, and then tunnel it under the skin until it exited my chest. The catheter would have two plastic lumens, or tubes, attached. That would allow large flows of blood to exit from one lumen, enter the dialysis machine, be filtered, and returned to my body via the other lumen.

~

"Don't worry," the doctor said. "You're going to feel much better once this is over."

I just wanted it to be over.

Though I had been given medicine to help me relax, I was still awake during the procedure. The area where they inserted the catheter and tubing was numbed, but I could still feel them tugging at the tubing under my skin as they slid it in. It wasn't painful, but it made me clench my fists. It was like a rope being pulled through a hole—a hole that was never meant to have a rope go through it. It made a distinctive grinding sound each time they tugged on it.

I felt them working on my neck, and I could tell things weren't going well. There seemed to be lots of bleeding. Several times the doctor and nurses just stopped working. It was as if they were trying to figure out what to do next. Their voices grew tense, but I didn't dare ask what was happening. I lay as still as possible, afraid that even taking a deep breath would cause something, or someone, to slip. I tried to not think about what was happening to me.

Before I even realized it, the surgery was over. "You did great," said the doctor. The doctor seemed more relaxed now that his work was done and he started a conversation with me. "I hear you're quite the musician."

"Yeah, I just returned from London where I studied music," I said. Though I was still groggy, I felt better when I talked about the things I loved, so I kept the conversation going. "I studied classical, but I just put out a new pop CD with original material called *Somewhere Else*."

"Really? I enjoy many types of music. I'll order a CD from your website and then listen to it during surgery."

My mind flashed back to all the times I'd played piano in the Mayo lobby, praying that my music would inspire patients and help in their healing process. It was weird to think that now he would use my music in the operating room.

Someone wheeled me out into the hallway. I was still pretty out of it, but I remember us stopping to talk to Mom and Dad, and the doctor updating them on the surgery.

"We had some trouble getting the catheter in the right place. He lost a lot of blood during the surgery, so we'll have to keep an eye on him. But he did great. They'll take him to dialysis now, and you can go with him."

~

As they rolled me into the ICU dialysis area, Mom described what she saw to me. "You're entering a big room. It's like an intensive care ward. There are lots of dialysis machines and beds along the wall. It looks like there's a nurse for every couple of patients."

The orderlies backed my bed into the bay. A nurse introduced herself and asked, "Is this your first time having dialysis?"

"Yes."

I could feel her lifting the tubes that protruded from my chest and connecting them to more tubes. She injected something into the tube to keep the blood from clotting and told me I might smell or taste something funny. But instead I was caught off guard by a weird sensation in my heart. My heart started beating rapidly beating and it felt like an air bubble, or some kind of foreign liquid, had rushed through my heart. I had never felt anything like it before; I didn't even know it was possible to feel things moving through my heart but thankfully, the feeling passed quickly.

As the nurse continued to work, I could feel her connecting my lumens to the tubing from the dialysis machine. "I'm going to turn the machine on," she said. I heard a gentle hum, followed by beeping noises that made it sound as if she was entering commands on a touch screen. Then a whirring noise started.

I was surprised when I didn't feel anything. But then again, I was still numb from the surgery. I heard soft voices across the room and the whirring, humming, and beeping of the other machines. Mom and Dad were still near my bed. Occasionally one of them would touch my hand or rub my leg.

"You're all set!" said the nurse.

But as my blood made its way into the tubes, I felt like life itself was going with it. "I don't feel very good," I said, closing my eyes and touching my forehead.

"Do you want some water?" Mom asked.

"Sure. But I don't feel very good."

I felt her place a cup in my hand. I raised it to my lips. Then everything went black.

∽

I don't remember what happened next, so what I am about to describe was pieced together from what I heard later.

As soon as I said, "I don't feel very good," I dropped the cup, spilling the water on the floor. The nurse tried to help me, but I had become unresponsive. When I didn't respond to her questions, she frantically pushed buttons on the machine and tried to adjust the tubes. It was immediately obvious to my parents that she couldn't figure out what to do. They could tell something was terribly wrong as they watched the nurse's demeanor grow more panicked. Another nurse came over to help. "He's coded," the first nurse said.

Mom, who was already standing close to my bed, moved in closer. She didn't know exactly what had happened, but she knew it wasn't good.

The nurses continued to talk amongst themselves.

"Check his vitals."

"I can't get a reading."

"BP?"

"Falling."

Mom started praying out loud. A social worker suddenly appeared by her side as if she had been notified of an impending crisis. Mom looked to Dad for help. He was sitting about ten feet away from her on the other side of the bed. With all of the medical people moving around, she couldn't see his face at first. But as more people rushed toward the bed and Dad stood up to make room for them, she finally got a glimpse of his expression. He was staring at me with horror in his eyes.

By now, loud alarms were beeping and everyone in the room knew something terrible was happening.

About that time, the nurse in charge of the ward rushed around the corner.

"His blood pressure's falling and we can't stop it," one of the nurses told the charge nurse.

"Lord, protect him," Mom prayed out loud. "Please protect Scott."

The charge nurse took my vitals and then adjusted some of the controls on the dialysis machine. Using a syringe, she inserted medication into the lumen. A tense minute passed while everyone waited to see what happened.

"It's coming up!" said the nurse closest to the monitor.

The tension seemed to lessen, but it was still a few minutes before I started moving my eyelids and eventually opened them.

Everyone breathed a sigh of relief. Slowly the nurses returned to their post, leaving the charge nurse, my original nurse, and the social worker at my bedside.

"You're an angel," Mom said to the nurse in charge. "We almost lost him. I can't believe we almost lost him."

"I'm just glad I was here," she said.

It was a terrifying moment for my parents. For weeks they had slowly watched me get sicker. Now, just when the life-saving treatment was administered, I had crashed. So far things had not gone well, and I think we were all worried about the future.

~

I woke up and sensed a crowd of people around my bed, though I wasn't sure why. But even in my sleepy state of confusion, I could tell the mood around me had changed dramatically.

The dialysis continued for four hours with the charge nurse, several other nurses, and my parents hovering over me. When it was finished, they put me in a private room where I would stay for the next couple nights.

Though I was recovering from surgery, my appetite returned quickly. Even the hospital food tasted good.

Todd came to visit after his rehearsal. He knocked softly and said, "Scott?"

I recognized his voice immediately and was glad for the company.

"He-yo!" I said.

He walked in, and I heard him pull a chair across the linoleum. "Scottio! How are you doing?"

"I'm good," I said. "I've been eating a lot again, and I feel like I have more energy."

"How was the surgery?"

I lowered the sheet that covered my catheter and showed Todd the doctor's handiwork. "They had to open up my neck right here, and then they inserted the tubing under my skin until it got to right here in my chest, where it comes out."

"Wow!"

"I was awake the whole time! I could feel them tugging on it as they tunneled it under my skin. Can you see it?"

"Yeah. It's like a ridge underneath your skin."

"It's pretty crazy," I said, rather proud of myself. "And these things coming out of my chest are the two tubes that they use to hook up to the dialysis machine."

"Does it hurt?"

"No. But I might still be numb from the surgery."

Todd asked more questions and I was happy, even excited, to discuss the details. It was like I was the tour guide on an exciting adventure.

I was thirsty, and there was a cup of water on the table to my right. I reached my left arm across my body to the table, but I couldn't get the cup. Todd grabbed it for me. "Can't you move your right arm?" he asked.

I stopped to think about it. "I can. At least I think I can. But I don't want to mess up the catheter."

"Well, how will you play piano?"

That's when I realized I hadn't been using my right side at all since the surgery. When they had hooked me up to the dialysis machine, I felt them pulling and tugging on the catheter and tubing. Sometimes I could also feel it pull when I moved my right arm or some of my shoulder and neck muscles. I didn't like the feel of it tugging beneath my skin. So to avoid it, I had just kept my right arm in the same stiff, awkward position. Likewise, the lumens were attached to the tubing in my chest, and I was afraid that if I accidently touched them, they'd pop off and my blood would drain out before they could stop it. I felt like I needed to do something to protect it, so limiting my movement on that side had seemed reasonable. But now that Todd had asked me about playing the piano, it no longer seemed reasonable.

How will I play piano if I can't use my arm? Will I be this way forever?

∼

I was released from the hospital on Wednesday, the day before Thanksgiving. Before they let me go, the nurse gave me a long list of dos and don'ts.

"Keep the catheter area clean and dry at all times. No showers. Be careful not to bump it or cut it with anything. Don't wear tight clothing or jewelry. And be sure to weigh yourself and check your pulse and blood pressure every day."

Mom brought me a button-down shirt to wear home. I wasn't ready for all the arm movement that putting on a T-shirt required.

Though I still had a lot on my mind, I did my best to ignore it for the rest of the day. Grandpa and his wife, Ann, would be there to celebrate Thanksgiving with us, and I didn't want my mood to affect the holiday.

We parked in front of our house, and as we walked in, I smelled pies baking in the oven. I went into the family room and sat down on the couch. Katelyn sat with me and asked me questions about the hospital and how it felt to be home. I answered them, trying to make my voice sound normal, but even I could tell it was a little subdued. By then, the medication from the surgery had worn off, and I felt a dull pain in my neck and chest. And I was emotionally drained from the experience.

It was so odd getting used to the catheter tubes dangling on my chest. I had associated the catheter with the hospital, as if I was going to leave it there when I returned home. But now sitting on the couch, in my own home, where I'd sat for so many healthy years, I had to try to figure out how to integrate the pieces of plastic into my everyday life. Not only was I extremely conscious of the tubes—I felt them dangle and slide across my chest each time I turned my head—but I was also extremely cautious. As I spoke, I gestured as little as possible and I still avoided using my right arm.

Ann entered the room and sat to my right. She asked if it was good to be home. "Yeah, it's good to be back," I said.

I sensed Ann shifting in her seat, and I expected her to speak again. But without warning, I felt her arms tightening around my neck in a hug.

Before the catheter tubes pressed against my chest, I knew what was going to happen and I reacted instantly.

"Ahhhhh!"

Even I was startled by the shriek that came out of my mouth as I shrank back in fear, drew my knees up to my chest, and bent over into a fetal position to protect myself.

Ever since the surgery, I had feared someone accidentally pulling out my catheter. It was attached to my vena cava and provided open access to my major blood vessels. It was my lifeline, and now it had been touched.

CHAPTER 19

Thanksgiving Realities

I'm so much stronger
Than I would be now
If it weren't for You, Lord
You've been my strength in every trial
—FROM "SO MUCH STRONGER," SCOTT MACINTYRE

Had I been sighted I would have seen Ann coming to hug me, and I would have stopped her or protected myself in some way. But I couldn't. Of course, she had no idea her innocent gesture would cause me to react so traumatically. "Oh! I'm so sorry! Did I hurt you?"

I immediately burst into tears. In the hospital, the medication had temporarily suppressed my emotions, and now they all came flooding out.

"Scott! Are you alright?" Mom rushed to my side to see what was wrong.

"I am so sorry," Ann kept repeating.

As I gingerly unfolded myself from the protective posture, I could tell that nothing bad had happened. I hadn't been hurt. The catheter was still in place, and the tubes still dangled from the hole in my chest.

"I'm sorry, Ann," I said, my voice still shaking and tears still falling down my face.

When she had reached out to hug me, she had only the best of intentions —to show her love for me and to welcome me home. She had no idea how concerned I'd been about moving my arm in the wrong way or accidently pulling a tube loose. I had been so scared of something bad happening that I had simply overreacted to her hug. Until that moment, I hadn't consciously realized how terrified I was. Now Ann was the terrified one, terrified that she'd done something to hurt me. Listening to her apologizing over and over, I knew I'd really made a mess of things. She felt bad, but I felt worse.

Am I destined to spend the rest of my life like this? Not able to be touched? And who would want to hug me after the way I just acted? It was a crazy mixture of emotions. I was embarrassed at having overreacted, and truly sorry for how I'd treated Ann, but at the same time, I had a tremendous sense of relief knowing that nothing happened. Ann's hug had snapped me back to reality. It broke me out of my protective shell and reminded me that I wasn't as medically fragile as I'd thought.

My protected hospital world had collided with my real-life world. But despite the rocky start, I now felt like both worlds could coexist. Things weren't perfect, but they weren't dire either. I *could* live with the tubes in my chest

~

My health. My future. My joy. As each of those things were stripped from me, instead of clinging to them more tightly, I felt God asking me to willingly give them up, to trust him. That wasn't easy. I was used to taking charge and making decisions about my future. Now that I was sick, each time I let go of something it seemed even more was taken. When you lose your health, your future, and your talent, you also lose your pride. I had gone from the blind musical prodigy who overcame any obstacle to someone who was sick in bed with no guarantee of a bright future. There was no pride in that.

But as those things were taken from me, I found myself turning to the spiritual things in my life. My faith had never been tested to the degree it was being tested now. I had never prayed so much or so fervently, individually or with my family. Without a doubt, I knew that if my health was ever restored and if I were able to play music again, I wouldn't take those things for granted. During this time, I promised God that I would praise him as much during the good times as I had called out to him during the bad times.

I believed that God had a plan for my life and that for reasons unknown to me he allowed both good and bad to come into it to fulfill his purposes. So if I truly believed that, it meant that I should be thankful for everything that happened to me in life—even the worst trials. *Could I do that?* Looking back over my life, I could see how God had used bad things in life, like my blindness, for my good. But now that I was swimming in the worst of the worst that life could offer, did I have enough faith to thank him even for this too? *Could I be the kind of man who praised God during the bad times?*

On Thanksgiving Day, I had a chance to find out.

~

I woke at five o'clock in the morning and Mom took me in for my second dialysis session. Though I had coded in the hospital during the first session, doctors had told me that a medication adjustment would hopefully prevent that from happening again. So for four hours I sat in a recliner and listened to the low hum of the machine that cleaned my blood. Since the diagnosis, I had been holding on to the hope that there would be some kind of cure or reversal of my situation. Though I still believed it was possible, I also realized it now was not very likely. Dialysis was my foreseeable future. *Could I thank God for dialysis?*

I thought about some of the events in my life that I initially labeled as bad—like the rescission letter from Cambridge—but that later turned out to be very good for me. When that letter came, I didn't stop and thank God. In fact, if someone had suggested it at that time, I probably would have asked incredulously, "Why?" But looking back at the time I'd spent in London and the ways I had grown personally, musically, and spiritually, I knew it was one of the best gifts God had given me. If I had gone to Cambridge, I would have missed out on so many wonderful experiences in London. By the time I left England, I was thanking God for the opportunities he had given me.

Though emergency dialysis didn't seem like a praiseworthy thing in the moment, I had to consider that perhaps in hindsight, at some later date, I would find a deeper appreciation for my current circumstances. And if I knew that was a possibility for the future, I had to admit it was possible to be thankful in the moment. But I didn't feel grateful for my situation. If I was to be thankful for my situation, it would take outside help.

So just as I had many other times when my strength fell short, I closed my eyes and asked God for help: *Dear Lord, on this Thanksgiving Day it's tempting to say, "Why should I be thankful?" I don't know how long I'll be on dialysis, or if or when I'll have a transplant. It's hard to imagine playing and performing like I once did, and without music, my future looks bleak. But you've already showed me so many times how you work all things together for good. Please, show me today how to be thankful, even in the darkness I am facing.*

As I sat in the chair, listening to the dialysis noises around me, I made a mental list of things I was thankful for. First, I thanked God for leading me to the dialysis. Without it I wouldn't even be alive. I was grateful for making it through surgery safely, and grateful for the nurse who saved my life when I coded. I was also thankful for the return of my appetite, especially as I thought about all the great Thanksgiving food being prepared at home. Since the surgery just a few days earlier, I had already felt better and had more energy than I'd had over the past few weeks, and I was extraordinarily grateful for that.

Of course, there had been many disappointments over the last year and a half: the "cures" that didn't turn out as we'd hoped, my inability to return to England, and losing my passion for music. But I was thankful that, even during those bad times, I could always feel God's presence with me.

I appreciated my family and all they'd been doing to support me. And despite the drama of the day before, I was so thankful that Grandpa and Ann had joined us for the holiday. Grandpa wasn't as active as he once was (he mostly sat and read the newspaper or a book), but when he did speak he was as sharp as he had always been and engaged each one of us in interesting conversation. He was a wonderful calming presence, as was the rest of my family. They were all a huge blessing to me.

I thought about how much dialysis must cost, and I was thankful for Dad's job and his insurance. Other things came to mind, like my appreciation for the nurses and technicians who were working on Thanksgiving and missing their families.

As I thought of each thing I was grateful for, ten more things would come to mind. Grateful thoughts are like rabbits; they multiply like crazy. When my four hours were up, I felt like I could have sat there for another four hours and not run out of things to be grateful for. But I was also ready to go home.

And I was thankful I could.

~

After a few dialysis sessions at the Mayo Hospital to make sure everything was working smoothly, I started going to a private center near our home in Scottsdale. Dialysis soon became as routine as going to school or going to work. Three times a week I got up before dawn and Dad or Mom drove me through the dark roads to the center. Unlike the car rides to ASU, which were filled with laughter and music, these rides were more somber. We would talk about my latest blood tests and pray for my protection during dialysis.

For the first few weeks, Mom or Dad would come in with me and stay around for an hour to make sure everything was going smoothly. Then Dad would head off to work or Mom would head home to drive Katelyn somewhere. Todd could drive himself, but Katelyn, just like me, needed rides anywhere she had to go. Mom would run her to community college classes, homeschool co-ops, or lessons, and then rush back to the dialysis center to pick me up. If we couldn't get the schedule worked out, and there were many days we couldn't, I'd call a taxi to take me home.

As the weeks wore on, I started to listen to music and books on tape during dialysis just to make time pass quickly. I filled eleven hours a week with Victor Hugo's *Les Misérables*, Jason Mraz's music, and recorded episodes of my favorite TV shows, *American Idol* and *24*. Soon I found myself looking forward to my next dialysis session just so I could find out what happened to Jean Valjean or Jack Bauer. I'd find myself lost in the book or show I was listening to, and they were good distractions until a technician started unhooking me from the machine and I was once again reminded of my illness.

I'm sure many people think that just sitting in a chair for four hours would be relaxing, but it was exhausting! My feet had to be raised, and I could only sit in a limited number of positions so I was often uncomfortable even when I used pillows from home to prop me up. By the time I finished each session, my body ached and I was drained physically and emotionally. I just wanted to go home and lie in bed.

Each day of dialysis was a lost day—not only because of the time I spent hooked to the machine, but because I couldn't do anything but sleep after I got home. I started pushing the doctors for less dialysis. At times, I was able to get it down to three hours a day, or on rare occasions I came two times a week for four hours. But then I would start to feel the toxins build up on my days off, so I'd have to again increase the frequency or the time I spent hooked to the machine.

But in general, I felt a lot better. I enjoyed my new appetite and energy level. And I gradually started playing the piano again. Without a doubt, I knew God had put me on earth to share my music with others. So when opportunities to do that came up again, I took them seriously. One day a representative from Guardian Insurance called and wanted to hire me to perform for a convention in Florida. At the time I was having dialysis on Monday, Wednesday, and Friday. Mom and I discussed it and we figured it was possible to do a three-day trip if I left after dialysis on Monday and returned home Wednesday night. Then I could have dialysis again first thing Thursday morning and push Friday's back to Saturday.

On the week of the performance, I finished my Monday morning dialysis as usual, but instead of going home to rest, Mom and I rushed to the airport to catch a flight to Orlando. Traveling was hard—much harder than I expected it to be. I was so tired that all I wanted to do was sleep. I tried to nap on the plane, but I was too stiff from the hours sitting in the dialysis chair that morning. By the time we got to the hotel I was ready to sleep.

Tuesday at noon I had a quick soundcheck at the venue. During the rehearsal, as I moved my arms at the piano, I could feel the catheter moving under my shirt and rubbing against my skin. It was the first time since starting dialysis that I was going to perform publicly and I was suddenly nervous about it. I took another nap that afternoon before performing that night.

Standing backstage with Mom, waiting for my cue, we prayed as we had prayed so many times before—that God would use my music to bless those who heard it. But we also prayed for something new—the strength and stamina for me to make it through the performance.

Fortunately God answered our prayers. As soon as I got up on stage, I forgot all about the catheter. I sang and played my heart out, pouring every ounce of my strength into the performance. Only a few people knew what I was going through; the other fifteen hundred people in the audience just seemed to enjoy the performance.

The next morning Mom and I headed back to the airport to catch our flight home. As I sat on the plane, I could feel the toxins building up in my body. It was similar to how I felt before I started on dialysis. As the day wore on, I felt worse. I didn't sleep well that night, and when Dad woke me in the morning, I couldn't wait to get to the dialysis center to start my treatment.

Experiencing the discomfort after missing a day made me realize the importance of the life-saving machines that cleaned my blood and returned it to my body. On that Thursday morning, I could wholeheartedly say I was thankful for dialysis.

~

Dialysis changed things around our house. Everything revolved around getting to and from my appointments and giving me enough time to rest after each one. But everyone else's life went on too. Dad still had to work. Todd was in college, playing tennis, and rehearsing for his latest musical. Katelyn was attending several classes at the local community college, taking horseback riding lessons, and rehearsing with her clogging group. And as for Mom—well, we were her work. She drove the freeways for hours each day trying to get everyone where they needed to go. And when she wasn't on the road, she was homeschooling, running the house, and helping take care of me.

Though I was thankful for dialysis, it wasn't something to be enjoyed; it was something to be *endured*. Each day I entered the facility and a new technician would ask me a few questions and then hook me up to the machine. Although technicians came and went, I was there every other day. Soon, it seemed that I knew more than they did.

"The doctor said he wanted me to receive half the dose of Procrit I got last time," I told a new technician.

"Well, this is the standard dose everyone gets."

"No. He was supposed to have faxed the order last night."

"Oh, lookey here. You're right!"

I tried not to dwell on how unpleasant dialysis was. Instead, I tried to accept it and be content with the circumstances. But even my attitude didn't help relieve the boredom. Every day was the same.

Dull.

Monotonous.

Mundane.

I had nothing new to look forward to. And no idea how long it would all go on. My life seemed to be made up of two things—dialysis and sleeping off the effects of dialysis.

During my days off, I tried to talk more with my family and live vicariously through the activities they were involved in. Growing up, Katelyn, Todd, and I had been as close as any siblings could be—closer than most—and we enjoyed spending time together. But now, as a group, we couldn't do many of the things we once enjoyed. We couldn't swim together because I couldn't get the catheter wet. I could only go to the third step of the pool, and they had to be careful not to splash me. Katelyn had always been affectionate and was a big hugger. Now when she wanted to hug me, she often didn't—she was afraid she'd accidently hurt me. Todd and I could no longer wrestle. And of course, the infamous MacIntyre tickle fights were out of the question.

My social life also suffered. Fewer friends came over to the house. I never knew how I'd be feeling by the time they got there, so it was just easier to not invite them. And my dating life came to a complete halt. I had always been a romantic, falling head over heels "in crush" with the slightest encouragement. My exuberance often scared girls—I'd say too much about how I felt at the wrong time or I'd write a serious love song for someone I barely talked to and frighten them away—but I couldn't help it. I had often wondered if anyone would ever be able to match me in the feelings department. I would dream about the perfect girl, someone who loved me as much as I loved her, but I doubted that she existed. Though I had gone out with several girls in the past—friends mostly—I hadn't had a serious relationship yet. Now I wondered if I ever would. I was twenty-one and in the prime of my life, but I was also trapped in a failing body propped up by dialysis. *Who will want me now?*

I spent a lot of time wondering what my future would look like and if it would always be like this. I couldn't do anything to change my condition on my own, but I continued to pray, believing God had a plan. But prayer didn't answer the question of what the plan looked like, or how long it would take to unfold. *Months? Years? Decades?*

Day after day, it was the same thing. Days rolled into weeks that felt like months. I had no idea if things would ever get better and nothing on my calendar to look forward to. But still, I did what I could to hold on to my dreams. I didn't have the health to travel and perform, but I started writing music again. Many times I would sit in my dialysis chair and just write music in my head, and on those really good days when I had extra energy, I recorded them in my studio. But even those times weren't much of a respite from the repetitive monotony that each day brought.

Then, during the depths of my mundane existence, I got a phone call.

It was Jerry Lindahl.

CHAPTER 20

A Very Mrazy Christmas

We won't be long
We won't be long here
We still belong
We still belong here

—FROM "STARS," SCOTT MACINTYRE

When I heard Jerry's ringtone start playing on my cell phone, I quickly answered the call. I was exhausted from dialysis that morning, but a conversation with Jerry was the perfect thing to break me out of my monotonous routine. Jerry and I chatted briefly before he asked the most unexpected question. "So how would you like to spend Christmas with Jason Mraz?"

I was stunned.

"Wow . . . Are you serious, Jerry?" I said, trying to sound calm, but not believing what I'd just heard. Since July, Jerry and I had exchanged e-mails and talked on the phone a number of times, and during those conversations he occasionally mentioned what Jason was up to, but he had never suggested my getting together with him. Now I was being invited to his house *for Christmas*?

"Jason's having a small Christmas party on the twenty-third. I thought maybe I could fly you in for the party, have you spend the night at his house, and still get you back in time for Christmas Eve with your family."

"Sure, I think that would work. Thank you so much for thinking of me!"

I had replied with heart, but now my head was screaming, *Are you crazy? You're on dialysis! How are you going to do that?* I didn't know how, but I didn't care. I had to make it work somehow.

"Jason has a rule about never performing for friends at parties because that's his job," Jerry said. "So I want to make you my Christmas gift to Jason. I want you to play at his party."

"That sounds amazing!" I was ecstatic. I wanted to run and jump and shout, but I did my best to hang on to my composure until I got off the phone.

I get to play for Jason Mraz at his house? I was overcome by Jerry's invitation.

A few minutes earlier I had nothing to look forward to; now the most exciting thing to happen in my pop career so far would take place *next week*! I couldn't wait to tell my family. The hope that Jerry had just given me shined brighter than a gold record.

By the time Mom got home from picking up Katelyn, I had thought through the details. I would have dialysis on the morning of the twenty-third before I left. Then Mom could drive me to the Phoenix airport and Jerry would pick me up in Los Angeles. We would hang out that night, and then Jerry would take me back to the airport the next day. I'd be home in time to sing at church on Christmas Day. Then I could have my next dialysis on the day after Christmas, only missing my usual appointment by about twenty-four hours.

Still, I knew there would be risks, and once again, those old fears arose. Although I had traveled back and forth to London by myself many times, I hadn't traveled alone since they'd put the catheter in. *What if something happens while I'm traveling and I need help? What if something goes wrong while I'm at Jason's house?*

I decided the best thing to do was fill Jerry in on the details of my health situation. A few weeks earlier I had casually mentioned my kidney failure to him, but now I'd have to tell him enough specifics to handle any kind of emergency. If something happened and I wasn't conscious for whatever reason, he would have to be the one to seek medical help. I wasn't sure I was ready to reveal that much of my condition yet, and I knew he might not want to take on that responsibility. Like Cambridge, he could rescind his offer. But if I wanted to go I had to take that chance.

I called Jerry to give him my travel plans and told him about my medical issues. I was pleasantly surprised to find out he wasn't concerned. "Don't worry. We're going to have a great time. I'll see you at the airport."

I could hardly contain my excitement. I wondered what it would be like meeting Jason and if he would be anything like I imagined him to be based on his music. Though I would go on to meet many famous pop musicians, Jason was the first, and I couldn't stop thinking about the trip.

After my dialysis appointment on December 23, Mom drove me to the airport and guided me to my gate. Sitting alone on the plane, I felt a bit vulnerable, but I pushed away those thoughts and concentrated on what was to come. When I arrived at LAX, Jerry and his friend Alicia were there to meet me.

Once we got into the car, Jerry said, "It's a bit of a drive to Jason's, and we're starved. Since dinner will be waiting, let's not tell anyone, but I think we need to make an unscheduled stop." I laughed when I found out it was the In-N-Out Burger drive-thru.

We ordered burgers and drinks. As Alicia finished her drink, she noticed the notation on the bottom of the cup. "John 3:16," she said.

"What?" Jerry asked, not knowing what she was talking about.

"On the bottom of the cup. They always have it printed there."

"I think it's a Bible verse."

Before I could stop myself, I interjected from the backseat. "For God so loved the world, that he gave his only begotten Son, that whosoever believeth in him should not perish but have everlasting life."

There was an awkward pause, or maybe a stunned silence. I wasn't sure if I should say anything more at all. I wasn't shy about sharing my faith, but this was a new situation for me. I had no idea what Jerry did or didn't believe, and for a moment, I worried that I had offended one or both of them.

Fortunately Jerry broke the silence. "How'd you know that? Alicia and I just looked at each other with our mouths hanging open."

What should I say? I could tell Jerry about my faith—why I believed what I believed, and how I knew so much about the Bible. *But you don't know him well enough to have that conversation*, I told myself. *This is your career. You don't want to mess it up on the first visit. Wait until later to talk about that.* So I didn't. I took the easy way out.

"I just happen to know that verse pretty well."

The conversation continued about other things, and the moment was lost. But as we drove, I replayed the conversation in my mind. I couldn't help wishing I had just told Jerry I was a Christian, but now I had missed my opportunity. Despite my desire to praise God in the good times and the bad, apparently I could still choke when I had the opportunity to tell others about my faith.

When we got to Jason's house, Jerry parked the car and then came around to help lead me into the house. As we walked through a courtyard-like area to the front door, butterflies filled my stomach. Meeting Jason was a huge deal, and I wanted to make a good impression. We entered the house and walked through the entryway into a larger space, which I gathered was the dining room and kitchen area. I immediately sensed that it was going to be a difficult situation to navigate socially. Like a cocktail party, people were spread out around the room and talking in small groups—maybe a dozen people total. I could hear everything they were saying, but none of the voices sounded like Jason's.

Typically one of my family members would have filled me in on the situation. "There's a table to your left with two guys and a girl and there are three guys sitting on stools to your right." But Jerry was probably not used to guiding a blind person, so he didn't know how helpful it was to make me aware of the context. Had I entered the home of an old friend, I would have said something like, "Hey, how's everyone doing?" and then waited for them to respond. But since I didn't know anyone, it seemed a little presumptuous to just start announcing myself. So I stood there for a moment listening and trying to figure out where Jason was so I could introduce myself.

"Scott brought a gift for Jason," Jerry said to someone else. Then he turned to me and said, "Do you want to give it to him now?"

"Sure," I said, hoping that would finally lead to an introduction.

We walked about ten feet over to the kitchen sink where apparently Jason was chopping carrots. Jerry introduced me, and I handed Jason the gift bag I was carrying.

"It's Prickly Pear Cactus Jam," he said as he opened the bag.

"All the way from Arizona," I joked.

"Looks dangerous," Jason said. I could hear the smile in his voice.

I'd also given him a copy of my latest CD, *Somewhere Else*. He thanked me for the gift and we chatted for a few minutes while he continued with the carrots. Jason struck me as very calm and understated. We didn't discuss music or songwriting or a whole host of topics I would have liked to ask him about. This was his vacation from work, so I decided I'd stay away from those topics unless he brought them up.

Jerry introduced me to some of the other guests, including Jason's keyboardist and percussionist. I had a good enough time talking with Jason's friends, but at times the conversation seemed forced or stiff. We discussed the weather, my flight, and the difficulties of trying to fly during the holidays. I understood; I was the newcomer among an intimate group of close friends.

At dinner about twenty people gathered around the long wooden dining room table. I sat between Jerry and one of Jason's friends. I was taking a bite of Grandma Mraz's sweet potatoes when the front door opened and the conversation stopped.

"Hi, Bill!" said someone at the other end of the table.

"I didn't know you were coming," a female voice said.

Chairs moved as several people stood up to greet him. Then I heard the man greeting Jason at the far end of the table. Jerry leaned over and whispered, "My boss just came in."

Bill Silva.

Not only did Bill manage Jason Mraz and several other notable artists, but he also produced concerts at the Hollywood Bowl. This was the best thing that could've happened. I was supposed to perform after dinner, and now Bill Silva would be there to hear me!

Bill made his way around the table, and Jerry introduced us and told Bill I would be playing after dinner.

"I'm looking forward to that," Bill said.

After dinner we all walked over to Jason's studio, which was separate from the main house. Everyone else took a shortcut through thick avocado trees to get there, but Jerry led me down the driveway and around a path to the studio so we wouldn't have to try and navigate the tangled roots and branches. When we walked into the studio, from what I could tell, everyone was already seated on couches or chairs around the room. Jerry showed me to the piano and I sat down. I took a breath and started with "Keep the Lines Open," the song I'd written in London. Then "Hard to Be Away" and "Who Am I" followed. It was a dream opportunity. Not only was Jason Mraz listening to my original music, he was listening to it in the same room as Bill Silva. It was my first showcase of sorts, though no one had really planned it that way. At Jerry's request I played "The Luckiest" by Ben Folds and I closed with "Piano Man" by Billy Joel. On the final song I heard someone tapping lightly on the drums—it was Jason's percussionist joining in.

I should have been exhausted from the dialysis and the travel, but playing for Jason and Bill Silva in Jason's private studio kept my adrenaline pumping and my energy up through the set. When I finished, I felt great about my performance. I stood up by the piano and Jason's friends came over and shook my hand or patted me on the back.

"Your voice is so beautiful!"

"Jerry said you were amazing, and he was right!"

"Thank you so much for playing for us."

Later, back in the kitchen, both Jason and his percussionist came up and complimented me on my performance. While it always felt nice to hear people say good things about my music, hearing compliments from music industry veterans made it that much better. I appreciated each of them and their words. The problem was that, being blind and new to this group of people, I didn't always know who was saying what. *Had Bill Silva said something to me and I didn't know it was him? Or had he not said anything at all?* I didn't know.

~

For performers who write their own music and lyrics, performing can be especially intimate. It's like opening a window to your heart, and exposing your innermost thoughts and feelings. I made myself vulnerable when I sang about my deepest emotions. But just as I experienced in London, Jason and his friends seemed to draw closer to me after I sang and played for them. The conversation that had earlier seemed stiff was now different. It was warmer and friendlier, like we'd known each other for a long time. By sharing my music, I had shared a part of myself, and now people reciprocated by opening up and talking about their families, their girlfriends, and their lives outside of music.

It started to get late but the party wasn't over yet. Since it was a sleepover, everyone changed into their pajamas and then we exchanged gifts. We'd each brought a wrapped book, and when it was our turn, we picked one from the stack and unwrapped it. I had brought *The Fellowship of the Ring*, and the book I received was a book on Eastern religion—not exactly the trade I was hoping for, but the book swap was a fun way to get to know the others, and I enjoyed discovering what books they liked.

After the gift exchange, it was late and I needed sleep. Jason had to get up early to catch a flight first thing in the morning, so I thanked him and said my good-byes before going to bed. "It's been great having you, Scott," he said as he hugged me. "We'll do it again."

I stopped in the kitchen for a drink of water and someone asked me about the T-shirt I was wearing.

"It's from *Les Mis*," I said.

"I really enjoyed your performance tonight."

"Thank you so much. Glad I could be here."

"So what else is going on with your career right now?"

I still didn't know who I was talking to, but he was obviously interested, so

I briefly talked about some of my performances in the States and abroad and my recent TV appearance in the UK.

"That's the best thing to do. Keep performing every chance you get. People will start to notice, and eventually you'll get your break."

Instantly I knew who the voice belonged to—Bill Silva. I couldn't help laughing to myself—I'd always pictured having that kind of conversation in someone's office. I never imagined I would be talking to Bill Silva in Jason Mraz's kitchen while wearing my pajamas!

It was a wonderful evening, and I was sorry to see it end. But by the time I got to bed, I was exhausted.

As I flew back to Phoenix the next day, I couldn't help but bask in the glow of all I'd experienced. It was so exciting to be a part of an evening like that. I felt like it was a Christmas present from God that said he remembered me and still wanted me to use my talent despite my circumstances. Although I was sick and limited in what I could do to promote my career, it reminded me that he had no limitations. When I was unable to do it on my own, he could still do abundantly more than I could imagine. God had given me a shiny ornament of hope I could hang on to and know that my dream was still alive.

∼

The adrenaline immediately wore off after I got home. The trip had really taken a toll on me. I was supposed to sing with Katelyn and Todd at church Christmas morning, but they had to do it without me. For the rest of the day, I went through the motions of participating in Christmas as best I could, but I wasn't my usual self. I spent a lot of time lying on the couch. Later I overheard Katelyn in the kitchen talking to Mom. "Christmas is supposed to be joyous, but with Scott not feeling well, it just seems kind of sad."

Despite the joy of meeting Jason Mraz, Katelyn's words were a stark reminder that I wasn't getting better. The one or two trips I had taken during my dialysis treatment were good for my musical soul, but I still felt chained to my dialysis chair. Although each dialysis treatment made me feel better for a day or two, even skipping one treatment would leave me feeling very ill. If I intended to travel and perform for more than a day or two, I had to come up with a better solution. I needed a plan that would allow a career and dialysis to coexist.

One option was to travel with a portable home dialysis machine. For a while, I considered that approach. The doctors would remove the tubing from my neck and chest and instead graft a fistula into my arm. The advantages were obvious—it didn't require major surgery, and since the dialysis machine would be with me, I wouldn't ever miss a treatment. In addition, the AV graft was safer than the central venous catheter I was currently using.

The other option was to push for a transplant. I'd learned that long-term dialysis could shorten a person's life by decades. And, just as important, not having to be tied to a machine every other day would give me more freedom and I would have more energy.

On the other hand, having a major organ transplant still sounded drastic to me. I would have to be on anti-rejection drugs for the rest of my life, which not only have side effects like hand tremors that could affect my piano playing but also meant that my immune system would never be the same. I would be more susceptible to all kinds of illnesses. *How would that affect my career?* I was always interacting with the public, whether it was a CD signing after a concert or while traveling through an airport. *Would I still be able to travel?*

Most importantly, I'd been told that a transplant wasn't necessarily a cure. Whatever caused my first kidney to fail could cause the transplanted kidney to fail. Even if it didn't fail, transplanted kidneys didn't last forever. The average life expectancy of a cadaveric kidney was typically fifteen to twenty years. One of my doctors summed it up nicely: "If you get a transplant, you're still going to have problems. They're just different problems."

My parents didn't always agree on which option was better for me—the transplant or portable dialysis. I was open to both options but dreaded making such a lifelong choice with permanent consequences. The truth was none of us had answers. All we could do was research and listen to the experiences and recommendations of others. Of course, the doctors were again recommending a transplant. But even if I wanted a transplant, it wasn't that simple. I had been put on the national transplant waiting list after my initial diagnosis, and we hadn't heard anything in more than a year. The median wait time was four years, but many people died while waiting to get the organs they needed. If I wanted to get off dialysis any sooner, I would need to seek a match with a live donor on my own.

We spent a lot of time discussing the pros and cons of each option. One day I'd hear a compelling case for long-term portable dialysis, and I'd think that I should just stick with what was working. Then I'd hear a statistic or have an appointment with a doctor who recommended a transplant, and I'd reconsider. I was grateful for those honest discussions. That meant we were looking at all sides without dismissing any option.

Most of the professionals we talked to thought transplant was a better option than long-term dialysis, but in the end, a transplant was still a major operation, and that was the bottom line for me. If I had a transplant, no matter how it turned out, there was no going back. As long as the catheter held, I knew I could continue doing what I was doing and still have some semblance of a life. Some might have even called it a good life. Although I couldn't do everything I wanted to do for my career, on the days I didn't have dialysis, I could still do many of the things I'd always loved, like writing and playing music.

Despite the temptation to be complacent, I also realized I needed to keep my options open regarding a transplant. It was time to explore finding a live donor.

CHAPTER 21

A Rough Climb to the View

The view from above is hard to believe
When you're driving uphill on a one-way street
It's a drag to keep moving
When only assuming
The view from above

—FROM "VIEW FROM ABOVE," SCOTT MACINTYRE

Being blind, I was much more vulnerable than the twenty-nine other patients in the dialysis room. Typically there was only one nurse and a couple of technicians. The technicians weren't highly trained medical professionals; their job was specifically to hook and unhook patients from the machines. Sometimes I worried what would happen if there was an emergency. After the holidays, I found out.

I had just finished listening to an audio book of Charles Dickens's *A Tale of Two Cities* and had taken off my headphones. I still had over an hour of dialysis left. Familiar sounds were all around me—the steady whizzing and beeping noises of the machines doing their work and technicians talking to patients as they arrived and were hooked up.

Suddenly the room went dark and the machines stopped. The entire room fell silent. *A power outage?* I had never expected anything like this to happen and I was horrified wondering if I was safe or if something was happening to me. My anxiety grew as I listened for a minute, but I couldn't hear a nurse or any of the technicians who should have been near me.

A door opened and another technician walked in. "What happened?" she asked.

"The power just went out," the nurse said. "It's a brownout."

A brownout? We're without power? Why don't they have a generator? I was strapped into my chair and hooked up to the machine. I knew this couldn't be good. *My bloodline is wide open!* Though the blood in my body was circulating, without the machine working, at least part of my blood was just sitting there, stagnate. *Is it coagulating in the tubes?*

I couldn't see what anyone was doing, and the nurse and technicians seemed to move around the room as if nothing was happening. I wasn't a nurse, or even a technician for that matter, but from what I knew, this had to be serious. *Why isn't anyone doing anything?* My stomach tensed as my anxiety grew. Thoughts of my stagnating blood made me squeamish. I took deep breaths to try to calm down. I couldn't get up; I was trapped into the chair, and I had no idea how to close the bloodlines or unhook myself. Even if I could, that was a drastic measure and not safe at all. Everything had to be clean and sanitary whenever the machine was touched. A single germ in my bloodline could cause a fatal infection. I didn't know what to do, so I did the only thing I could. I called out for help.

"Hold on! I'll be there in a minute," one of the technicians snapped.

I sat there, helplessly waiting for someone.

Eventually the nurse came over. She had been going around the room, patient by patient, showing them how to crank their machines until the power was restored. Apparently you could manually keep your blood flowing through the lines, and many of the patients picked up on this by observing others. But I couldn't see what was happening so the nurse had to guide my hand to the handle, and as soon as I got the hang of rotating it around, she moved on to the next patient.

I cranked that handle as if my life depended on it—for forty terrifying minutes until the power was finally restored.

When Mom picked me up and I told her what had happened, she was concerned. "They know you're blind. They should have helped you first instead of letting you sit there for so long, wondering what was happening."

They also should have been better equipped to handle an emergency like that. The brownout reinforced my belief that staying on dialysis forever wasn't the best option for me. I was even more vulnerable than I'd thought. There were so many things that could go wrong, and there was very little I could do about any of them. What if there was a fire? Even if there were enough technicians to unhook all thirty people at once, I couldn't find my way out of a burning building on my own. I'd need someone to guide me. The brownout was an extremely unsettling experience, but I began to consider lots of other reasons why a transplant might be my best option.

Even though I was on dialysis, I was still having chiropractic treatments several times a week, hoping that the misalignment in my spine was the cause of my kidney failure. We had met someone who was able to get off of dialysis after the chiropractor realigned his spine, so we felt it was worth continuing the treatments in case they could help me. My friend Larry often drove me to the appointments. One night, after hanging out at my house following a treatment, Larry got up to leave. He hugged me and then moved to hug my dad. But as I drew my arm back after hugging him, it got stuck inside his arm as he hugged Dad. Typically, when something like that happened, the other person would just lift their arm so I could reposition mine. But I realized from the way my arm was pressed between Larry and Dad that Larry couldn't feel my arm against his at all. He still had a large graft in his arm from when he had been on dialysis before his transplant, and somehow that had affected his sense of touch. It seemed that he had lost all feeling in that part of his arm. That scared me.

For my own safety, and to prevent infection, I wouldn't be able to keep the catheter in my chest forever. If I remained on dialysis long-term, I would eventually need a permanent graft in my arm. Though the hug with Larry only lasted a few seconds, the memory of his inability to feel stayed with me. As a blind person, and a pianist, my sense of touch was one of my best assets. I didn't want to lose it like Larry had. I knew then that if a kidney ever became available, I would take it.

I wanted a transplant.

~

So many people wanted to know about my medical condition that my parents sent an e-mail to all our friends and family. In it, they wrote about how I had needed emergency dialysis, and how I'd been placed on the national transplant list but it didn't look hopeful. Finally, they mentioned that we were praying for a living donor.

Within days, six people responded that they were willing to get tested, and if they were a match, to donate a kidney. I was overwhelmed. The first person who responded was Patricia Cosand, the wife of Walter Cosand, my piano professor at ASU. I had only met her a couple times, and I didn't know her that well, but I did know that Patricia, like her husband, was also a talented performer and music teacher. Much of what she knew about me I assumed she had learned through

Walter, and it touched me deeply that someone I barely knew would make such a generous offer.

There were others who offered, most of whom we knew better than I knew Patricia, but my gratitude was equal. As Mom and Dad read the list of potential donors, I realized that it wasn't just my family and me who wanted the world to hear my music. Others wanted that for me too—so much so that they were willing to donate their kidneys to help me live. It was humbling.

But it also left us with a dilemma. At the time, the Mayo Clinic would only test one donor at a time. Only after the first person was disqualified could the next person be tested. It was a difficult decision as to who should go in what order. There was a lot to consider: blood type, age, health, and even location—one of the donors lived out of state, which would add complications to the surgery and his recovery.

We prayed about it, but we also realized we needed to get moving. The longer I was on dialysis, the more harm it could do to my body. And if I was going to be on dialysis much longer, Dr. Grant would no doubt recommend an AV graft in my arm, and I didn't want that.

After much discussion and even more prayer, we eventually chose Stefan, a friend of mine who was approximately my age, height, and weight. The testing was scheduled to take two months, during which time they would test his blood and tissue types, his protein antigens, and other markers. He would also go through a lot of counseling with a transplant coordinator from Mayo Hospital where he could ask questions and learn more about the risks. Although they never tried to scare people away, they did want to separate those who were serious from those who were likely to pull out at the last minute, or those who were offering their kidney for the wrong reasons.

Stefan started the testing, and we kept up the praying.

Two months later we found out Stefan had been disqualified. We were never sure of the reasons for someone's disqualification; we only knew what the potential donor was willing to share with us. We went back to the list and selected another friend who we thought was a good physical match. Charles lived out of state, and when we warned him about the difficulty of having surgery and then not being able to recover at home, he didn't care. He was still willing.

Unfortunately, he was also disqualified.

The third donor, an older man, seemed promising and we thought for a while he was a match, but he got disqualified when his wife told the interviewers she didn't want him to do it. We understood, but it was still hard to keep get-ting our hopes up only to have them dashed.

After getting the news of each disqualification, Dad called the next person on the list of volunteers to carefully ask if they were still willing, or if their circumstances had changed and they no longer wanted to be considered. Each time Dad made that call, we knew a lot of time had passed since our initial request, so we were prepared for one or more of them to say no. But each one of them was still willing.

It was surprising how invested they each became during the testing pro-cess. Sure, we were disappointed with each disqualification, but many times the disqualified donors were even more distraught that they couldn't donate. While we would certainly have understood if someone had backed out, the commitment of my potential donors was a hopeful sign that assured us that once we did find a match, the donor would be willing to go through with the surgery. In the meantime, I just felt so thankful that so many people had stepped forward and offered to be tested.

The fourth potential donor was Marie Sellers. She was a mother of four, and we knew her family through homeschooling. By now we had learned not to get our hopes up, but we still continued to pray for each potential donor and that we would find the right match—the one God had in mind.

One afternoon, several weeks after Marie had started the testing process, I was home alone and thinking a lot about God's sovereignty. I knew he was in control, but I longed for guidance and direction in our search for a donor, which at times seemed to be endless. On that day, I prayed a little differently than I had prayed before. *God, I trust you with this. If Marie isn't the donor you have for me, then please just have her be disqualified.*

A few minutes after I finished praying, my phone rang. It was Mom.

"I have some news," she said. "Marie's been disqualified."

I was disappointed, just as I had been with all of the others. But in this case, I was completely at peace with the outcome. It was a sacred moment that affirmed that God was in the midst of my situation. In a way, he had used my prayer to show me his presence.

It was easy to think prayer was just a mechanism for petitioning my requests to God, but the truth was, prayer changed me. The more I prayed, the closer I got to God, and the more I felt like I was in communion with him and his will for my life. Part of me still wished Marie had qualified so I could have some certainty about my future, but I trusted that God had a plan, and I was willing to let it unfold.

By then we'd been through the first four people on the list and it wasn't looking good. The next person was Patricia Cosand, my piano professor's wife. When Dad called to see if she was still willing to be tested, she simply said, "Of course. I'm ready."

It was almost May when we asked Patricia to be tested. It would be two more months before we knew if she would be a match. Although experience had taught us that the chances of a donor being disqualified were much higher than being a match, I still clung to hope as each donor got tested. Now it was Patricia's turn.

⁓

As we went through the months of donor rejections, I tried to find new social outlets so I wasn't always stuck in the house. Todd, Katelyn, and I started going to my friend Christina's house to watch TV. Christina was the long-time friend I had been interested in for several years. We liked to watch the weekly exploits of Jack Bauer on *24*, and occasionally we watched *American Idol*. Christina had never really watched the show, but it didn't take long to get her hooked on it.

Watching *Idol* was one small way for me to stay connected with what was happening in pop music. I continued to write songs, and although the inspiration didn't come as often or as quickly as it did in London, I still found hooks in the most unusual places. Early one morning, my neighbor Randy was driving me to dialysis when he started telling me about what he'd done that weekend.

"A friend and I took a drive up Mogollon Rim. I'd never been up there before."

"I haven't either."

"We drove on this road that went straight up the ridge. It was so steep, we didn't take our eyes off the road for fear that we'd drive off the side. I don't know how many miles it was, but it seemed to take forever because we were going so slowly. When we got to the top, we parked the car and got out to look back, and . . . well, it was like the earth just seemed to fall away in front of us. There were limestone and sandstone cliffs. There were forests full of Ponderosa Pines. And there were so many flowers, some I'd never even seen before."

"Wow! That sounds beautiful," I said.

"It took our breath away. We had no idea how far up we'd gotten until we saw the view from above."

We pulled into the parking lot, and I thanked Randy for the ride—but I should have also thanked him for the inspiration. While I sat in my dialysis chair, I kept thinking about what he'd said, and I started to write a song called "View from Above." It was about having faith that the eventual outcome would be worth the struggle to get there. In life, we're often so concerned about the hardships of the climb that we forget about the beautiful view that awaits us at the end. I wrote the song to encourage and inspire others on their own tough roads and to remind them that it would all be worth it once they reached the top and looked back.

Maybe I was writing it for myself too—sometimes I would do that and not even realize it. The meaning of "View from Above" really spoke to me. Though I couldn't see an end to my struggles, I clung to my faith, hoping there would be one.

God had stripped away so many of my options, and with the disqualification of each potential donor, he'd left me with fewer and fewer alternatives. But that wasn't a bad thing. I knew that God was doing something, although I couldn't see what. This was my opportunity to trust in him alone. There was nowhere else to turn. I couldn't cure the kidney disease or find a matching, willing donor on my own. Whether God healed me or left me on dialysis for the rest of my life, the power was in his hands, and I needed to believe that someday I would look back and see that the view was worth it.

I believed it would be, but that didn't mean the waiting was easy.

When I first started dialysis, my newfound energy motivated me to be more productive, but the longer I stayed on dialysis, the more my drive and motivation slipped.

Jerry Lindahl and I continued to talk about projects we could work on together, but either they never materialized on his part, or my health prevented me from doing the necessary travel. I worried that I was losing my drive, and with it, the career I'd worked so hard to build. While I still focused on music— mostly through composing—I lost my ambition for the business side of things. I knew there was no way I could tour, even if I was handed the opportunity. Likewise, there was no way I could fly to a studio and spend days recording.

As we waited on the matching results for Patricia Cosand, my health declined even further. My creatinine levels were increasing to higher levels on my off days, and I needed treatments more frequently. My levels would go down immediately after dialysis, but as the highs got higher, the lows got higher too. My motivation was shot. I was stuck in Scottsdale, counting the days of dialysis, two months at a time, while I clung to the hope of a match.

I prayed that God would intervene soon.

CHAPTER 22

The Miracle of a 1.5

The moment you see it
You know why you needed
The view from above

—From "View from Above," by Scott MacIntyre

It looked as if I could be on dialysis for years rather than months.

So many potential donors had been disqualified that I'd taught myself not to get my hopes up as we waited to hear the results of each new volunteer. Of course, that also prevented me from being crushed by the disappointment when each one didn't work out. Perhaps that's why I don't remember much about the day we got the call saying Patricia Cosand was a match.

Dad called us from work. "I've got great news! Mayo just called and Patricia is a match!"

"Praise God!" Mom said, her words overflowing with joy.

I don't remember what I said, but I know I was stunned. The news seemed too good to be true and I wasn't sure how to process it. In one phone call, having a transplant went from an intangible idea to an event we were scheduling on the calendar. It was amazing and frightening at the same time. It was really going to happen; I was going to have a transplant.

As soon as we were all together that night, my family and I gathered in the living room to thank God for this amazing turn of events. Dad prayed, "Lord, we are so grateful for Patricia and the incredible gift she is offering to Scott. Thank you for providing a donor when we least expected it. We marvel at how you knew it was going to be Patricia all along and your steady hand kept guiding us toward her. We pray that going forward everything will move smoothly and we ask you to bless Patricia beyond measure for the sacrifice she is making."

It's hard for me to describe the sense of wonder that I felt once the news finally sank in. Patricia was the first person to volunteer and the fifth person to undergo testing. While we'd been looking around for other donors, she'd been right there the whole time. I couldn't believe someone I barely knew, someone who was completely healthy, was going to give me one of her kidneys. I was overwhelmed by her selflessness and filled with reverent awe for how God had worked to bring all of this about.

What if we had never moved from California to Toronto to Arizona? What if I hadn't gone to college at fourteen? What if I'd studied with another piano teacher and never met Walter? Looking back over my life I could see God moving in ways that I'd never noticed until now.

There were risks involved in the surgery for both Patricia and me, and if I had allowed myself to, I could easily have been overwhelmed by the fear of what was yet to come. Yet, when I saw how God had orchestrated the events of my life to bring Patricia and me together at the very moment he knew I needed her most, I couldn't help but trust him. How could I dwell on the fear of the surgery when he was so obviously in control of even the smallest details of my life?

~

Jerry Lindahl and I continued to talk. He knew how much my health had deteriorated during the previous few months, so we had postponed any projects until after I got a transplant. Though we hadn't yet worked together, he promised me that we would soon. One day he called and told me about a four-million-dollar recording studio in San Clemente he was working with. "I'm thinking it would be so cool to get you in there to record. I just think about everything you've produced yourself, in your own studio, and I can only imagine what you could do in a studio like that." He promised he would arrange everything and we would do it as soon as I recovered from my transplant. I didn't want to get my hopes up, since other things we had enthusiastically planned together had not always panned out in the end, but this time he assured me it would absolutely happen, and I believed him.

I called him in July, not long after hearing about Patricia. "She was just approved as a donor for me, and it looks like the transplant will take place in August."

"That's great news!" said Jerry. "Get through your surgery and then as soon as you're ready to travel, we'll set something up. I've already talked to the studio. This is definitely going to happen. We just need to find dates that work for everybody."

I could only imagine what my music would sound like with expensive microphones, top-of-the-line mixing consoles, and high-end guitar amps at my disposal. I'd even heard that the studio had several drum sets I could choose from to make sure I got the exact sound I was looking for. Dreaming about the studio gave me something to look forward to—I could have my transplant and then immediately move forward with my career. God had given me another ray of light to keep me going.

~

The surgery was scheduled for August 22. During the weeks leading up to the surgery, there were lots of tests and doctors' appointments to make sure everything was ready to go. We met with the surgeon who would be performing the surgery and we immediately liked her. She was reassuring and put us at ease.

Patricia didn't waver at all. After she was identified as a match, we spent time getting to know her better. Walter had been my piano professor, but in the five years I'd worked with him, he'd said very little about his family. Now we would be forever linked as a family through his wife's selfless gift.

The night before the surgery, Walter and Patricia came over to our house for dinner and we prayed together. There was no sense of foreboding or anxiety; instead we all felt very connected. It was a warm and intimate evening. Later Mom told me that Walter and Patricia held hands a lot that night. I had felt the love between them, and I hoped they felt the love we had for them. Before they left, we took a few pictures to remember that very special evening.

Lying in bed that night, I felt happy and surprisingly free.

There were no more decisions to make. And there was no time for second-guessing. The path had been long, but it had led irreversibly to this day. An incredible sense of calm came over me as I realized that this was the moment I had thought about, dreaded, and yet longed for during the past couple of years. I had been diagnosed with kidney failure more than two years earlier, and I'd spent ten months on dialysis. I'd been through four potential donors before the fifth one was a match. The next day I would finally have the transplant that had loomed so large in my mind for so long, and in less than twenty-four hours I would be lying in a hospital bed with someone else's kidney inside of me. It was hard to wrap my mind around the thought.

The next morning I once again got up before the sun, but instead of heading to the dialysis center, we went to the hospital. As we drove through the dark streets of Scottsdale, I felt closer to God than I ever had. I thought about how many people had prayed for me to get here, and how many were praying for me at that moment—countless family members and friends across the United States, Canada, and England. I had a friend who was teaching in China, and she told me her entire class of children was lifting me up in prayer. It seemed as if I could feel each of their prayers. Our faith united us across distance and time, and that comforted me.

At the hospital, Patricia and I started in different rooms. Since her surgery would happen first, she was already there, prepped and ready to go by the time I arrived. As soon as I was ready, they wheeled my bed next to hers so both families could be together. As my parents stood around me, and Walter stood by Patricia, I turned to her and struggled to once again find the right words to thank her. It was an impossible task. How could I ever thank her for literally giving me a part of herself?

In the weeks leading up to the surgery, I had tried on many occasions to tell her what I was feeling, but each time I had tried, my words never seemed to carry the depth of emotion and gratitude I wanted to express. Each time I'd tried to say thank you, she simply and graciously responded, "Well, it's something I can do to help." Now, like then, I just had to trust that, despite my inability to articulate what I was feeling, she could still feel and understand my profound gratitude for her sacrifice.

A nurse came in and said it was time for Patricia to go. We said our good-byes, and the nurses wheeled her off to surgery with our prayers flowing after her.

~

Had things been a little different, I might never have studied with Walter Cosand. Acceptance into the ASU School of Music required a separate audition and application from the rest of the university. At the time, Walter was the department head. After moving to Arizona from Toronto, Mom and I met with him to learn more about the audition. Seeing how young I was, he thought I would be better served in a different program. "I'm going to refer you to Jane Johnson," he said. "She runs the piano preparatory program for high school students. I think that would be a good place for Scott to be."

That sounded good to us. My piano teacher in Toronto had highly recommended Jane, and I would've been thrilled to study with her. A few weeks later, I went to Jane's studio and auditioned for her. I played several pieces and then she asked me a bunch of music theory questions. I figured she wanted to see if I could think and communicate as well as I played. After she finished, she walked me out into the hall where Mom was waiting. "Well, I just gave him my masters' student theory exam. And he passed." After we left her studio, Jane called Walter. "I'm sending Scott back to you. He really needs to be in the university-level program." Walter took her word for it, and he met with me a couple of times to help select music and to prepare me for my audition.

Mom was with me the first time I entered Walter's studio, and she described the setting. Straight ahead was a window that let in a lot of light, making the room feel airy and bright. Although most teachers had two pianos side by side, Walter had set up his studio so that the pianos faced each other, nestled together like shoes in a shoebox. Over the years I would look up while playing some long passage and catch a glimpse of him sitting across from me. When my pinhole glimpse caught sight of his lower face, it seemed that I always spotted a sort of half smile.

Walter carefully thought about everything he said, and when he spoke, he spoke deliberately. He was a quiet and humble man. One day, during my second or third year in his studio, a freshman asked him if he was a Christian.

"Well, I try to be," Walter replied in his understated way.

I thought that was a clever answer and the most humble thing he could have said. If being a Christian meant being a follower of Christ, the best we could do as imperfect people was to *try* and follow Christ in everything. I don't know if the student who asked the question understood his answer, but I thought it was beautiful.

The night before my junior-year recital, Walter listened to my rehearsal in an intimate concert hall. The adjudicators and a large audience would be there the next day, and I was meticulously practicing the passages that gave me the most trouble. When I finished, Walter simply said, "It sounds like you can do things I can't even do." Coming from him, it was the greatest of compliments.

Despite my young age, Walter always made me feel comfortable in his studio. His master classes brought together undergrad and grad students alike, but because he never looked down on me because of my young age, neither did the other music students. When students in my academic classes saw the music students treating me as a peer, like Walter, they also looked past my age and accepted me based on my academic and musical abilities. That in turn led to many friendships, and eventually to being accepted throughout the ASU community. Walter's kindness, friendship, and musical training were priceless gifts that I will always carry with me.

Now his wife was giving me a priceless gift too.

~

The nurses came in and hooked up an IV to my wrist, and they took some blood so they could check my creatinine level one last time, as well as check my potassium and electrolyte levels. After they walked away we took a moment to talk and pray together as a family. They must have been listening, because as soon as we finished, they walked back in and said, "It's time to go."

I knew things might not go well. I could wake up to discover that my body was already rejecting the kidney or that it never took at all. Complications could occur while I was on the table. During the past few days, and hours, I'd had to sign waivers to protect the doctors and the hospital. But the one that scared me the most was the living will. What did I want to do if I ended up in a vegetative state? I didn't even want to think about that.

The surgery involved cutting through nine layers of skin and muscle in my abdominal wall. A metal pipe would be inserted down my throat, and as a vocalist, that concerned me. The slightest damage to my throat or vocal chords could forever change the direction of my career. But there were also more painful concerns, like the necessity to insert a catheter in a place that made me want to cross my legs and sing soprano. Fortunately, they weren't going to do that until I was under anesthesia. The anesthesia worried me too. What if I got too much or too little?

But there was nothing I could do about any of that now. I was ready to accept whatever the outcome would be. That acceptance gave me confidence. I was glad we had tried so many other options first. I had fought a valiant fight to avoid a transplant, and now that I couldn't, I would never have to look back and wonder, *What if?* It had been a slow progression, but I was thankful for the time I'd been given. As they pushed me through the operating room doors, I fully surrendered to the transplant team and to God's will for my life. From the beginning of time he had known who would be my donor. I had an overwhelming sense of peace, not only because I was sure this was God's plan, but because people all over the world were now joining in prayer—for me, for Patricia, and for our doctors. I only expected to wake up to good news.

~

The surgery was expected to take up to four hours. After a little more than two hours, my parents were notified that I was already in recovery. Both surgeries had gone well. There were no complications. In fact, the minute they put Patricia's kidney in my body, it immediately became red and they could see the blood pulsing through it.

I found out later that after Patricia woke up, Mom and Dad went in to visit her. When they asked how she was doing, she simply said, "Oh, I'm fine." Mom handed her a card we'd written, and once again on behalf of our family, she tried to find words to say thank you. But Mom's tears said it all.

In the recovery room, I woke up and felt something on my stomach. It was a huge bandage. That was my first clue that the surgery had happened. A nurse saw me stirring and came over. "You did great. Your new kidney is working just fine." That was a huge relief to hear. The weight I had carried for so long had finally been lifted off me, but still, it was hard to comprehend that my nightmare was now over.

While I was still in recovery, Mom and Dad were brought in. I was still a bit groggy as they took turns holding my hand and telling me how well the surgery went. As my mind became clearer, I suddenly realized I had neglected to do something. "Can I borrow someone's phone? I need to call Jerry!"

When I said that, Mom and Dad laughed. If I was already thinking about music, they knew the surgery had been a success.

A nurse came in. "I have your latest creatinine level. Do you want to hear it?"

We knew that was the true test. It had been higher than twelve before the surgery. If the kidney was truly working, then the number would be lower than that by now.

"What is it?" I asked cautiously.

I could hear the smile in her voice when she said, "It's a four! Congratulations."

"That's amazing!" I couldn't remember the last time I'd had a four—probably over a year ago when I was in London. Over the next twenty-four hours, it kept dropping, from a 3.0 to a 2.4 to a 2.0.

When it hit two, Dad couldn't believe it. "Wow! Praise God!"

That's how I felt too. It was astounding to think that, within a day, my level was already lower than it had been when we first started monitoring it in May 2005. But it continued to drop after that. We saw 1.9, 1.8, and then 1.7, where it seemed to hold. By the next day it had dropped to 1.6 and stabilized at 1.5, with only slight variations above or below that. It was a beautiful thing to watch and tangible proof that Patricia's gift was doing its job.

Although I couldn't visit Patricia in the hospital—and once home it wasn't recommended that I go out of the house for the first six weeks except for doctor's appointments—I followed her recovery via e-mail and phone calls. She was not supposed to do anything strenuous for thirty days, but within a week she was back at work, giving viola lessons and lifting her viola case. Her quick recovery wasn't an indication of what she went through—she should've been out of commission for several weeks—but it was a testimony to her strength, God's goodness, and the many prayers for her rapid recovery.

True to their personalities, the Cosands resumed their lives as if nothing had happened. I do my best to stay in touch with them, and I always try to call Patricia on the anniversary of our surgery. But anytime I or anyone else thanks her for the sacrifice she made, she simply says, "I'm glad I could help."

But it was more than help. It was everything. The gift of her kidney meant that not only could I have my life back, but I could also have my music, my career, and the chance to fulfill so many of my dreams.

God had given me two years to warm up to the idea of having a kidney transplant, and during that time I learned that his promises are true even when his answers aren't always the answers I'm looking for. God had answered our prayers for healing. It wasn't an instantaneous healing, but watching those creatinine levels fall in the hospital, I knew without a doubt that it was he who had used doctors and medical science to heal me. In my mind, that didn't make it any less miraculous.

CHAPTER 23

Slow Business Recovery

I like the brand new look you have
Our glitter text and colors match
And it never felt so right
—FROM "I'LL TAKE TOM," SCOTT MACINTYRE

Though I was freed from the chains of dialysis, I still had a lot of doctor's appointments—six to nine appointments a week—for the first six weeks. Some appointments were for examinations, others were just for lab work, but their intent was the same—to make sure everything was functioning properly. During those six weeks, the doctors didn't want me going out into public because my immune system was being severely suppressed so my body would accept the foreign kidney; they didn't want me exposed to any more germs than necessary because I might not be able to fight them off. Even when I went to see the doctors, they wanted me to wear a mask over my mouth and nose. Soon they gradually lowered the dosages of my immunosuppressive drugs, making my system less compromised and allowing me to once again go out in public.

The doctors continued to be pleased with my progress, but the recovery wasn't easy. Basic things like standing up and lying down required use of my stomach muscles, including the ones the doctor had cut through. I had a nine-inch scar from the surgery that one doctor described as "beautiful." I described it as painful. For a while I slept in a reclining chair because getting into bed hurt too much. It even hurt to sit up and watch TV. I was home five days when I first sat down at the piano, and it burned so much that I couldn't stay longer than a few minutes. Muscles I didn't know existed screamed for me to stop. I didn't take the high-powered painkillers that doctors prescribed because I didn't like how they made me feel; instead I opted for Tylenol. But, day by day, as I healed and regained my strength, I was able to stay at the piano a little longer each time.

Too much time had passed for me to return to England, and although

I was sorry I wouldn't be attending Cambridge, I was excited about pursuing my pop music career. During those first few weeks after the surgery, I arranged and produced seven original songs. It was exciting to have the energy to attack a new song and complete it in just a few days, rather than the weeks or months it had been taking. My voice still sounded a bit frail, but it was good to be doing what I loved again.

Though the physical recovery was extremely painful, overall it actually went pretty fast, but the emotional recovery took longer. I wasn't motivated to promote my music or book performances, and that was unusual for me. Though the artistry and the business side of music were two separate things, I'd always done both. Without a manager, I had to be the go-getter. But even after most of my physical healing had taken place, I still lacked the emotional drive to find and book performances. Over the past year, as I became used to the limitations of dialysis, I hadn't felt ambitious. And though I was now healthy, my ambition hadn't yet returned. I was starting to wonder if it ever would.

~

When the initial six weeks were up, I was once again allowed to go out into public. My first night out was to see Todd perform in a musical theater production at ASU. I was glad to finally get out of the house, but even happier to support Todd in something he loved doing. I asked Christina if she would join me for the evening and she agreed.

Christina and I had an easy friendship. We could see each other several times in a week and enjoy each other's company, or we could not talk for several months and still pick up right where we left off. I suspected she had some feelings for me, but I was never sure. With all that I'd had going on the past two years, I wasn't surprised that nothing had happened between us. This would be the first time the two of us would be alone in a very long time. I was so eager to check in with her and see how she was doing.

At the theater Christina and I took our seats. I told her it was the first time I'd been out since the transplant.

"Really? You haven't been out of the house at all?"

"Just to the doctors and back."

"Wow! It's so sweet of you to invite me!" Her melodic voice sounded sincere, and it made me feel warm inside.

Ever since we met while performing in *The Music Man* four years earlier,

I could picture Christina and me going out. Now that I was healthy, and we were both older, I wondered if the timing might be right for us to start seeing each other. As the lights in the theater dimmed and the curtain rose, I took a chance and reached for her hand. This could have been a really awkward move, because I couldn't see where her hand was. *Is it resting on her knee or folded in her lap?* If I reached for the wrong area, I could be in a lot of trouble. It had happened before.

I tried to be natural as much as possible, and when our hands finally met, I was relieved to not have embarrassed myself. As I held her hand through the first song, I hoped that she was enjoying it as much as I was and that this would be the start of something more.

When the song ended, we broke apart to applaud the performers. But as soon as I finished, I moved my hand back into position so she could grab it again. But to my disappointment, she didn't. For the rest of the show, I wondered what she was thinking. Did she like holding my hand, or did it make her uncomfortable?

As we walked to the car after the show, I decided that I needed to be direct. It was the only way I'd know what she was thinking.

"I know you're planning to go off to college next semester, so I don't know how we'd make it work, but I feel like there might be something between us, and I wondered what you thought about it?"

"Well, you've always been a special person in my life, and I really like you as a friend, but . . ."

As she paused I already knew what she was going to say. *Special* and *friend* were words of doom for a potential dating relationship.

"I don't know if now is the right time, and I wouldn't want to ruin our friendship if things didn't work out."

It wasn't what I wanted to hear. Holding her hand I was sure I'd felt more than friendship from her. *Is she still denying her feelings for me?* Though her words were clear, I clung to hope where I found it, in the touch of her hand during that first song, and on the front of the program from the show—the name of the musical we saw together that night was *She Loves Me.*

⌒

Suddenly it was October, and just like the previous year, I had another doctor's appointment scheduled for October 31. During the drive over, my parents and I couldn't help but talk about the appointment exactly one year earlier on Halloween.

"Remember that appointment?" I asked. "That's when the doctor said I would need a transplant before Christmas." At the time the news had seemed so shocking, but I didn't even last until Christmas. I had to start emergency dialysis just a few weeks later.

I wondered what this year would bring. So far everything about my recovery had looked good, but bad news had surprised me before. I said a quick prayer that the news this Halloween wouldn't be as frightening as last year's had been.

The appointment couldn't have been more different from the last. Dr. Grant came in with a bounce in his step and a lilt in his voice. After looking at my test results and reviewing the stability of my creatinine levels, he gave us the good news. "Your prognosis looks great for the long term. You're going to have a really good run with that kidney." For the first time in a very long time, a doctor had given me unqualified good news.

On the way home we reflected on how far we'd come during the past couple of years. Mom told me how proud she was of how I'd handled everything.

"I remember days when Dad or I had to wake you up for dialysis at five in the morning. We hated to do it because we knew how tired you were and how awful it was for you to sit in one place for so many hours. But you always had such a good attitude about it. In some ways, you've been the wind beneath our wings."

"Thank you for saying that, but how was I the wind beneath *your* wings?"

"Instead of complaining about having to go, you would jump out of bed, throw on your clothes, and say, 'I can't wait to go to dialysis today.'"

"I said that?"

"Yes. And when I asked you why, you said you were at a really good place in *A Tale of Two Cities* and you wanted to hear what happened next."

I laughed because I remembered the day she was talking about. She was right; I couldn't wait to finish it. At the time, I didn't know that finding joy in little things would help me deal with the big picture, but looking back, I could see it was one of the ways I had coped. I was thankful she shared that moment with me. Despite the ups and downs, I did always seem to have some measure of peace. I always felt like God was with me—no matter how bad the circumstances.

Now that I had a clean bill of health, I was ready to record in the San Clemente studio with Jerry. Mom drove me to Los Angeles to meet him, and I spent the night at his friend's house. The next morning Jerry and I drove to the studio. On the drive over, I learned that Jerry had traded favors with the owners of the studio; in exchange for them working on my EP, he volunteered to do a bunch of free promotional work for them. It was a wonderful thing for him to do for me, and I wanted to make the most of his generosity.

I had been in recording studios before, so the environment was familiar. But now, instead of being there to work for someone else, everyone in the studio was working for me. I couldn't believe it. Musicians, technicians, audio engineers, and a host of other people were all there just to help me. We only had three and a half days in the studio. That wasn't a lot of time, so I came prepared with a list of what I wanted to accomplish, and I'd broken it down by the hour so we could make sure we stayed on track.

Each day started early in the morning and went until after midnight. If I wasn't playing piano, strumming the guitar, or singing, I was coaching the drummer, bass player, or cellist. And I spent a lot of time analyzing the play-back of the most recent recording. The first day passed so quickly I barely had time to catch my breath.

We left the studio that night and headed to Jason Mraz's house, where we were staying. Jerry seemed pleased with the day's work, and that made me feel even happier than I already felt. We drove with the car windows down and the warm California air blowing our hair. I asked Jerry if we could stop by a Starbucks. I wanted to celebrate our work with an Iced Mocha Frappuccino. I went all out and ordered the largest size they had—a venti—and slowly savored it the rest of the way home.

We got to the house and unloaded our stuff. Jason wasn't there—he was out on tour—but Jerry had a key. Once inside, Jerry went straight to bed, but I wasn't ready to let go of the moment. I pulled a chair up to the dining room table—the same table we'd had Christmas dinner at the year before—and continued to sip on my Frappuccino and bask in the overwhelming joy of the day. I was so pleased with the way things were working in the studio. I knew what a miracle it was to be there and how fragile life could be, and I was determined to make the most of every minute that had so graciously been given me.

I recorded four complete songs during the next few days in the studio. The first two were "Easily Broken" and "Fire in My Soul." I also recorded "View from Above," the song I'd written in the dialysis chair, and "Autumn Leaves," which Jerry thought was my best song. It was an incredible amount of work in a very short period of time, but I was proud of what we accomplished. Three of the songs ended up on my *View from Above* EP, which I later released on iTunes, and "Autumn Leaves" and "View from Above" reappeared on my *Heartstrings* album.

One day, during a break, Jerry asked me if I was seeing anybody. I told him about Christina, and how the timing had just never worked out, but despite all that, we'd remained close friends. But something had happened between Christina and me right before I came out to California. It had been bothering me, and before I knew it, I was telling Jerry.

"Christina took my picture off of her MySpace top friends list and replaced it with a picture of Tom." Tom was Tom Anderson, MySpace's founder.

"Why'd she do that?"

"I have no idea. I'm hoping it was an accident, but I don't know. It's like the ultimate MySpace dis. When you join MySpace, Tom is the first friend you automatically start with and everyone has to have him. But Tom never interacts with anyone on a personal level. His profile is completely utilitarian. It's as if Christina were saying to me, 'Tom is more important than you, even if I'll never talk to him.'"

"Exactly," Jerry laughed. "So did you call her and ask her why?"

"No."

"What'd you do?"

"I removed her picture from my top friends and replaced it with a picture of Tom."

Jerry and I both laughed as I realized how juvenile that sounded. But then Jerry got serious. "I think you should write a song about that."

"Really?"

"Yeah, I think that could make a great song. Maybe we could even get Jason to co-write it with you."

"I think you may have something there!" I knew it could be a really cool opportunity and tried to picture myself co-writing with Jason Mraz. But there was a part of me that wanted it to be my song alone since it was my story.

Later that week, he again brought up the idea of doing a MySpace song. "After thinking about it, I think you should do it on your own."

"Really? Why?"

"I want to see what *you* come up with."

I appreciated Jerry's confidence in me. When I got home I thought up as many MySpace puns as I could and made a list of the best ones. Eventually I wrote "I'll Take Tom." It's a song about going through a breakup or having a friend who ticks you off, and then giving them the ultimate dis online—replacing them with Tom. The last part of the song says:

> *Tom will listen to my problems*
> *Wait around until I solve them*
> *Hear me out and never say a word*
> *Tom will never treat me badly*
> *Tom won't spit my words back at me*
> *Tom won't make me wish I never knew him*
> *And that's because I knew him first*
> *It really looks like you forgot me*
> *Ever since you went to block me*
> *I don't give a click*
> *Watch my feelings float away*
> *Till they're lost in cyberspace*
> *You don't need to hide your face*
> *Guess I win the breakup*
> *Time to clean my space up*
> *I'll take Tom any day*

When I finished it, I sent the song to Jerry. He loved it. I loved the song too. After pouring my emotions into it, I booted Tom off of my top friends list and put Christina back on top where she belonged. I later recorded a produced version of "I'll Take Tom," and it also ended up on my *Heartstrings* CD.

And as for Christina, to this day I don't know how or why she replaced me with Tom. I asked her once, but she didn't remember it happening. I suspect it was just an accident. But now it was a happy accident—because Christina and I had a good laugh, and I got a great song out of the experience.

~

Whether making strategic decisions about the music or turning ideas into marketing plans, I had always been the guy heading up my career. Through the years, I enlisted my parents to help, and between the three of us, we not only negotiated the performances, but booked the flights, pitched my story to the media, maintained my website, scheduled photo shoots, started a mailing list, and set up CD tables to sell merchandise after each concert. There was no agency or record label working for me. If I wasn't on top of it, it didn't get done.

Writing and recording was going well, but the business side of my career had stalled. Dialysis had stripped away the motivation and drive that had previously fueled my ambition. Although I could always find the energy to work on music, I could no longer muster the initiative to proactively promote myself and book gigs. My health had taken priority above my career for so long that I was stagnating professionally, unable to seize each day the way I wanted to.

Around the time of my graduation from ASU, my career had achieved its highest level in terms of number of bookings and pay per performance. I was in demand for concerts and performances—as a soloist and as part of the MacIntyre Family Singers. But then I disappeared for two years. After such a long break and having to turn down so many opportunities, I had completely fallen off the radar. Now that I was ready to perform again, no one was asking me to. I knew it would be a difficult task to build back up to the notoriety I once had, but it was even harder to muster up the energy to begin the climb back.

My family and friends didn't quite understand. They saw that I was feeling better and had more energy, but they knew I wasn't quite myself. Mom and Dad noticed that I had stopped keeping a calendar and wasn't working toward any future concerts.

Dialysis had taken a mental and emotional toll. For the past year, every day had been a repeat of the same monotonous day before it. Now the world was open to me again, and I could chase any dream I wanted; all I needed was my professional zeal. It was as if my body had healed, but my mind was still stuck in that dialysis chair.

I needed something to break it loose.

CHAPTER 24

Coming Full Circle

I'm still here
Standing where I shouldn't be
It's up to me this time
—FROM "I'M STILL HERE," SCOTT MACINTYRE

In November, VSA—the international organization on arts and disability—was holding their annual International Young Soloists Competition, and Mom encouraged my siblings and me to apply. I knew that entering and winning the competition could help me move ahead musically, but at the time, I had no idea that it also held the potential to restore my motivation to get back into the business side of things.

Ambassador Jean Kennedy Smith founded VSA in 1974 to provide artistic and educational opportunities for people with disabilities. As part of their mission, VSA held an annual International Young Soloists Award to recognize outstanding young musicians with disabilities and to encourage them in their pursuit of a musical career.

Applications were posted on the VSA website in September and musical submissions had to be entered by mid-November. Musicians could enter as either soloists or ensembles, but at least one person in the ensemble had to have some kind of disability, whether mild or severe. After talking with my family, we decided to enter the MacIntyre Family Singers. Since both Katelyn and I had been blind from birth, we would meet the disability qualification. The only downside was the age qualification, so Mom wouldn't be eligible to participate; it would just be the three of us.

An advisory committee comprised of music professionals and educators would choose two American and two international award recipients. Winners would be announced in January and each of the four acts chosen would receive five thousand dollars. But more important, they would also be invited to perform in a ticketed concert at the Kennedy Center in Washington, DC.

We filled out the application and worked hard to select the best recordings of the three of us together. Then we wrote the required biographical narrative and sent the package off. We had submitted our best work, but I had no idea if it was enough to win.

~

That Thanksgiving and Christmas were some of the best holidays we'd ever spent together. We were so thankful for my renewed health and energy. The previous year I had started dialysis just before Thanksgiving, and when I returned from Jason Mraz's house on Christmas Eve, I didn't have the energy to participate in all of the family activities. But this year I was part of everything that was happening.

Music and joy once again filled the house. Not only were we singing together, but we also did the other things we enjoyed. Once again I could swim with Katelyn and Todd in the backyard pool. They made up for lost time by beating me at "noodle wars," a game in which we launched foam projectiles back and forth at each other in the pool. In the past when we had wrestled, I had nearly always beaten Todd, but now he beat me more often than I cared to admit. It seemed Todd had grown physically stronger, or perhaps I was weaker, since the last time we played. And Katelyn no longer had to give me side hugs to avoid the catheter; now she was free to hug me any way she wanted.

During Christmastime we talked about taking a family skiing trip in March. At first I was a little concerned if I would be ready, but doctors assured me that I would be seven months out of surgery by then, and I'd be fine. I was excited! I hadn't been skiing in several years, and it was one of my favorite winter sports. When I first learned to ski while living in Canada, we worked out a system where Mom or Dad would ski thirty to forty feet ahead of me, shouting verbal cues and wearing dark pants. As I followed behind, I had to keep my eyes fixated on their legs, which contrasted against the white snow. If I tried to look at anything else even for one second, I would lose track of where my guide was and be completely disoriented—not a good thing when speeding down an icy mountain. So I had to stay focused and implicitly trust my guide to keep me away from trees and other obstacles. I also had to be prepared for the terrain to change at any moment since I had no depth perception of the white snow. But I didn't worry. It was exhilarating to feel the wind in my face and hear the crunch of the snow beneath my skis as we descended.

I was so thankful for the holidays. I was healthy, the family was happy, and with the upcoming travel plans, we all had so much to look forward to.

~

In January, the seventh season of *American Idol* started airing on FOX, and once again we watched as a family. That spring, as I started performing at churches and other charity functions, people would often say to me, "You should try out for *American Idol*. I'd vote for you!"

Like the rest of America, I thought *American Idol* was great entertainment. I laughed at the judges' comments during the auditions, when people who couldn't sing begged for another chance to show their lack of talent. But in the back of my mind, I wondered if some of them were accomplished singers just having an off day. Some people seemed truly stunned by the judges' harsh words.

I had never thought *American Idol* was something I wanted to do. They didn't allow contestants to play instruments, and as a singer and songwriter who considered the piano a crucial part of his performance, I didn't think it would offer me the best place to showcase my talent.

Fortunately, performance opportunities were starting to trickle in, and I hoped to build my schedule back to where it had been. I didn't want to throw it all away on a reality show looking for a few laughs. I felt I had too much to lose by taking that risk. Some people would do anything for their fifteen minutes of fame, but I needed to be true to myself, even if it meant missing my fifteen minutes.

But as the season continued, I softened my thinking. For the first time, *Idol* let contestants play instruments while they sang. The night the top 16 performed, David Archuleta, an early favorite, began his solo from behind a grand piano. Though he only played it for about thirty seconds before walking to the front of the stage to sing the rest of his song, it made a strong impression on me. Mom noticed it too. "Wouldn't it be amazing if you could play and sing for the judges?"

The following week Brooke White sang "Let it Be" while accompanying herself on the grand piano. It was a beautiful moment for her, and she was very emotional when it was over. During the critique that followed, Paula Abdul said that America could feel Brooke's heart through her music. I began to wonder if *Idol* could help me share my heart and my music with a larger audience.

Singing my heart out while playing in front of a live studio audience seemed the perfect way to do it. With that thought, auditioning for *Idol* some-day suddenly went from a non-starter to an interesting possibility.

~

In late January we received the news that we had won the VSA International Young Soloists Award! That meant we would be performing at the Kennedy Center. It was quite an honor, and we were thrilled. Once we knew the date of the performance—May 29, 2008—I decided to set up as many concert dates around it as I could. Perhaps the four of us could make a tour out of it?

Putting together a tour wasn't easy. Most established bands have a tour manager and a travel agent to handle all the bookings and logistics. But if the MacIntyre Family Singers were going to go on tour, I had to make it happen. I still didn't have my drive back to do all the business things, but I hoped that forcing myself to plan for this trip would help me recover some of what I'd lost.

I started by reaching out to people we knew. We had some connections in Toronto, California, and Chicago, so I asked if any of their churches would be interested in having us perform. Performing at the Kennedy Center was like having a magic key that opened every door. Once decision makers learned about that event, they were eager to get us on their calendar too. In addition, the Kennedy Center performance helped garner a lot of media attention. I was able to book TV and radio interviews for days we weren't performing. Those interviews helped advertise our local performances and increased attendance and CD sales at our concerts.

Within a few weeks I had put together our first international tour, book-ing performances in California, Arizona, Ontario, Illinois, Virginia, and Washington, DC (in addition to the one at the Kennedy Center). But by far, my biggest accomplishment was negotiating the honorariums and fees. By the time we left for the first show, everything was paid for, with money left over. We didn't have to worry about breaking even, and any CDs we sold were pure profit. Mom never wanted to take any of the money we made. She was just happy to be singing with us. So, everyone agreed that I would take half since I had booked the tour, and Todd and Katelyn would split the other half. It was a lucrative tour for an independent group no one had heard of. And it also gave me a lot of business experience.

Seeing it all come together lit a fire inside of me. I was ready to once again grab the marketing and promotion reigns and proactively take control of my career. I realized that God had been faithful—not only in restoring my health, but in allowing me to share my musical talent in a bigger way than ever before. It was confirmation that he wanted me to get back out there and share my music with new audiences. I had restored my faith in myself and fueled my desire to do more. When something is successful, you *want* to do it again. This was the success I needed.

Once we were on the road, I continued to pray for the details—that I hadn't overlooked anything. One wrong flight could upset several performances and then we would be in trouble. Fortunately, most everything went as planned, and what didn't was easily rectified. After each performance, we would fly to our next destination, then we would be picked up by a limo or Mom would drive a rental car to the hotel where we would rest up and prepare for our next concert.

Since churches typically wanted us to perform on weekends, we did media events during the week and occasionally had a couple of days off to visit friends. While in Canada, we stayed with our friends the Feinbergs. The day we arrived, none of us were feeling well. By the next day I had almost completely lost my voice. Every time I tried to sing, nothing came out but air. I didn't know if it was laryngitis or something else; it had never happened to me before. But the worst part was that I had a big television interview and performance early the next morning for *100 Huntley Street*, Canada's longest-running daily talk show. Though I wasn't feeling well, I had promised to appear and I knew I couldn't let them down.

With a few musical adjustments (I had to sing half an octave lower than usual), I did all right. I sang "No Fear," which was the same song I played for Laurie Z. the last time I saw her. She had predicted the song would do well, and she was right. The YouTube video of the "No Fear" performance became my most-watched video of all time.

We went back to the Feinbergs' house after the show, and Dad called to see how everything was going. "It's so exciting!" he said. "This is what you've always talked about."

He was right. Ever since I was a kid, I had dreamed of going on tour and now it was happening. It wasn't an arena tour, but I was on the road, sharing my music with people all over North America. "It feels great," I said, as I tried to take it all in. "Even better than what we talked about."

Later that week, while still in Canada, we watched the *American Idol* season seven finale with the Feinbergs. Like the rest of North America, I was pretty sure that David Archuleta was going to win (he was favored in the media and popular among the pre-teen set). However, a couple of hours later, to everyone's surprise, David Cook was crowned the winner. But as I watched the celebration, I realized it didn't really matter who came in first place. Anyone who was in the top ten on *American Idol* had already won. They would leave the show with name recognition and an unparalleled musical platform that could help them take their careers to the next level. The top ten also went on tour, performing in arenas while tens of thousands of fans cheered them on. As I thought about the tour I was on now and how amazing it would be to tour on the level that *Idol* offered, the seed of interest that had been planted earlier began to put down roots.

～

I didn't think much about *American Idol* after the finale ended. I concentrated on my own pinnacle moment—performing at the Kennedy Center. It was so exciting to think we would be on the stage of one of the best-known venues in the world.

When we arrived at the Kennedy Center, I felt a bit like Dorothy—we weren't in Kansas anymore. Because we had typically played in churches or smaller venues, we were used to working with volunteer soundboard operators on how to best mix our voices and the piano. We were a do-it-yourself kind of group. If we needed a monitor moved, we moved it. If there was no one to turn on the mikes or plug in the cords, we did it ourselves. During rehearsals, one of us would leave the others on stage to walk out toward the seats and do a sound check. In fact, we felt very lucky on those rare occasions when Dad traveled with us because we could all stand on stage and let him check the sound for us.

But the Kennedy Center had the best sound crew I'd ever worked with. They were amazing and knew exactly what to do to bring out the best in our voices—individually and as a group. It was also the first time in several years I'd worked with union stagehands. When I leaned down to adjust a monitor, I was told that I couldn't do that—someone else would take care of it for me.

Before the show that night, we rehearsed in one of the large orchestral practice rooms. There were windows on one side and mirrors on the other, so a lot of natural light reflected off of the stately walls and wooden floor. We were practicing one of our a cappella songs when Todd stopped singing and said, "Can you believe we're singing this at the Kennedy Center?" It really was hard to take in.

Earlier we had been given the "celebrity" treatment. A car service picked us up from our hotel and delivered us to the Kennedy Center via a secret back entrance reserved for artists. Two of the four acts performing that night were soloists and two were groups. The other ensemble was an African hip-hop group. The producers had arranged the order of the acts so that the groups essentially headlined the show, giving a little extra kick to the end of a great night of performances.

It felt amazing to stand on that stage with Todd and Katelyn, and to sing before such an appreciative audience. I will never forget the experience. We had worked it out with the VSA executives to include Mom in one song. After singing our third song, Todd said, "Normally there are four of us in the MacIntyre Family Singers, so we have a surprise for you tonight. Ladies and gentlemen, please welcome our mother, Carole!"

The audience applauded like crazy, and on cue, Mom came out to join us. Dad was in the audience, along with some other family members and friends who'd flown across the country to see us perform. It just didn't get any better.

After the show there was a large reception for the performers. At the party, a member of the British consulate came up and told me how much our singing had impressed her. "I'm not sure you remember me," she said in her distinguished accent, "but we met a couple of years ago."

As soon as she said that, I recognized her voice. "Yes, in Washington, DC, during the Marshall orientation. I remember."

It had all come full circle. Though the Marshall experience hadn't worked out exactly as I had hoped, I was now back in Washington, DC, and once again meeting incredible people and sharing my talents. Performing at the Kennedy Center was the proudest moment of my career, and it reignited my dream to perform in front of large crowds.

CHAPTER 25

Idol Auditions

I'm a man of second chances
Place the blame on circumstances
I know I can't expect a love without pain
—FROM "SOMEWHERE ELSE," SCOTT MACINTYRE

"*American Idol* auditions will be in Phoenix in three weeks," Mom said. She was sitting at the computer in the family room.

"Really?" Todd said, walking over to the computer to see for himself.

"You guys might want to all try out together."

Todd and Katelyn immediately loved the idea, but I was hesitant. I still felt like I had a lot to lose. When I first started getting regular gigs, I was paid about fifty dollars a performance. Over the years, I'd worked my way up to earning one hundred dollars, then five hundred dollars a performance. Now I was regularly making two or three times that amount. What would happen if I went on *Idol* and the judges' comments took a toll on my musical reputation? Would everything I'd worked so hard for disappear?

I was confident in my musical ability. In fact, I had no doubt that if the judges heard me sing and play the piano, I would have no trouble making it far in the competition—even to the top ten. The upcoming season would be a better fit for me than any previous season. I remembered the contestants from the last season sitting behind that grand piano, and I imagined myself doing the same thing. But it was that first audition in front of the judges that concerned me; there would be no piano and I would have to win merit for my voice alone.

Before I could say yes or no, Mom spoke up with an idea. "The San Francisco auditions are next week. Maybe you guys should audition there first so you'll know what it's like before they come here. That way, if you don't get through, you'll have a second shot when they come to Phoenix."

"So we're going to San Francisco?" Katelyn asked.

"We'll make it a road trip!" Mom said.

And so it was settled.

While Mom phoned relatives to line up places to stay—first in Redondo Beach with Grandpa and then at my cousins' house in San Francisco—Todd, Katelyn, and I started selecting music. There would be more than ten thousand people auditioning in San Francisco, so we needed to stand out. Song selection would be an important part of that process. During the next week we each picked out several songs and then practiced them for each other and for my parents, narrowing down the list until we each found the perfect song.

A few days later we were in the car, headed to California.

~

Though we'd known that *Idol* auditions would be a cattle call, we laughed when we discovered the venue was appropriately named Cow Palace Arena. It was home to herds of hopefuls.

On the first day of the San Francisco auditions, we went to the arena and picked up our wristbands. The wristbands told us what section to sit in the next day when we returned. The next morning, it was still dark out when we arrived at the arena. But we weren't the first to arrive; we quickly discovered contestants had camped out overnight just so they could be first into the arena. As we watched the sunrise, our hopes rose too. We had no idea what to expect once we got inside, but after all of our preparation and more than a thousand miles in the car, we were excited to see what the day would bring. When the doors opened, we were ushered to our seats to wait for further instructions.

Our anticipation grew with the crowd. The arena held sixteen thousand people, and it soon sounded like every seat was filled. Listening to various vocalists warming up, it was clear the contestants ranged from those who were serious about their music to those who were serious about getting their fifteen minutes of fame. According to Todd, some even wore outrageous costumes. The crowd was loud and enthusiastic, and the producers encouraged the frenzied atmosphere. From the middle of the arena they'd say things like, "On the count of three, we're going to yell, 'San Francisco!'" And the entire arena would yell.

"Next time, scream louder. If you guys want to be on the show, we need you to look and sound excited," the voice said over the PA. Then, "Okay, we've got to do it again. This time, give it everything you have!" Each time the crowd yelled louder and louder. I could hear girls screaming at the top of their lungs, shredding their voices.

Mom described what was happening: "There's a camera on a big crane, and every time they tell the crowd to scream or cheer, the camera sweeps across the crowd and films everyone cheering."

They did that over and over until they got the footage they wanted. Each time my family and I stood, jumped, and acted enthusiastic with the rest of the crowd, but we never screamed. We only mouthed whatever they asked so that we could keep our voices intact for the audition.

After the *Idol* producers got the shots they wanted, they asked the crowd to sing a couple of songs. Once again, we looked like we were singing, but we were only lip-syncing. So many people were using up their voices that it gave me hope. Most of them weren't going to be in it for the long haul, and that gave me confidence that we might make it through the first round.

Once the actual auditions began, they called one section at a time down to the arena floor. Todd described how there were twelve tables spread across the floor and two evaluators behind each table. Later we would learn those people were producers or staffers from one of the companies behind *Idol*. They were the ones entrusted with finding the best talent each city had to offer. They'd been doing that for a while and knew what they were looking for.

Our section was one of the earliest sections called. We walked down to the arena floor where we were directed to a line in front of one of the tables. We stood four across. Obviously, Mom wasn't auditioning, but she didn't want Todd to have to lead both Katelyn and me at the same time while trying to focus on his audition, so she helped guide one of us. It was a nerve-rattling wait, but the line at least seemed to keep moving forward.

When I sensed the line growing smaller, I asked, "How many groups are ahead of us?"

"About seven," Mom said. "It looks like they'll call you up in a group, and then each of you will step forward and sing individually. But they don't make their decision until after everyone in the group has gone. They make up their minds quickly, so it doesn't take long."

I was impressed that the *Idol* staff took the time to listen to *everyone*, and that they did it so efficiently. But I also realized it was more important than ever to stand out. With producers listening to so many people, we had to do something to tickle their ears and make them notice us. With so much ambient noise, no microphones, and at least eleven other vocalists singing at the same time at other tables, I was glad we'd put so much thought into our song choices.

When our turn came, Mom helped us line up in front of the table, and then she stepped away. Katelyn sang first, then Todd, and I went last. I sang "Mandolin Rain." I didn't hear all the noise in the arena as I sang; I was completely focused on my performance. As soon as I finished, I stepped back in line with my brother and sister.

The decision took much longer than I expected. The group directly before us had immediately been dismissed. I hoped it was a good sign they were taking so long. Finally one of the evaluators told us to step forward. I took a deep breath and held it. I couldn't see their faces, but I knew this was the moment of decision—hopefully the first of several rounds of decisions.

"We're not putting you through. I'm sorry," said the evaluator. "Next four, please step up."

What? I couldn't believe I heard her right. None of us had made it? Though it was unlikely we would all end up on the show, I thought we'd at least make it through the first round together. But not even making it through the first round? Not one of us? It was hard to comprehend.

At first I didn't feel anything at all. I think I was in shock. I just stood there thinking, *What could we possibly have done wrong?* I felt Todd's arm, indicating we needed to leave, and it snapped me back into the moment. I put my fingertips on his elbow and followed him past the table, across the arena floor, to the exit. Apparently, there were two doors leading out. One door was for the people who were advancing. The other was for people who weren't. We were shown to the losers' door.

Once we got outside the arena, the disappointment set in. I said, "That's so lame! What happened?"

"They spent a lot of time deliberating over you," Mom said. "I thought that was a good sign. Everyone else was done so quickly."

"I think the people at the table liked us," Todd said. "They were nodding and smiling as they talked. I thought for sure we were in. But then some other lady came swooping over. She started whispering in their ear, and when she left, the two evaluators didn't look so happy anymore. That's when they said we weren't going through. I blame the swooper lady."

"Did the swooper lady even hear us sing?" Katelyn asked.

"No. She wasn't even there when we sang."

We were all disappointed. It was a bum ending to a long week of rehearsing and driving, and it wasn't at all what I'd hoped for. I had been convinced we'd make it through the early rounds at least.

We drove away from the arena, went back to our cousins' house, and tried to make the best of it. We didn't get to see our cousins often, so spending time with them was fun. They helped us feel like the trip wasn't a total waste.

~

On the way home we started talking about the Phoenix auditions. Katelyn and I were all for trying again, however, Todd was not convinced things would be any different in Phoenix. "I don't want to audition again. They're just going to say no. Why be disappointed twice?"

I understood his hurt feelings—mine were hurt too—but having been through the experience once, we'd learned a lot and now knew what to expect. Perhaps there were things we could do differently to stand out more.

"I think you should all try again," Mom said. "What if they were going to let you in and the only thing that stopped them was the swooper lady?"

It was a good point. We all suspected she had been the one to change their minds. Without her, what might have happened? Todd relented, Katelyn was excited, and my competitive streak came out. I wanted one more shot to prove that I could do it.

So the following week in Phoenix, we followed the same procedure as the week before. On the first day, we went down to the arena and picked up our wristbands. The second day, we showed up in our designated section, but this time, instead of being nervous, we just tried to have fun.

When it came time for our section to go to the arena floor and line up, I debated my song choice for the last time. In San Francisco I'd sung "Mandolin Rain," but this time I planned to sing "Nobody Drinks Alone" by Keith Urban. Todd joked it was because I was depressed from being shot down, but the truth was, it had a long soaring note in the chorus, and I hoped it would show off my voice better than "Mandolin Rain." I decided to stick with it. It was nerve wracking to be on the floor again, but being there with Katelyn and Todd helped take the edge off. We would all share in the outcome.

When it was our turn, Katelyn again sang first. She sounded great, and I wanted her to make it if only to validate the incredible voice I knew she had. Todd sang, and he was totally in his element. Then I sang. The soaring note came off just as I'd hoped, and I was pleased with myself. There was another pause while we awaited their verdict. Todd had told me these weren't the same evaluators, yet the situation seemed so familiar, I was sure we were all headed back out the losers' door.

"Step forward," one of the evaluators said.

I held my breath.

"We're really impressed with all of you. The three of you are through to the next round."

By then I was so convinced it was going to be another no, that when I heard the unexpected yes, my heart jumped. A big smile spread across my face and I thanked the evaluators. Todd gave me his arm and Mom stepped back in to help Katelyn. As we walked past the table and across the arena floor, I felt like I was walking on air.

It felt so good to walk through the "winners'" door. We had made it through the first round, and the "San Fran swooper," as we affectionately called her, was nowhere to be found. They took us to a room with other successful contestants and had us fill out paperwork. We would have to come back at a later date to sing for more producers before singing for the judges, but we were excited to have made it that far. Our last duty of the day was to go back into the arena with the other contestants who were still waiting so we could cheer for more camera footage. That time we really did cheer.

～

A couple of months later we returned for more auditions. This time they held them at the W hotel in Scottsdale. We went through another producer-judged round and made it through again. Finally, we were asked to sing before Ken Warwick, the executive producer, and other top-level decision makers. They were going to have us go in one at a time, but we asked if we could go in together. We hoped that perhaps the sibling angle would make us unique. Plus, we knew they loved the drama of siblings having to part ways in the later rounds, so we hoped that by staying together, we could all get to sing for the judges. They yielded and we were ushered in.

We sang an a cappella version of Bon Jovi's "Dead or Alive" I had arranged. Then we each sang our individual solos. From the mood in the room, it seemed they liked what they heard. But after we finished, the executive producer, Ken Warwick, gave us the bad news. "We can only send one of you through."

As he huddled with the other producers, I thought about what it would be like to proceed without Katelyn and Todd, or to have Todd or Katelyn proceed without me. We'd talked about that possibility at home. It was extremely unlikely that all three of us would make it to the end. Although each one of us wanted to be the one to go through, we just hoped that one of us would. As siblings, we had an unusually tight bond, and a victory for one of us still felt like victory of all of us.

The whispering at the table stopped, and I strained to hear the words that would decide my future. "As I said, we can only send one of you through," Ken said in a clipped British accent. "We've decided to pick . . ." I was prepared for anything. "Todd . . . I mean, *Scott.*"

As I let out my breath, I was simultaneously ecstatic to be chosen and sad for Katelyn and Todd.

"No!" Todd said. "You can't take it back now."

When Ken had inadvertently said Todd's name, I thought for sure I wasn't going on. For that split second, I felt the disappointment that Todd and Katelyn were now feeling. But I heard the humor in Todd's voice as he tried to convince Ken that he should go. As everyone laughed at Todd's words, I knew it was going to be okay.

"You're all very talented," Ken said. "But of the three of you, we just think Scott has the most pop-sounding voice."

There was nothing we could do now to persuade them otherwise. We thanked them before leaving the audition room. Outside the door, Todd hugged me and said, "I'm so happy for you!" I knew he meant it.

The next stop for me was the one I most looked forward to and the one I most dreaded. From the moment the *Idol* seed had been planted in my mind, I worried about what the judges would say to me if I got to sing for them. The next audition could be the stuff of dreams or the stuff of nightmares.

I was about to find out which one it would be.

CHAPTER 26

A Golden Ticket

Win or lose is all the same
As I watch you play your game
I regret that I can play it too
—FROM "HEARTSTRINGS," SCOTT MACINTYRE

"Mind the gap" is a warning used in London to remind Underground passengers to pay attention to the gap between the train door and the station platform. I had bought a T-shirt with "Mind the Gap" emblazoned on the red-and-white logo of the Tube at the Tower of London gift shop. It was the last purchase I made before leaving London. It seemed a bit touristy at the time, but as I prepared for my audition in front of the *American Idol* judges, I thought perhaps it would connect me with Simon Cowell, the notoriously difficult British judge.

My goal was to get far enough in the competition that I could sing *and* play the piano for the judges. That's where I would shine brightest. I believed that if I could do that, I *could* get all the way to the top ten. But would I? That was up to the voting public that hadn't met me yet, and to find out, I'd first have to make it through my auditions with the judges.

The auditions were held at the Boulders, a resort near our home in Scottsdale. Once again we arrived early and stood in line outside the resort, eagerly waiting for the day to begin. The local FOX affiliate was there, and they interviewed me in line. Once we got in, contestants were escorted into a large holding room filled with chairs where we were seated until it was our turn to perform in front of the famous judges. Producers, followed by cameramen, roamed the room, stopping to chat with contestants and film anything that looked interesting.

My family and a few friends were there to support me—there were nine of us total. We spent a long day waiting in the holding room. While it was comfortable at first, after being there for hours, the room got hot and contestants started to become restless in their chairs. At various intervals someone would come in and announce five or six contestant names. Those contestants and their families were escorted to another room. When it was my turn, we followed the staffer to a smaller holding room where each competitor was assigned a seat. As contestants were called to audition before the judges, we were told to slide over one chair. This gave me an opportunity to take in the sounds around me, and as I listened, I heard a familiar voice.

Ryan Seacrest stood outside of the judges' room and interviewed each contestant before they went in. Hearing his voice in person made everything suddenly seem so real. After listening to him so many times on television, I could practically reach out and touch him. It was an exhilarating feeling to think about how close I was to making it on the show.

As each contestant exited the judges' room, the conversation in the holding room would pause for just a split second. Depending on the outcome, it would be followed by either lots of cheering or a reverential silence. Then the conversations would start back up and the whole cycle would repeat. I was lost in the sounds around me, when it was suddenly my turn. I talked briefly to Ryan before Todd escorted me into the audition room, squared me off, and then stood to the side while I faced the judges. They started talking to me, and I asked how they were doing. I knew there were four judges in the room. Simon Cowell, Randy Jackson, and Paula Abdul had been around since the creation of the show. But this year a fourth judge had been added—Kara DioGuardi. Though she was a singer, she was probably best known for her songwriting. When I had learned that Kara was joining the judging team, I was excited. Being a songwriter myself, I knew she'd relate to what I was trying to do musically.

Surprisingly, they didn't ask me to sing right away like they seemed to on television. Instead they continued to talk, asking me a lot of questions. I told them a little bit about myself, how I went to college so early, and how important the piano was to me. When I told them I had studied piano in London, I pointed to my shirt and said, "Actually, I was wearing this shirt for Simon."

"It's the subway, right?" he said.

"I thought you'd recognize it."

We talked a few minutes longer, which helped me to relax. Finally Simon said, "What are you going to sing?"

"'And So It Goes' by Billy Joel."

"Oh, I love that song," Paula said, giving me an extra boost of confidence.

I wanted to do something different from the original, so I had arranged my own version of the song. It was a tender rendition, keeping with my desire to communicate emotions and tell a story.

After I finished, the judges were quiet. I couldn't see expressions on people's faces, so I couldn't tell if the judges were smiling during my performance or not. I had no idea what they would say next, but I sensed that one or two of them might be undecided about me, so I jumped in.

"I can sing something more upbeat," I offered. Without waiting, I started snapping my fingers and singing "You and I Both" by Jason Mraz. It didn't take long before they stopped me.

"Okay, Scott," said Simon. "You're a cool guy. I like you."

"I love your voice, especially when it goes into the softer tones," said Paula. "I like you. I think you're very talented."

"I think it's a courageous thing for you to come out and sing not with your instrument, which probably makes you feel more comfortable," Kara said.

At that point, things seemed hopeful, but no one had said yes or no yet. Finally Randy broke the tension with the first vote.

"I'm going to say yes."

Kara quickly followed with, "I'm going to say yes."

"Absolutely, yes!" Paula said.

With three yeses, I was through to the next round in Hollywood. But I really wanted to hear what Simon had to say. He was the hardest judge to please, and I knew many viewers of the show respected his opinion. There was a brief pause and then he said, "Scott, you've got four yeses."

Four yeses? It was music to my ears. "Thank you!" I said. I was so excited that I had made it through to Hollywood Week. If the previous year's show was any indication, I was now one step closer to playing the piano and singing for the judges. At the same time, I felt proud of myself for making it this far on my voice alone. To stand in front of the judges and not be ridiculed was a feat. To stand in front of them and get four yeses and several nice compliments was amazing! I'd been worried they would hurt my musical reputation, but instead they had confirmed my talent.

I felt Todd's hand on my back, and I turned and hugged him. I was proud to have him there to share in the moment, and I could tell he was just as excited as I was. I thanked the judges again, and then Kara said something that helped me know she was rooting for me. "I think we really need to see you with your instrument to see how great you really can be." Her words added an extra glow to an already shining moment.

Todd handed me my cane, and I followed him out of the room, but before we got out the door, he stopped. "Grab the ticket," he whispered, reminding me that I needed to get that vital piece of golden paper from the producers before I left.

As we exited the audition room, I couldn't hold back my smile and my heart was beating like crazy. My family and friends must have immediately seen the ticket because they erupted in applause, screams, and hugs. It was another amazing moment, and it felt so good to share it with my loved ones.

~

We decided to go out to dinner to celebrate. Despite the craziness of the day, we picked a restaurant known for its great Italian food *and* it's noisy atmosphere. Once we were seated, Katelyn spoke up, trying to be heard over the background noise. "I can't believe this is happening, Scott. You're going to Hollywood!"

"You're that much closer," Dad said.

"I hope you get a chance to play piano for the judges in Hollywood Week," Mom added.

"That would be a dream come true!" I said.

Later my phone rang. I didn't recognize the number, but I answered it anyway. It was one of the *Idol* producers calling to ask if they could bring a film crew to our house at nine o'clock the next morning. It was already dark and getting very late. We were out celebrating, and I knew the house wasn't clean.

"Yeah, that would be fine," I said. "But is there anyway it could be pushed back a little later in the morning?"

"No, we need to come at nine. Is that a problem?"

"Hold on for one second."

I turned to Mom. "It's somebody from *Idol*, and they want to come over at nine o'clock tomorrow morning. Is that okay?"

"That's fine."

"We'll be ready for you at nine," I told the producer.

We finished our dinner and then hurried home to get the place looking as nice as we could.

The next morning they showed up on time. They asked us about some of our normal activities as a family. They filmed Todd and me playing guitar and singing in an old barn that we'd converted to a rehearsal space. And then they filmed Katelyn and me swing dancing by the pool. They also took footage of me playing the piano.

By that point in my life, I'd already experienced quite a few unbelievable moments, but that had to be the most surreal. The show I had watched from my living room was now in my living room filming *me*.

Christina was at college in Los Angeles, and since I hadn't talked to her in a long time, she didn't even know I had auditioned. As it got closer to Hollywood Week, I decided to call her.

"I've got big news," I said.

"What?"

"You can't tell anyone."

"What is it?"

"Do you remember that show we used to watch a couple of years ago?"

"*American Idol*?"

"Yeah. Well, I auditioned, and I made it to Hollywood Week."

"Wow! That's amazing! I'm so proud of you."

I knew Christina didn't fully understand how big of a deal it was; she'd missed the first few weeks of the show during the season we had watched together. But I had another reason for sharing my news.

"Maybe I'll see you when I come out to Los Angeles."

～

Hollywood Week was the final series of auditions before the live shows. Though Hollywood Week wouldn't air on TV until the following February, they were filmed in November. Five days before I was supposed to show up for Hollywood Week, the producers called and said I needed to bring eight unique performing outfits. I'd never worn fancy clothes as a kid, and our family never paid much attention to the latest trends in fashion, so suddenly I needed to become a fashion expert. I called Aunt Ellen and asked her for advice since her husband worked in the film industry.

"What kinds of jeans are in right now? The ones with the striped patterns and designs on the pockets—are they still in? How about ripped jeans?"

I had a closet full of suits, and even a tux left from my days in London, but the rest of my wardrobe pretty much consisted of tired T-shirts and stiff-collared shirts. My aunt gave me lots of good advice, and everyone pitched in to help me find what I needed. Mom scoured several stores for clothing that was trendy and unique. She came home with jeans, vests, T-shirts, and even shoes with rhinestones on them for me to try on. Todd would compare them against the current fashion trends and give them a thumbs-up or thumbs-down, and I would model them for my whole family for final approval. By the time I left, I felt comfortable that we'd put together enough good looks to make it through Hollywood Week.

I showed up to Hollywood Week looking pretty hip, but it wasn't just about looking good. It was about surviving the most intense, strenuous week of my life. A better name for the experience would have been "*Idol* Boot Camp." The week was designed to break you down and see what you were made of—whether you could handle the pressure or not. They wanted to separate those who were in it for the long haul from those who couldn't deal with high stress. During the week I witnessed several contestants decide that a music career wasn't worth the struggle, and they dropped out. They just turned their backs and walked away. Others broke down in tears from lack of sleep. It made me so sad to see people give up—there had been stadiums full of hopefuls who would have given anything for the chance those contestants had just thrown away—Katelyn and Todd being two of them. Each person had to make their own decisions based on their personal circumstances, but I don't think they fully understood what an incredible opportunity they were giving up.

The pace of Hollywood Week was grueling. I was just fourteen months out of my transplant surgery, and although I felt great, I still needed to take good care of my body. I was passionate about competing on *Idol*, but I also knew it was important to pay attention to my body's signals and make sure I got as much rest as I could. It would be hard to balance all the demands.

The first round in Hollywood Week was a cappella, and it should have been a slam dunk. Just go up, sing a song, stay on pitch, smile, and don't forget your words. Nothing to it, really. But many people were so nervous that they sank their performances. One poor guy was shaking so bad that he couldn't stay on pitch. By the end of his song, he sounded like he couldn't sing at all. Unfortunately, I was a little too confident. I decided that I should do a little body drumming while I sang. It was something I'd done for many years. As a kid, when I got tired of drumming on the muffin tins, I learned that I could simulate an entire drum set on my body by slapping my chest and stomach, and flicking my fingers across the fabric of my shirt. Sometimes I would do it when writing a song or just walking around the house. That day, I thought I'd give it a try on stage in front of the judges.

I started to sing "Music in the Night" by Jamie Cullum, and halfway through I brought in the percussion section full force. As soon as I finished, Randy said, "Dude . . . what's going on? I was like, why is he hitting himself? Are you trying to keep the beat? It was a little weird for me."

"I don't think you can hear it from there," I struggled to explain. "But Randy, I've got my bass drum here"—pointing to my upper left rib cage—"my snare drum here"—pointing to my stomach—"and my toms and hi hat all mapped out on my body."

My attempt to make myself unique and set myself apart worked—but in the wrong way. Randy was confused. Simon hated the song. Without a mike to pick up the drumming noises, the judges couldn't hear what they were supposed to hear. It probably looked like I was having some kind of musical convulsion. Playing the judges' comments over and over in my head, I walked off stage to wait until everyone in my set finished. *The judges probably think I'm crazy.*

After everyone finished singing, they lined us up across the stage in a single line. Simon said, "Scott, step forward," and I joined a few other people who'd also been told to step forward. After all the names were called, Simon said, "Back row, you're going home." It took me a moment to realize I was in the front row. I had made it through to the next round!

~

They had split the contestants into two groups. My group sang the first day, and at the end of the day, the staff gave us each a CD, but they didn't tell us what the songs were for. I suspected it was for the group audition round, and I thought about finding other contestants to form a group with ahead of time, but the producers specifically told us, "Don't form your groups yet. You're just going to waste time if you do it now." Having watched the show before, I had a hunch we would all be asked to form groups at the last minute so as to create drama and chaos as contestants frantically joined forces on a whim. Because I was blind, I knew any relationships I could form before that moment would help tremendously, since I wouldn't be able to spot talented singers from across the room or navigate through a crowd. So the next day I strategically positioned myself at a grand piano I'd found in a hall off the lobby in hopes that some other contestants would hear me playing and stop by. Soon I was jamming with several guys around the piano. Derek, who was also from Arizona, was one of them. I asked if they had listened to the CD yet and would they be interested in forming a group.

"Yeah, but they said not to worry about forming groups yet," Derek said.

"Well, we don't have to set anything in stone. Let's just keep singing. Do you guys know this one?" I asked as I started to play and sing "Get Ready" by the Temptations and they all quickly joined in.

Later that night, after all the second-day contestants finished singing, and the remaining contestants from both days had gathered back at the hotel, the producers instructed us to walk back to the Kodak Theater and await further instructions from the stage. As they led us through the back hallways of the theater, I had a horrible feeling that as soon as we were seated, we would be asked to form groups. It would be virtually impossible to form a group with anyone other than the people sitting immediately to my left and right. I didn't want to end up in a group that couldn't harmonize well, or that lacked work ethic.

Mom spotted Derek and Chris, another one of the guys I had jammed with at the piano. "Let's try to stay close to them," I said, as Mom did her best to maneuver me through the moving crowd of contestants.

We caught up to them and I called out, "Guys!" I couldn't see either of them in front of me and didn't know where to point my voice. "Want to be in a group together?"

"I want to wait and see what they say when we get in there," Chris said.

"But I think we're going to have to form groups as soon as we sit down." I was getting worried. We had all clicked so well earlier that day, but now it seemed I was of no more interest to them than anyone else.

Though it took some jockeying on her part, somehow Mom managed to get me a seat next to where Chris and Derek were sitting.

As soon as all of the seats were filled, the producers made the announcement I expected. "For the next round, you will need to form groups, but you must have at least one member of your group from the day one singers and one member from the day two singers. Start forming your groups now." This was a surprise twist, and the producers' way of preventing us from forming groups made up of only people we already knew. It was a good move on their part, but it also made it more difficult since Chris and Derek had sung on the first day like me.

As soon as the producers stopped giving directions, I turned to Chris on my left. "Come on. Do you want to form a group? I can bring a lot of creativity, and I'm really good at arranging four-part harmony. I think we can do a great job with this."

"I don't know . . ."

"Well, let me know soon, because I'm going to form another group if you're not interested." I then turned to my right and started asking someone else. Thankfully, my bluff paid off.

"Okay, let's all get into a group, and we'll find a fourth person from day two," said Chris.

"I met this kid, Von, who would be great," Derek said. And it was settled.

Not only did we each have to sing a solo in the group round, but we also had to come up with background harmonies to sing behind the person soloing. And in addition to all of that, we had to create our own choreography as a group and dance as we sang.

I took the lead arranging the song. Chris had some dance training, so he took the reins in choreographing and teaching the rest of us the dance. Everyone in the group was familiar with singing harmony, so it was easy to work with them. Of course, dancing was the hardest part for me. I knew my ballroom dance experience would come in handy, but, unlike the other guys, I couldn't watch a series of moves and then just do it. Someone had to explain each part of the choreography to me. I felt so blessed to be in a group with Chris. He was patient and kind and spent a lot of one-on-one time teaching me the moves. Sometimes he would have to take my arms and hands and position them in various ways, walking me through the motions of the dance. Once we all had it, we worked late into the night to perfect each element while we sang. There was a lot of pressure on all of the contestants. Simon had already warned us that if we forgot the words, we would be going home. We knew there were no second chances.

It was an interesting situation because we had to work together as a group, but we also were individually competing against every other contestant there. About three thirty in the morning, I realized just how cutthroat it could get. We had stopped to take a short break, and I went to get some water. Chris had been helping me with some of the dance moves, and I had worked up quite a thirst. After I returned, I heard Chris talking with someone from another group. The guy was trying to speak quietly so I wouldn't hear.

"Why are you helping him?"

"What do you mean?" Chris asked.

"Why are you helping him learn the dance? You should just let him fail. It's a competition."

My face warmed with embarrassment as I waited for Chris's answer.

"Hey man, I know he would do the same for me," Chris said with confidence. "Besides, he came up with all the harmonies for us."

I didn't know much about Chris, but to me, in that moment, he was the picture of grace in the most competitive environment I'd ever experienced.

We had to wake up early the next morning, only to sit in the Kodak Theater for hours as other groups performed on stage. I had only gotten two hours of sleep and I was exhausted, but I had to look alive because at any moment, one of the many cameras could be getting a shot of one of us reacting to what was on stage. But with so little sleep, I was having a hard time keeping new lyrics, new melodies, new harmonies, and new choreography straight in my head. We had learned so much the night before, and I could barely wrap my mind around it now. It wasn't like me to have trouble retaining new information either. I heard Ken Warwick talking to someone as he walked down the aisle. He stopped next to me, and I said to him, "I'm so tired. I don't think my mind is working at full capacity."

"It's not," he knowingly replied.

I would've laughed if I hadn't been fighting to keep my eyes from closing. But the way he said it made me realize the lack of sleep and intense pressure was all by design. Hollywood Week was a boot camp. Although talent was necessary to continue in the competition, the ability to withstand pressure, learn music quickly, and survive on little sleep were equally important.

It wasn't till late that afternoon we were finally called to perform. Chris, Von, and I each made it through to the next round. Unfortunately, Derek didn't.

Making it through the group round meant that I had finally arrived at the moment I had been waiting for. In the next round, I would finally be able to play an instrument when I sang for the judges. From the CD, I chose "Home" by Daughtry, and then I asked to play the piano, but I was told that only the staff accompanist could use the piano. However, I could play the keyboard. I was a little disappointed, but I chose to make the best of it.

When it was my turn, I felt ready. I'd memorized the song from hearing it; I can typically play a pop song if I've heard it played once or twice. I was also used to leading worship in church, so performing on stage with a keyboard in front of me felt very comfortable. It was my first real chance to show the judges who I was. As I started singing, I felt like I was performing a mini-concert just for the judges, but as soon as I hit the first long note, I heard the other contestants in the audience start to cheer. To my surprise, they continued to cheer throughout the song, which gave me great confidence that I was doing well. By the time I finished, I felt like I had nailed the piece, and I was ecstatic. It was my big moment in front of the judges and the last chance to prove that I deserved a spot in the top 36. I hoped it would be enough.

Backstage someone told me that Paula had given me a standing ovation. Of course I hadn't seen her, so learning that she had responded so enthusiastically put me over the top. Week one of Hollywood was done, and I had made the top 50, and I felt I had done everything I could to prove that I deserved to be in the top 36. The decision was in the judges' hands.

I headed home for the holidays, knowing I would return in January to see if I made the final cut.

CHAPTER 27

Second Verse, Same as the First

I've been here before
Recognize the signs
—FROM "AUTUMN LEAVES," SCOTT MACINTYRE

I returned home to Scottsdale after Hollywood Week in November. I was one step away from the live show, which was exciting. On the live show, my future would no longer be in the judges' hands; instead, my fate would be up to the voting public. How would they feel about a blind contestant? No one with a severe disability had ever been a finalist on *Idol* before. But I welcomed the opportunity. Whenever I had performed in the past, at least one person would come up to me and say, "You are an inspiration!" I hoped I could be an inspiration to America too. If I made it, I just planned to be myself and let America see who I really was. Let the votes fall where they may.

Until then I had planned to enjoy the holiday with my family. Of course, everyone was busy doing their own things—Katelyn was working on college entrance materials, Todd was performing in *A Christmas Carol*, and Mom was busy prepping for the holidays.

On Christmas Eve I sang for three candlelight services at church. It was a special moment for me considering how dangerously sick I'd been two years earlier after returning from Jason Mraz's party. But now Katelyn wasn't feeling well. She'd been struggling with a bad cold for several weeks, and she ended up laying her head on Mom's lap during much of the service.

After we got home, I needed to wrap my presents. My room was such a mess that I didn't have enough space to lay out everything, so I asked Katelyn if I could wrap presents in her room. Her room was always pristine—nothing was ever on the floor, and each morning she made her bed so perfectly she could have passed a military inspection.

After an hour of wrapping, Katelyn came in. "When are you going to be done? I'm so tired. I want to go to bed."

"I'm almost finished. Just a few more minutes." I knew why she wanted to go to bed. Katelyn loved to get up early on Christmas morning to open presents. Todd and I preferred to sleep in and open them later. Mom and Dad didn't care either way, but it was up to us to work out a time we could all agree to. That Christmas we'd agreed to get up at nine o'clock.

As I lay in bed that night and waited to fall asleep, I realized I didn't care what was under the tree in the morning. I already had everything I needed—my health, the love of my family, and now I was in the top 50 of *American Idol*. My dreams were so close I could taste them, and they tasted sweet.

~

"Scott. Scott. Scott! Wake up!"

Todd was shaking my shoulder, but I was never one to wake up easily. That morning it felt like I was fighting through a thick fog.

"What's going on?"

"It's eleven o'clock. We overslept."

I sat up and rubbed my eyes. *Eleven o'clock? Why didn't Katelyn wake us up?* Usually she would come bursting into our room as soon as it was time to open presents. Todd threw some clothes at me and I got up and put them on. We raced out to the living room, but no one was there. The presents were still under the tree, but the lights were off and no one was around.

We called out and no one answered. Todd looked in my parents' bedroom and checked Katelyn's room and determined that they'd all gotten up and dressed. "Maybe they're helping Katelyn feed her chickens," I said.

Todd went out the back door to check. He returned a few minutes later. "The car's gone."

I picked up my cell phone and called Mom. When she answered, I could tell something was wrong.

"When we were in the doctor's office with Katelyn yesterday, he ran some blood tests to see why she was so tired and not feeling well. We got a call at six o'clock this morning. It turns out she only has a third of the blood that she should have in her body. We had to take her to the hospital immediately. They're giving her a transfusion now. She's severely anemic."

As soon as Mom said "anemic," it was like an icy wind blew through my insides and left everything shaking. Anemia was a by-product of kidney failure, and though Mom didn't say anything about that, I knew she was thinking it.

"Do you want us to come down there?"

"No, you and Todd just stay there. We don't really know anything right now. I'll call you as soon as we do."

Later that afternoon Mom called back. "They've completed her first transfusion, and she's feeling a little better. Why don't you and Todd come down and at least we can all eat Christmas dinner together in the cafeteria."

"Do they know what's causing the anemia?" I asked, afraid to hear the answer.

"They think it has to do with female-related issues. They say it's common in teen girls this age. That, plus her cold. She's just really run down."

I breathed a sigh of relief.

Todd and I drove to Phoenix Children's Hospital. Mom and Dad had tried taking Katelyn to Mayo first, but because she was only seventeen, they wouldn't treat her without special permission from a hospital executive—permission no one seemed to be able to get on Christmas Day. When we arrived, we learned that they planned to admit Katelyn overnight so they could continue to give her blood. Her room wasn't ready, however, so we all went to the cafeteria to eat. Katelyn wasn't hungry, and it was obvious she wasn't feeling good. All she did was lie with her head in Mom's lap.

Because the final round of *Idol* was in a few weeks, I had worn my mask to the hospital, knowing the air could be filled with germs. I untied it and laid it on my tray so I could eat the congealed Jell-O salad and made-from-powder mashed potatoes—not exactly the Christmas dinner we'd planned. It reminded me of all the days and nights I'd spent in the hospital, and once again, it made me appreciate Patricia's gift to me. Good health was everything.

We got Katelyn settled into her room, and we prayed together as a family before Todd and I left. The doctor planned to give Katelyn another bag of blood overnight and a third the next day. Hopefully she would feel better after that and be able to return home.

The next morning Todd was at his rehearsal for *Annie Get Your Gun*, so I was home alone when the phone rang. It was Mom and she was crying. "I kind of had this unsettled feeling this morning, so I asked the doctor if he could check Katelyn's kidney function. He just came in and told us her creatinine level is 7.1. They've put her on the transplant list."

Suddenly my head felt light and heavy at the same time. I know I continued to talk to Mom on the phone, but I don't recall anything I said. I was in such shock. *How can this happen twice?* It was the worst case of déjà vu ever.

No one knew better than I did what Katelyn would face during the next few months—the fear, the pain, the denial, and the bleakness. I wanted to comfort her, to say something that would help her feel better, but I knew she needed to process things on her own first. I thought about how, for her, the knowledge that her kidneys were failing had to be even worse than it was for me. I had been blessed with ignorance. I hadn't known what would come next—I didn't even know what dialysis was the first time it was mentioned.

But Katelyn knew.

She knew how the disease progressed. She knew the pain, the lethargy, and the monotonous and tiresome days of dialysis. She had shared in the hope of each new potential donor and the disappointment that came with each disqualification. But she had also shared in the joy of my successful transplant. I hoped that knowing I had survived my kidney failure would somehow be a small comfort to her. As I stood in the kitchen, separated by a few miles and a disability that wouldn't let me drive to see her, I longed to wrap my arms around her and tell her that I would always be there for her just as she had been there for me.

But I was supposed to leave for *American Idol* in a few weeks. If that happened, I wouldn't be by her side. Once again I felt like I was on the top of the mountain experiencing the highest of highs and in the valley with the lowest of lows *at the very same time*. It was graduation day all over again.

∽

Christmas came and went, and the presents still sat unopened under the tree. Katelyn came home from the hospital, and despite the bad news, we did our best to celebrate the fact that she was feeling better. In between Todd's rehearsals and performances, we found time to open presents and enjoy each other's company. Todd performed at a New Year's Eve gala, and we all got dressed up and attended the event. Though my parents thought Katelyn looked pale, she felt better than she had earlier, and the party was a nice distraction for all of us. We were a family who enjoyed making music, and there was no better way to bring in the New Year than with Todd's voice ringing in our ears. As the clock struck midnight and guests toasted the New Year, I think we all felt a little more optimistic, like maybe it wouldn't be that bad.

But that optimism was short-lived. On January 5 we met with Katelyn's doctor. I had joined Mom, Dad, and Katelyn because, with my experience, they thought I could add something to the conversation. The doctor laid it all out. Her kidneys were functioning at 13 percent, and her creatinine level was 7.4. Though the level had decreased slightly after three bags of blood had been transfused, the doctor didn't expect that dip to last long. The transfusion had essentially done the same thing as dialysis—it had given her clean blood. But it wouldn't last. She'd soon be feeling sick and tired again. The doctor recommended a transplant but said that if it didn't happen soon, Katelyn would need dialysis.

As I sat in the doctor's office, I felt like I was watching scenes play out in a movie—a scary movie I had once starred in. It was so sad to see my sister having to go through this horror. I also grieved for what Mom and Dad would have to endure once again. While I was sick I watched them make me, and all of my medical appointments, their top priority. Yet they still had to juggle two other kids, a marriage, a house, a job, homeschooling, and lives that didn't stop just because someone was ill. Although I knew they'd find strength through God, I also knew their wells had to be dry—they'd have to dig deeper than they ever had before. It seemed unfair they had already given up so much to take care of their two blind children, and then they had to watch their oldest son suffer through undiagnosed kidney failure followed by ten months of dialysis. Now the same thing was happening again; only this time, it was to their little girl.

How could one couple go through so much?

How could I leave my family at a time like that?

Idol allowed me to have a sighted guide throughout the competition, and Mom had volunteered to help me. But how would she do that now that Katelyn was sick and needed her? Todd couldn't go—he had a contract with Arizona Broadway Theater and was performing in shows for the next several months. Dad, of course, had to keep working—his job paid for our medical insurance and was our primary source of income. As much as I wanted to be on *American Idol*, I didn't want to make things harder for my family. But I couldn't do *American Idol* alone. I needed Mom. Yet I didn't want to take her away from Katelyn or have my family preoccupied by anything I was doing when Katelyn needed to be the priority. At the same time, Katelyn was more excited than anybody that I had made it so far on *Idol*. *How can I disappoint her by not continuing?*

We drove home in silence, each of us lost in our own thoughts about the doctor's prognosis. As we neared our neighborhood, Dad broke the silence. "Can we stop by the post office? I haven't checked Scott's P.O. box in over a month." Most of my business correspondence was sent to the P.O. box, and

Dad would often check it on his way home from work. But with the holidays and the news about Katelyn, no one had been by the post office in weeks. Mom needed stamps, too, and Katelyn didn't want to stay in the car alone. So we all went in together.

As we walked in, Mom spotted Marianne, Katelyn's horse mentor and riding instructor. Katelyn loved animals and had been in a therapeutic horse-manship program since she was nine.

"Well, Katelyn! How are you doing?" Marianne asked. I could hear the two of them embracing.

"I'm okay," Katelyn said, but she couldn't hold back the emotion of the truth, and she burst into tears. Marianne tried to console her, and my parents sniffled in the background. I tried to swallow the lump in my throat.

"What's wrong, honey?"

Katelyn told her what was going on as best she could.

"Do you need a kidney?" Marianne asked Katelyn. "You can have my kidney."

Mom tried to tell Marianne how we'd already listed Katelyn on the national waiting list, but Marianne interrupted and said, "You don't want a kidney from somebody you don't even know. I'll give you mine." There was no reservation or hesitation in her voice. Marianne's mind was made up. Katelyn could have her kidney.

As Mom and Dad told her more about the process and the testing, I couldn't believe what I was hearing. I remembered how Patricia had imme-diately offered to donate a kidney to me, and now Marianne had done the same for Katelyn. It wasn't a coincidence—God had arranged that meeting. Marianne confirmed my thoughts when she said, "I *never* come to this post office. I don't know why I stopped here today. It was just meant to be."

On the way home we all marveled at how, after such a discouraging doc-tor's appointment, we now had a ray of hope. We wouldn't know for at least two months after Marianne started testing whether or not she would qualify to be a donor, but that almost didn't matter. God had used her to give us peace during very trying circumstances. It was a reminder that he knew our pain, he was working his plan, and we were in his presence.

~

A few days later Katelyn and I were lingering at the table after dinner when the subject of *American Idol* came up.

"You don't seem as excited as you used to be about *Idol*," Katelyn said.

"I'm still excited," I said, choosing my words carefully, "but I don't know if I should go."

"Why wouldn't you go?" She sounded shocked.

"Well, with you being sick and Mom needing to be here with you . . ."

"Why would you give up this opportunity? I mean, I love having you here, but you need to do this."

"I just don't want to take Mom away from you when you need her. And if you need me to be here for you, then I want to be here."

"What could you do for me if you stayed here?"

"Well, moral support for one thing."

"Scott, I would rather be lying in my hospital bed watching you on TV then having you standing next to my hospital bed holding my hand."

I laughed. Mom had been listening and now she came over and sat down. "Scott, you need to do this. There will be times when I need to be with you, and times when I need to be here with Katelyn. Todd can come out to be with you or Dad. We'll work it out somehow."

"I know you love me and I know you care," Katelyn said. "But the truth is, it would be a lot sadder if you're just sitting around the house worrying about me. If you go back to Hollywood and make it onto the show, that would be the best gift you could give me—something to distract me from thinking about all of this."

I reached out my hand, found hers, and held it. "I love you," I said.

"I love you too."

And so it was decided.

~

In early January I went back to Hollywood to learn my fate. The judges had made their decisions during the break. There were no more auditions. This time they took us to the "Judges' Mansion," where, one by one, we would be brought in and told our *Idol* destiny. Mom was with me, and I had invited Jerry Lindahl to be there too. When it was my turn, Mom guided me up a lavish staircase and down a long, wide hallway. I listened to my footsteps and cane echo off the hardwood floor. I could feel my heart beating faster with every step.

Mom helped me get seated in front of the judges, and then she stepped out of the room. The judges asked me questions about Hollywood Week and how

I thought I'd done. I figured they did that with every contestant. It was a way of making the contestant remember their mistakes and increasing the tension for the viewing audience before the big reveal.

I answered honestly about the things I thought I'd done really well. There was no point in mentioning the things I hadn't done so well. The judges said kind things about my artistry and my song interpretation, and they also said that the other contestants really seemed to like me. That was great to hear, but I wanted to know if I'd made it into the top 36. The judges may have been drawing things out to try and make me second-guess myself, but the longer we talked, the more comfortable I became. Finally Kara said, "I think it's pretty unanimous that—" She paused.

Randy interrupted. "Go on, Kara, give it to him."

After another dramatic pause, Kara said, "We want to see you again. You've made it to season eight!"

Yes! I smiled and the smile grew bigger as I stood up, thanked the judges, and hugged each one of them before I left. On the way out, I threw my arms up in the air and pumped my fists.

I was now officially in the top 36 of *American Idol*! On one hand, I couldn't believe it was happening, but on the other, I had always believed I could do it, ever since that first audition in San Francisco more than six months earlier. I had made it this far because I had managed to impress the judges with my talent, but now I had the chance to inspire the voting public with my music and my life story.

I couldn't wait to get started.

CHAPTER 28

The High Five Heard 'Round the World

But out here we can make history
No one will contest

—FROM "STARS," SCOTT MACINTYRE

Season eight of *American Idol* premiered on January 13, 2009, and because I didn't have to be back in Hollywood until February, I was home in Scottsdale to enjoy it with my friends and family. We had a viewing party at a friend's house, and though the Arizona auditions weren't the first to happen in real time, they would be the first shown on the program. An associate producer tipped me off that my story would be featured on that first episode. It was a two-hour show that started with a magnificent shot of the Grand Canyon and Ryan Seacrest saying, "This is where it starts." My heart swelled and excitement pumped through my veins. That was where it all started for me too.

Suddenly I was on the screen and everyone in the living room started yelling, "Yay!" Then someone said, "Shhh! Listen, listen everybody!" and immediately we all got quiet so we could hear what was said about me. But it was a false alarm. They were headed to a commercial break and were just teasing the audience that my story was coming up. When the show cut to commercial, we all started talking.

It was hard to contain my emotions. Not only was I excited to see my story, but I knew they'd feature the best stories of all the contestants from the Arizona auditions. From watching past seasons of *Idol*, I knew that they often saved the most compelling story for last. I wondered who it would be and if perhaps it was someone I had met during the audition process.

"It's back on!"

"Shhh."

We quieted down as soon as the show came back on. From the tease, we expected my story would be next. But it wasn't. For nearly two full hours, they teased my story, leading the audience on by saying things like, "The only thing more incredible than his story is his incredible voice." But each time they would cut to a commercial and then return with someone else's audition.

"Maybe they're saving the best for last," Todd said.

Could that be true? There was only ten minutes left in the program.

Whether it was or not, I was flattered by how many times they had teased the audience that my audition was coming up. Finally, in the last few minutes of the show, they started to tell my story.

It turns out I was the last contestant they showed auditioning in Phoenix. Using dialogue from interviews taped during my first auditions the previous fall, they did a great job of telling my story through my own words. While I talked about my life, they showed footage of me walking with my cane, playing the piano in our house, and dancing with Katelyn. They allowed me to talk about my blindness and how my musical gifts had more than made up for my disability, and they included pictures of my playing the piano when I was young and from our ski trip the year before. Then they showed me being led into the audition room by Todd, handing him my cane, and facing the judges. Though they cut out a lot of my conversation with the judges, my song sounded good, and I was very pleased with what they had included.

They concluded the spot with my leaving the audition room with Todd and celebrating my golden ticket to Hollywood with hugs from my friends and family. And then they showed my interview with Ryan Seacrest.

Ryan asked me how it felt to get the judges' approval.

"I am pumped!" I said. Those weren't words I normally used, but in the excitement of the moment, it was the first thing that crossed my mind.

"As well you should be. And we will see you in Hollywood."

Next the television cameras showed something that I'd forgotten had even happened. Ryan raised his hand to give me a high five, but since I couldn't see him, his hand just hung in the air by itself. Then he realized his mistake and reached for my hand. "Well, I'm giving you a high five."

After hearing his words and feeling his touch, I raised my hand to reciprocate.

"Congratulations. There it is," he said as we made contact. He thanked me and promised to see me in Hollywood.

The whole thing lasted just a few seconds, and I hadn't once thought about it since then. Neither had my family. It wasn't an unusual occurrence, really. Similar humorous things had happened rather frequently. Someone would forget that I couldn't see them and hold out their hand to shake mine or to give me a high five, and since I didn't see them, I would inadvertently leave them hanging. Even watching it on the TV, we didn't pay much attention to the incident.

But the day after the premiere aired, it was as if the world had taken notice and everyone had an opinion on it. Some thought Ryan was rude and used it as an opportunity to make fun of the likeable host. Others realized it was an honest mistake and that it created a teaching moment for those who weren't blind. During the next few days, television shows talked about it, bloggers wrote about it, newspapers covered it, and even the glossy magazines ran still shots of me and Ryan with his hand hanging in the air. Mom showed me one weekly magazine that had a picture of the U.S. Airways plane that landed in the Hudson River, and across the fold was a picture of me in my "Mind the Gap" T-shirt and Ryan with his hand forever suspended in midair. I hadn't even been on the live show yet, and already people were talking about me.

I thought the whole thing was pretty funny. So did my family. I was the last person who would be offended by something like that. It never bothered me when someone waved to me or held out their hand to me forgetting I was blind. But as far as *Idol* was concerned, I thought the "high five heard around the world" was the best thing that could've happened to me. I'd soon be depending on the American public for votes, so the more people who knew my name and story, the more potential voters I'd have when it came time to keep me on the show.

I thought the hype would die down in a couple of days, but it didn't. Soon there were videos of the high-five showing up on YouTube and accumulating millions of views. It was the viral video of the week for two weeks. But as soon as FOX saw what was happening, they successfully got the videos taken down—which, interestingly, only resulted in more publicity as the media started writing articles about FOX's intervention and my "star potential."

TMZ and other celebrity blog sites began making fun of Ryan Seacrest, which didn't hurt his name at all, but continued to help make mine. Within days I realized how many people now knew of me. At one point, Mom and I were shopping for new clothes and a salesclerk came up and asked, "Can I get a high five?" I wasn't even buying anything from him, but he just wanted to say he high-fived me. That was the first time that happened, but it wasn't the last. Even now, years later, people still approach me in public and say, "Can I get a high five?"

~

While the hanging high five got a lot of media attention and opened up some discussions about disabilities, something else I did on that premiere had an even bigger effect on the blind and disabled community.

I had used my white cane on television.

When Andrea Bocelli or Stevie Wonder performed on stage, the lights would dim and when they came back up, the singer would be standing there. It was as if they just appeared without assistance. No one showed Andrea or Stevie using a cane to get on or off stage; it was all done in the dark. Likewise, I was not aware of any footage of either of them being led by a sighted guide. Perhaps there were many good reasons why it was done that way, but sometimes I wondered if it might cause a blind or disabled person to think the assistance they needed was somehow shameful and should be hidden. That was especially true in certain countries around the world where people were shunned in public because of their disability.

So when the videos started to go viral, and for the first time many people saw a blind musician using a cane, embracing his disability and not trying to hide it, there was an unexpected swell of support. The footage of my walking with my cane on *American Idol* showed a blind person on TV being treated with respect. I was treated like a human being, not like some character in a sitcom who was only there to get laughs.

Almost immediately I received letters and e-mails from people all over the world, even third world countries, saying things like, "I don't care how far you go on the show, even if you only last one day, because you've already changed my life just by being shown on TV with your cane."

I thought I'd understood the power of *American Idol* before, but as the messages kept pouring in, I realized that I had grossly underestimated the impact I could have through the show. Not only was the reach of *Idol* much broader than I'd expected—I was getting e-mails from places in the world where most of the population didn't even have TV—but it was also much deeper. I received personal and heart-wrenching e-mails from people who were seeing themselves through me. Their emotions ran high and spilled out all over their notes. They felt deeply connected to me in a way that I had never experienced before.

I realized that *American Idol* wasn't just some singing competition on the way to living out my dreams; it *was* the very way I could live out my dreams. The opportunity I had been looking for—to inspire as many people as possible—was available through this reality show. *American Idol* would give me a chance to reach out to millions.

It had been a treacherous climb to the top, but the view from where I now stood showed me a world of possibilities. God had brought me to that place of influence, and it was up to me to use it wisely.

~

Christina came home for the holidays, but she had to return to college before the premiere episode aired. With all that was going on with Katelyn, I didn't get to spend much time with her, but when I did, I found she was almost coy when I asked about her dating life.

"So I heard you're dating someone."

"Well, we're just really good friends."

"Really? I heard you were more than friends."

"Who told you that?"

"Does it matter?" I said with a smile.

It was almost like she didn't want me to think she was taken.

Although I was still interested in her, I didn't have much time to pursue her. The live shows started on February 18, but I had to be in Hollywood before that to begin rehearsals. Before I left, one of the last things I did was send Christina a Valentine's Day card. For some reason, I always found it easier to be more forward when there was distance between us. Maybe it was because if things got awkward, they could work themselves out before we saw each other again.

The pink-and-purple card came preprinted with the words "Roses are red, they have leaves that are green, and you're the cutest Valentine I've ever seen!" Underneath it I wrote: "Honest . . . You are! Christina, I still think of you a lot even though we're not together as often these days. Know that you're in my heart. Love, Scott."

I didn't care if she was seeing someone else or not. What was the worst that could happen? Whatever it was, it would blow over by the time I got back. I had nothing to lose and only Christina to gain.

~

One of the behind-the-scenes secrets of *American Idol* is that it seems as if the contestants can pick any song they want as long as it fit that week's theme. I found out the hard way that wasn't always the case.

To narrow the thirty-six semifinalists down, we were divided into three groups of twelve. One group would sing each week, and then the top three contestants with the highest votes that week would advance to the finalist round. That made nine finalists. Then the judges would select eight of their favorites from those who hadn't advanced. Those eight would sing again and the judges would choose the best three contestants to add to the nine chosen by popular vote. That would complete the top 12.

I was in the third group of twelve to sing, so my first performance wouldn't be until March 4, but I could begin preparing my song right away. The theme was "Billboard Hot 100 Hits." We could pick any song from the Billboard charts, but just because we picked it didn't mean we got to sing it. The producers could still veto our choices. And they did.

My first choice was "I Swear" by Boyz II Men, but the producers turned that down. My next choice was "February Song" by Josh Groban, but they also rejected that. Next I presented a song by Avril Lavigne, "When You're Gone," which I thought would be an interesting choice since Avril was a girl and, well, I wasn't. But producers said no to that one as well. The executive producer, Ken Warwick, recommended that I sing a Michael Bublé song. But I didn't feel like those songs really represented who I was.

I was getting desperate. Since I wasn't allowed to have a piano in this round—it would be just me and the microphone—I needed to find something that I could connect with emotionally and that I felt comfortable performing. But most important, I wanted a song that would showcase the kind of artist I was. That's when I thought of a singer I should have thought of before: Bruce Hornsby.

In 2002, right after I turned seventeen, I attended a Christian music conference and competition in Estes Park, Colorado. I was new to pop vocals and songwriting, but I had enough going for me to earn a spot in that conference. While I was there, I was selected to perform for a master class in front of an audience and receive feedback. I decided to perform "Your Father Is Waiting" from my soon-to-be-released CD, *My Guarantee*.

Someone in the audience said that my vocals, along with my piano playing and songwriting, reminded him of Bruce Hornsby. At the time, neither my parents nor I had any idea who Bruce Hornsby was. After I got home, I looked him up and started listening to his music. I fell in love with his lyrics. Hornsby had a way of telling a story in his songs without speaking literally, sometimes using ambiguous lyrics that danced around the topic rather than stating it plainly. In his song "Mandolin Rain," Hornsby encouraged the listener to hear things that we don't normally hear—music on a lake, tears rolling, and hearts breaking. It was a perfect song for me since I experienced so much of the world through my ears.

I picked up the phone and called the *Idol* office to suggest the song.

"Huh. That's an interesting idea," a producer said. "No one has ever done his music on the show before."

"There you go. I could be the first."

"Well, we've never done him because he's never given us clearance for any of his songs."

My heart dropped. I had been disappointed that my other choices had been vetoed, but I felt like those vetoes had led me to the perfect song. It would crush me if I couldn't do "Mandolin Rain."

"Is there anything we can do?" I asked.

"I'll try to get ahold of his people, but I wouldn't get your hopes up."

A few hours later, I got a call. "I have some good news. We talked to Bruce Hornsby's camp, and he personally approved you doing 'Mandolin Rain' on the show. We assured him you would do it justice." I was ecstatic. I knew what a privilege it was to be the first *Idol* contestant to do his music. Fortunately, I still had plenty of time to practice and get my performance just right. I hoped to make him proud.

CHAPTER 29

Moving in the Right Direction

Stop, lift your eyes
See the night that so surrounds us
It moves without a sound
—from "Stars," Scott MacIntyre

Although I was most comfortable performing from a piano, as I sat on a stool, center stage, I felt surprisingly relaxed. I held the mike in one hand, and the other rested gently on my knee as I waited. I had been playing and singing in front of people for as long as I could remember. Audiences at smaller venues across North America had already seen me perform. I wondered if any of them were watching *Idol* now and would remember me. If so, would they pick up the phone and vote?

As my package—the video story about each contestant—ended, and I heard the band start the intro to my song, I took a deep breath and softly sang the beginning of "Mandolin Rain."

"The song came and went . . . like the time that we spent . . ."

As I continued, I increased my volume and intensity, eventually standing and taking a couple of steps toward the judges. The crowd cheered as I built to a climax, hitting a long, high note and holding it. The song ended a couple of minutes later, and as I listened to the cheers of the audience, I knew I'd done my best. Now it was up to the judges.

Randy, Kara, and Paula each had nice things to say.

"You move mountains when you step on that stage," Kara said.

"I can feel the passion pouring out of you, how much you love this and want this," Randy said.

But I was curious about Simon's reaction. He was the judge that the television audience responded to the most. In his typical style, he got right to the point—he didn't like the lyrics. Although his comment wasn't personal toward me, it still surprised me. I identified with the lyrics, and they were one of the reasons I'd chosen the song. But before I could challenge him, he continued.

"Out of a sea of forgettable people, you are the only one I think I'm really going to remember."

I couldn't have asked for a better compliment from Simon. He was the judge who typically told contestants that they were *forgettable*. There would always be people who liked or didn't like my musical choices, but if they remembered me, if my presence and voice touched them in some way, what more could I ask for? I felt good about my performance, and I wasn't nervous the following night during the elimination show. That night I learned that I was one of the three contestants America had voted into the top 12. I smiled as I thought about how far I'd come since I'd walked through the losers' door at the Cow Palace in San Francisco.

~

Looking back, I wish I had stopped to soak in the feeling of making the top 12, because right after the show, the pace of things went into overdrive.

At three o'clock the next morning, the three of us started a national satellite tour. I sat in a studio in front of a camera, and remote television and radio hosts from across the country took turns interviewing me. Over and over I was asked the same questions about *Idol*, the judges, if I was going to play piano in the next round, and what I would say to encourage people who felt like giving up. With each interview, I talked about how grateful I was to be a part of the show and how amazing it felt to be the first disabled finalist performing on *Idol*. I wanted people to see how much I'd accomplished and the obstacles I'd overcome in my life as a way to encourage them to take on their own challenges and not give up on their own dreams.

The staff graciously allowed me to use a sighted guide during my days on *Idol*. There was no way I could get O&M training for every soundstage, warehouse, recording studio, and office building that I would work in, and unlike the other contestants, I had no way of knowing when cameras were filming my everyday activities. So I was grateful to have Mom with me during the frenetic months of being an *Idol* finalist. She was invaluable in helping me navigate the ever-changing environments and making sure I didn't miss out on important opportunities. We worked out a system so I could know when a camera was filming me during the day. She would say, "Super," and I'd know to smile.

Idol was a happy distraction for my family, but life-and-death decisions still had to be made about Katelyn's failing kidneys. Although arrangements had been made so Dad or Todd could take Katelyn to her appointments while Mom stayed with me in Hollywood, my mom was still very much emotionally with Katelyn. When she wasn't helping me, she was on the phone and often conferenced into medical conversations back home. By now Mayo had changed their policy and allowed multiple donors to be tested at once. Marianne was the first to go through testing. Not only was she willing, but doctors thought she had the perfect body type—small and petite, just like Katelyn.

So while Mom tried to balance the needs of both her kids, I tried to balance the demands of the *Idol* schedule. On that first day, the press interviews didn't end until the afternoon. Then it was time for the taping of the wild-card show. During that show, the judges allowed eight contestants who hadn't made it through the earlier round to sing again. I was exhausted, having only gotten a couple hours of sleep the night before, but I couldn't completely relax. I still had to look alert because we were always on camera. Even so, it was a nice change of pace to watch other people sing for the judges' votes, knowing that the viewing audience had already voted me through. Though the judges were supposed to choose three finalists to round out the top 12, they surprised us by choosing four. For the first time ever, *Idol* had a top 13.

The other contestants and I were all sitting on stools near the back of the stage when the announcement of the four new finalists was made. Suddenly I heard and felt lots of movement around me, but I didn't know what was happening. I tried to smile and look as if nothing was wrong in case the cameras were on me. Then Todd, who had been sitting in the audience close by, appeared at my side and whispered, "Everyone is congratulating the four who made it."

In a rush of emotion, they had all gotten up to celebrate the final four who made it into the top 13, but since I couldn't see what was happening, I was left sitting alone on my stool. I took Todd's elbow and he escorted me to the center of the stage. Although Mom was with me during the week, I had asked Todd to be my sighted guide for the live shows. I needed someone to help get me on and off stage and I hoped that his good looks would earn me a few swing votes.

After the top 13 was determined, I would've loved to have gone back to the hotel and get some sleep. But that's not how *Idol* worked. There was very little downtime. Ever. As soon as the show announcing the top 13 finished, we were whisked off to a red carpet event where hundreds of national and international media were waiting to take our pictures and interview us. I was getting a good taste of what it was like to have the eyes of the world focused on me.

After another short night of sleep, we packed up and moved out of our hotel and relocated to a mansion in a remote part of Bel Air. A camera crew filmed us moving in. On TV, the mansion looked posh. But the first person to use the bathroom quickly discovered that our new home lacked the basic necessities that came standard in a hotel. Things like toilet paper. There was no soap or shampoo either, and the remote location meant we couldn't buy some by just going downstairs to the gift shop or walking to the store. The cell phone coverage was spotty, and there was no Internet service. Soon we discovered that the roof leaked.

But overall, those things weren't too hard to deal with. What was tough to accept was the absence of a piano or keyboard in the house. And the *Idol* studios didn't have one either. We were all scheduled to sing again on Tuesday, and I planned to accompany myself on the piano. But I was dismayed that I would be playing piano in front of thirty million people in less than a week and couldn't practice. I talked to a few producers and my vocal coach to see if they could do anything about it, but nothing changed. I didn't want to be a complainer so I practiced the best I could—by imagining the piano in my head and moving my fingers as if I was playing. For the time being, it would have to do.

~

The theme for the top 13 show was Michael Jackson's music. I chose "Keep the Faith." It would be the realization of a dream for me to sit behind a grand piano, and for the first time, show millions of *Idol* viewers who I was as an artist. Our first rehearsal wasn't on the *Idol* stage. It was in a large, cavernous warehouse, and I found myself positioned in the midst of all the musicians in the band. So for my song, I was able to just lean over and tell the drummer or the guitar player what I wanted. I was one of the only finalists who had experience arranging music, and I always had a very specific vision for a song. I worked hard with the band to create my own unique arrangement—it was a special moment for me. (I didn't know it at the time, but for future rehearsals in the theater, I wouldn't have access to individual musicians because of where the band was positioned.) It's hard to explain how thrilling the experience was, and yet at the same time, how much pressure I felt.

At the red carpet event on the night the top 13 were announced, members of the media had asked me if I was going to perform with the piano. I had assured them that I was and that it would be worth the wait, and with the help of the band, I was prepared to deliver on that promise. It was the moment I had been looking forward to since the beginning of the competition.

The day before the live show, the stress started to get to me. I internalized how much was riding on each performance. After the show on Tuesday night, America would once again vote and two people would be sent home the next day. As I practiced my song, I obsessed over small details (like how fast the band should play when they joined in) that I later realized would have little impact on the outcome. But knowing that I only had one shot, I scrutinized every decision and my inner perfectionist came out. I was trying to take control of a situation over which I could never have total control. Looking back, I wish I had been more relaxed.

But I forgot all about my concerns on Tuesday night. When I started singing for the live show, the studio audience went crazy. They cheered me on during and after my song, and their passion for the music restored my confidence. In that moment, I knew that was why I made music—to share my God-given talent and to inspire and encourage people. Fortunately, the judges also liked it and had kind things to say.

Referring to the title of the song, Kara said, "It's your message. It's that hopeful message that you deliver."

Simon didn't like the fact that I'd chosen a lesser-known Michael Jackson song. But when Paula spoke she pointed out that the songwriter (who also wrote "Man in the Mirror") was in the audience and asked her what she thought. She said she loved it.

Having successfully navigated that experience, I felt more secure the next night as I awaited the results. I was confident I had done everything I could to earn America's votes. Still, relief surged through me when Ryan announced that I'd made it through another week. I was pleased and extremely grateful to my fans for their votes. It made me want to do it again. I was hooked, just like after that first Christmas musical at church when I was a little boy. I had caught the *Idol* bug.

~

Back during Hollywood Week when I was learning the dance moves, Ken Warwick must have been watching. At one point during that very long night, he pulled me aside and said, "Don't worry about the dancing, Scott. You don't have to do it."

"No, it's okay. I'll do my best." But I had no idea what I was getting myself into.

As a viewer of *Idol*, I assumed that after a live show the contestants went back to their home base and relaxed. Nothing could've been further from the truth. The show ended, and instead of going back to the mansion, we went right back to work—often for dance rehearsal. The dance during Hollywood Week was simple compared to the choreography we did for the live shows. It was unbelievably difficult and required three times the effort from me as it did from anyone else.

The first time I met the choreographer was during my final preparation for the top 36. Each week on elimination night, the twelve contestants who had performed the night before were expected to do a group number. Fortunately, that stage was much smaller than the stage we would use later on, so the choreography was more limited. But now the choreography was much more complicated and made use of the entire stage. There were three layers to performing the choreography of the group number, and for each one, I had to memorize hundreds of details.

The first layer was the dance itself. When you're blind, "Move your arm a little to the right," or "Bend your leg like this," doesn't mean as much as when you can see it demonstrated. Mom would be with me during rehearsals, so as the choreographer taught each part of the dance, Mom would explain the steps to me in detail. I had taken ballroom dancing, and I was used to moving on stage, but this was more complicated because it involved learning unique movements for every body part. Where was my right arm supposed to go? Was it straight or bent? Fingers open or closed? Palm up or down? Elbow in or out?

Once I got the moves down, I had to get the spacing correct. Sometimes I needed to be in a specific formation with other contestants, and I couldn't just look and see if I was in the right place. Every move I made was based on my ability to memorize angles and body positions, and I knew each new position I transitioned to would only be correct relative to my last position, so I had to be precise. I had to rely on my spatial memory to make sure I traveled just the right distance across the stage, and when I turned, I had to know how far to turn, and in which direction. A slightly inaccurate turn followed by several long steps could put me in the lap of someone in the front row rather than center stage.

In real life there were sometimes visual cues I could reference to supplement my spatial memory—a light border against a dark edge, for example. But on the *Idol* stage, lights glared from every direction, making it impossible for me to see anything at all. There were no contrasts of light and shadow either. Everything was lit, and the lights were always changing. Even if I could have found a visual focal point, the dance moved so fast, I'd never have time to scan around and find it.

Many blind people wouldn't have felt comfortable moving around on a stage without their cane for protection. But Mom and Dad had helped develop my spatial awareness from a very early age by letting me run on the beach, learn to ride a bike, ski with a sighted guide, and jump off the bridge at Trinity Alps. I wasn't afraid of those things anymore, and neither was I afraid of falling off the stage. Despite all that could have gone wrong, I trusted my instincts and memory to guide me. The choreographer also helped by occasionally building into the routine an opportunity for someone to give me a nudge in one direction or another.

Once I got all that under control, I had to take on the second layer—the television cameras. It wasn't enough to just memorize the dance steps; I also had to memorize where the cameras were and what they were doing. The studio had more than sixty cameras, and many of them were camouflaged or out of view so the television audience would never see them. Cameras on cranes, handheld cameras, and stationary cameras pointed at us from every angle.

Once the dance was set, the choreographer would then explain to me what the cameras would be doing. "On the second verse, third line, there will be a camera swooping down at a forty-five-degree angle, so when you sing that line, try to move your head and your eyes in line with where you think the camera will be."

To help me visualize what she was describing, Mom would lift my arm and point it in the direction the camera would be moving.

"And then on the next line, a cameraman with a handheld camera will be traveling along an arc behind you, so try to turn and smile at him, and then follow him as he moves around to the front."

Sometimes things the choreographer said made me think she forgot I was blind. I must have been doing a pretty good job. Her voice at least helped me guess where I should look, but she couldn't spend much time focused on me. Some of the other contestants had trouble with the dancing, and she needed to spend extra time with them too.

It was a lot of work to memorize the dance and the camera angles. But the third layer was the hardest. That was when they would change the steps we had learned. Sometimes it was because the choreographer came up with a better idea, but often it was because a producer didn't like something they'd seen in rehearsal. None of the contestants liked the changes. We all found them frustrating, but they were especially difficult for me. Instead of going to the right, I now went to the left, which meant I raised my right hand instead of my left and the camera was now on my left instead of my right. Or the camera arc that I thought was happening in the first verse of the song was now happening in the second verse. It was hard enough to learn it all the first time, but it was even harder to unlearn what I'd memorized and replace it with something new.

And I was supposed to sing during all of that!

But I am so thankful that the *Idol* executives ventured into that uncharted territory with me and allowed me to do it. I'm sure it would have been easier on everyone to sit me on a prop and have the other contestants dance around me. With more than thirty million viewers, they were taking as much a risk by allowing me to dance as I was taking by dancing. But together we broke a lot of paradigms. I proved that visually impaired artists didn't have to "just appear," wearing dark glasses and standing center stage when the lights came up. Instead, with a lot of work and patience, we could dance, move across the stage, and smile into the cameras just like any other singer.

Though it required a lot of extra effort, I was pleased with the way things turned out. Since leaving *Idol*, I've met a lot of my fans at concerts and talked with them afterward. Some of them have told me that while watching *Idol*, they didn't realize I was blind until someone else pointed it out. Those are nice compliments, but the best ones come from fans with disabilities who tell me that my presence on *Idol* inspired them to make bold moves in their own lives. If my ambition encouraged others to pursue their dreams, then the extra effort was definitely worth it.

CHAPTER 30

Desperate Prayers

It's hard to be away from you
I treasure all the memories I have to see me through
And I know there's nothing I can do
But pretend to end the story
That you'll be waiting for me
It's hard for me to be away from you
—FROM "HARD TO BE AWAY," SCOTT MACINTYRE

People are often surprised to learn I can send and receive texts. Navigating a phone isn't that different from memorizing a physical route—it just involves different cues. Instead of memorizing physical distances, I memorize the menus on the phone; and instead of using my cane to feel for a wall, I use my fingers to feel for buttons. If I get a text, I press the end button to make sure the home screen is showing, then the menu key, followed by the down arrow key twice. Because the phone is in my hand, I can locate it quickly, and then slowly scan it until I find the top left corner of the screen. I can scan down the left side until I see a dark icon, which indicates an unread text. Then I can move my eyes to the right to read who it is from. If I see K A T E, that is enough to tell me it is from Katelyn, and I hit enter to open it. Then I can read the message one letter at a time, occasionally moving through words more quickly if I guess their meaning.

Sending a reply is similar. I memorize the menus to get me to the right screen and then use the raised keyboard (which I've also memorized) to type a reply. I've gotten pretty fast at it, but it is still a laborious process that requires more time than it would a sighted person. Perhaps the biggest drawback is I can't use the new touchscreen technology. I have to have raised keys to feel my way around the keyboard.

Unfortunately, that constraint proved to be a vital limitation while I was on *Idol*. Other contestants used their iPhones or other smartphones to download and preview songs. Since I couldn't use that technology, *Idol* staffers had to burn songs to a CD so I could listen and select the best song for me.

Choosing songs each week was a stressful process. Even when a contestant found what he or she thought was the perfect song, the producers would weigh in with their opinions, which at best could affirm a contestant's decision. At worst they could decide it wasn't going to work for the show and just eliminate it. Sometimes they wanted us to sing something more upbeat than what we'd chosen, or perhaps permission for a song wouldn't clear in time for the show. We never really locked in on one song because sometimes songs didn't clear until the day before.

Good songs went fast too. For one show, someone else picked a Carrie Underwood song and the producers didn't want two contestants to sing songs from the same artist. There were also weeks when two or more contestants wanted the same song, so they'd put pieces of paper into a box. One had the song name on it and the others were blank. I only drew blanks. I remember Matt (the other piano player) and Anoop each beating me out of a song at least once.

Once we finalized a song, we still had to rehearse it. But it was tough finding enough time to practice singing because we were so busy with photo shoots, music videos, recording sessions, wardrobe styling, and choreography rehearsals. Because I was a songwriter, the time I had was divided between creating a unique arrangement of a song and practicing singing and playing it. Some Tuesday nights, as we prepared to go on stage for the live show, I'd ask myself, "When did I practice my song this week?"

The theme for the top 11 week was supposed to be "Country," but at the last minute they changed it to "Grand Ole Opry." That dramatically narrowed the range of songs I could choose from. I wanted a song I could frame with a contemporary pop feel, but it was hard to find anything that suited my voice and my vision as an artist.

The top 11 week was probably the most important week of my whole *Idol* experience. If I made it through, I would be in the top ten, which would secure me a spot on the *American Idol* tour. It would mean playing in arenas before tens of thousands of cheering fans. It was my lifelong dream, and suddenly it was close enough to touch. I wanted to be in the top ten like nothing I'd ever wanted before. Everything rode on that performance, and I'd do whatever I could to succeed.

But in addition to finding a song that week, there were other distractions.

First, several contestants had come down with the H1N1 flu. Ever since my transplant, I had tried to avoid sick people. Since my immune system was already compromised, I couldn't risk getting sick. I started wearing a mask to avoid breathing in anything contagious. As more people came down with the virus, I was surprised the contestant coordinators didn't do something to segregate the sick from the healthy. One day, as we were getting into the two vans that drove us back and forth to the soundstage, Mom made a suggestion: "Why don't we use one van just for the sick people?"

All week we'd dealt with the issue. Mom usually just tried to seat me as far away from the sick people as possible, putting herself between them and me to lessen my risk of exposure during the forty-minute drive. But as more contestants became ill, Mom worried about more than just me. She knew how important it was for the show to have healthy contestants putting forth their best efforts. I thought it was a great suggestion, but the idea went over like a bad song. "I'm not going to try and control that," said the contestant coordinator.

So Mom and I didn't bring it up again, but we still tried to sit away from those who were coughing and sneezing. Later in the week, a doctor prescribed antibiotics for all the contestants, even those who weren't sick. I was already on several medications for my new kidney, and I didn't want to create unnecessary drug interactions, but he insisted that I take the antibiotics. He said the pills would cause nausea, but instead, after just one dose, I broke out in hives on one of my arms and both legs. I never took another pill.

That week I chose to sing "Wild Angels," a Martina McBride hit. Though it was a country song, I thought it showed a bit of my contemporary singer-songwriter side, and I liked the arrangement I had worked out. Everything was going great. Randy Travis was the celebrity mentor that week, and he really liked what I did with the song. I felt good. I'd had some mild cold symptoms, but had managed to avoid the flu, and I was confident I'd done everything possible to prepare for the performance. I set my sights on earning a spot in the top ten. If I found favor with the voting public, I would be performing live in arenas across North America. If not, I'd go home.

Tuesday night, as I stood backstage and listened to the other contestants perform, I thought about Christina. She was in the audience that night. I was given four tickets to each performance, and usually I gave them all to my family, but that week, Katelyn wasn't feeling well so she and Dad were home in Arizona. I had two extras. I gave one to a friend in the industry, and since

Christina was at school in Los Angeles, I wanted her to have the other one. I couldn't wait to see her after the show.

During a commercial break, Todd walked me out on stage and helped me get seated at the piano to wait for my cue. As soon as the break ended, Ryan would introduce me, they would play the short video package, and then I would sing. As I waited, I played a few notes on the piano and tapped my microphone to make sure I could hear myself, but the sound wasn't on yet. That wasn't unusual; sometimes it took them awhile to turn it on.

"Thirty seconds," came the voice over the stage intercom. It was Annie the stage manager, and she was counting down the time we had left before the end of the commercial break.

"Test, test, test . . ." I tried again. Still nothing. "What's going on?" I asked, not sure if anyone was on stage beside me. "There's no sound coming through my monitor." I started to feel like they were cutting it a little close.

"We're trying to figure it out," said a voice from the other side of the piano.

"We're trying to fix it," said another voice.

"Twenty seconds," Annie said.

"Test, test, test . . ." Still nothing. Both the monitor and the house speaker system were dead. The entire sound system didn't seem to be working. Once we went live, I wouldn't be able to test it because the sound would interfere with the video package and Ryan's introduction. But if I didn't get any sound, how could I be heard? My life on the show depended on a vote from a television audience who had to hear me play and sing. My heart raced. I was alone in the middle of the stage and I couldn't see if anyone was doing anything, and if they were, how close they were to fixing the problem.

"Ten. Nine. Eight."

As soon as I heard Annie's voice, I prayed desperately. I didn't have time to think about my prayer, but I knew that instead of panicking, I should turn to God. *Please, God. Please fix whatever is causing this problem. There's nothing I can do. I need your help.*

"Seven. Six. Five."

"Test, test. One, two, three," I said in one last desperate attempt.

Then just as I heard Annie say, "Four, three, two . . ." I also heard myself. The mike was live, and I could hear my voice through the monitor and the house speakers. It was working!

Ryan introduced me, and as the video package played, I took a deep breath and tried to stop shaking. *The top ten is on the line. You can do this.* When my cue came, I started playing. I sang softly at first, but by the time I sang the second line, "It's a miracle in itself," I sang with conviction. I knew that one had just taken place. As the song continued, my intensity increased until I reached the climax of the song. The lights on the stage turned from blue to a bright yellow as I repeated the chorus about the wild angels watching over me.

It was a triumphant performance. God had answered my prayer and given me a working sound system for one of the most important performances of my life. The judges made their typical comments that night, but I don't remember what they said. I was just so excited to have actually pulled off a good performance after such a close call.

After the live show ended, all of the contestants gathered in the third-floor Red Room and waited to hear what we had to do next. I begged a producer to let me go see Christina, and they finally agreed to give us all five minutes before the choreography session started. As Mom led me downstairs, she explained what had happened with the sound system.

"When you first sat down and said the sound wasn't working, two guys came up. A few seconds later, two more came. By the time Annie started her final ten-second countdown, there were eight sound techs all crowded around the piano, jiggling things, disconnecting and reconnecting wires, and moving them around in a desperate attempt to get it back up. They barely made it in time for you to sing."

"I was worried. It was way too close," I said.

"I know. Great job holding it together. I'm so proud of you."

By the time we got downstairs, it had been forty-five minutes since the show had ended. I wasn't sure if Christina had waited around. But immediately after we opened the backstage door, I felt arms around me and knew they were hers. Mom stepped away to make a phone call while we talked.

"Ooh, you have lots of makeup on," Christina said.

I laughed. It was so good to hear her voice.

"Why are some of the other contestants wearing breathing masks?" she asked.

I explained how many of them had been sick, and how worried I'd been that I'd get sick too. She assured me that I sounded great, and she thought I'd easily make it into the top ten.

"We need to start heading back up in a minute," one of the wranglers said. "Wrap it up."

Mom came over, and it was time to go. I hugged Christina good-bye, and I promised to call her to get together if there was a break in my schedule.

～

As Mom and I walked back upstairs, I could tell her thoughts were somewhere else. It was challenging for Mom to be with me while Katelyn was at home dealing with doctors, feeling sick, and waiting to hear about a donor. For me, I mostly felt like I lived in an *Idol* bubble, a false reality that consumed everything around me and forced me to stay in the moment. It insulated me from thinking about anything else because it demanded so much of my attention. But when I had a chance to step back—to think for myself, and to notice Mom on the phone with Katelyn, Dad, or another doctor—the *Idol* bubble burst and the reality show gave way to the reality of life. Although I hoped to get enough votes to stay alive on the show, we were all praying Katelyn would get a kidney to keep her alive—period.

Katelyn had been out a couple of times to see the show, but she returned home immediately after each one, and I hadn't been able to visit with her. I remembered how awful I felt when my creatinine levels were that high, and I understood her need to rest and be at home. I felt guilty at times for not being with her more, but I also knew how much she wanted me to be on *Idol*. Still, I would have given it all up if it would help Katelyn get a donor.

～

Nothing was more nerve-wracking than standing in front of a live audience and millions of TV viewers and waiting for Ryan Seacrest to announce my fate. Would I make the top ten and go on tour?

"Scott, you are going to be packing your bags," Ryan said and then paused. For a second I felt like I'd been punched in the gut. "Because you are going on tour!"

Inside my mind, it was like midnight on New Year's Eve in Times Square. Horns sounded, confetti and tickertape showered down, and everyone cheered! I was going on tour! My lifelong dream would be a reality. I sat down next to my friend Matt who had also made it, leaned over, and whispered, "Piano men on tour, dude!" We had talked about doing a dueling piano number together, and now we could make it happen. I was thrilled beyond belief. I tried to just live in that moment and soak in the joy I felt. Five hundred thousand people would see me perform live on tour, and I couldn't wait.

After the show, Mom came up and I could tell she was excited for me. But her words surprised me. "Scott, I've got some great news! Marianne has been approved as a donor!"

"What?" Immediately, I was snapped out of the bubble and brought back to reality.

"I heard a couple of hours ago, but you were backstage and I couldn't tell you. Mayo called Dad, and Marianne has been approved!"

Katelyn's news put everything in perspective. Sure it was great that I was going on tour. It was a lifetime dream, and an achievement that I had worked hard for, but Katelyn's news was so incredible that mine faded in comparison. I hugged Mom and then reached for my phone to call Katelyn. But before I could dial the number, one of the wranglers stopped me with his announcement.

"*Idol* contestants, we need you to get your things and proceed immediately to the vans."

CHAPTER 31
The Search Is Over

I wake up every morning
To a picture of you
That sits on a table by the bed
The sunbeams bathe the faces
As it catches my eye
Taken on the last day we spent
—FROM "HARD TO BE AWAY," SCOTT MACINTYRE

The vans arrived at a small airport where we were ushered onto a private jet. Once we were on the plane, we learned that next week's theme was "Motown," and we were headed straight to the source for inspiration. After flying all night, with no sleep, we landed in Detroit and then toured Motown Records with its founder, Berry Gordy, and its long-time recording artist, Smokey Robinson. It was inspiring to be mentored by the same legends who'd been so influential in Stevie Wonder's life. I had always looked up to Stevie Wonder; his success as a blind musician in a very visual industry was an inspiration to me. As I pursued my own path in the business, I couldn't help but wonder what obstacles he'd faced and how he dealt with them as he climbed the ladder of success. I needed to keep Stevie's tenacity in mind as I dealt with my latest issues.

For several weeks I had heard through blogs, fan forums, and e-mail that people couldn't hear my piano on TV. I knew what the problem was. When the sound was mixed for broadcast, instead of treating the piano like a featured instrument, as they did with my voice, they mixed it with all the background instruments. They treated the piano like it was just one of the fifty instruments in the orchestra rather than its own entity, and therefore, the television audience couldn't distinguish the piano sound from anything else. Several times I'd asked to talk with the person in the sound booth, but I was never given the chance. My goal was to showcase my voice *and* the piano. I'd been performing long enough to know that this combination best represented me as an artist.

So for Motown week, I decided that if I couldn't change the mix, I would only use a small number of backup instruments in hopes that the piano would be more prominent. For my song that week, "You Can't Hurry Love," I envisioned a hip piano version that only used a few horns, a bass, drums, and guitars. The musical director wasn't happy with me. "Stevie Wonder would use the whole orchestra," he said, trying to change my mind. But I stayed true to my vision. I liked the arrangement and was excited about performing it.

Monday's rehearsal went great. The sound was perfect, and I couldn't wait to perform it the next day. On Tuesdays, we had a rehearsal around two o'clock in the afternoon. It was a full dress rehearsal with hair, makeup, clothes, and a live audience. Typically we ran through the whole show without stopping. I was expecting a repeat of Monday's smooth rehearsal, but when I started singing, I realized my monitor wasn't working right. The monitor was a dedicated speaker placed downstage and pointing back at me so I could hear my voice. It allowed me to hear what I was singing—helping me to know that I was staying on pitch and keeping up with the band. In essence, it was the feedback loop that let me know how I was doing. But the top half of the frequency range was cut off. I could only hear the bass sounds. I couldn't hear my voice. I was now singing blind *and* deaf.

I finished the song and the studio audience cheered, but instead of getting up to leave, I leaned into the mike and said, "Excuse me. There's something wrong with this monitor. Can we try to fix it?"

The show went live in a couple of hours, and I hoped they could just replace it with a spare from the back or something. They examined the monitor, and I kept talking into the mike so they could check their progress. But they couldn't hear what I was hearing.

"Sounds fine to me," said one technician.

"It's not working right. Can't you hear how it sounds all muffled?" I said.

"Not really."

It was soon obvious they weren't going to fix it. I would have to do the show without a working monitor.

"Could you please at least boost the higher frequencies?"

They agreed, but that night as I sang, I immediately discovered it hadn't helped much at all. After I finished my song and went backstage, I was frustrated. The flawed monitor sound had affected my performance. It was one thing to be judged based on my talent, but it was so discouraging to know that one of my performances had been affected by technology. Technology that could have been fixed or replaced if someone had cared enough to listen.

The next night I found myself in the bottom three, but Ryan Seacrest quickly told me that I wasn't the one going home. Being in the bottom three didn't worry me—I just didn't feel like it was my time yet. Still, it was a sign that I was vulnerable.

∽

Throughout the next week, I was very worried about the monitor going out again. I wasn't sure who I should talk to or what I should say. I could keep insisting that they try to figure it out, but if the professional sound crew couldn't hear anything wrong, why would the producers believe me? I knew that the *Idol* staff didn't appreciate complainers, but if there was ever something to complain about, maybe this was it. I lay awake in bed and played the scenarios over and over in my mind. *What if it doesn't work for Monday's rehearsal? Or what if it works on Monday but doesn't work again on Tuesday? Why do I even have to be the one worrying about the technical issues?* It was maddening that I couldn't focus completely on the music.

The theme for the week was "Popular iTunes Downloads," and I chose "Just the Way You Are," a song by my own idol, Billy Joel. The judges had pegged me as a contemporary Joel, and this was my opportunity to give them exactly what they wanted. I believed the song was a perfect fit for my voice and a great way to showcase the piano. I thought about doing the number with a string quartet, but in the end, I decided against it.

"I want to try something new," I told the musical director. "I want to do it with just piano and voice." But I was really thinking, *This malfunctioning monitor stuff is stressing me out, and I don't want to deal with it if I don't have to. This way I have total control over the music.* If it worked, I was responsible. If it didn't, I had no one but myself to blame.

Monday's rehearsal came and once again the monitor didn't work. Fortunately I wasn't the only one to notice. Finally one of the sound techs heard what I was hearing. They knew there had to be a loose connection, but when they couldn't find it, they discarded the monitor and brought in a brand-new one. As soon as they hooked it up, everything sounded perfect again.

During Tuesday's dress rehearsal, I took my place at the piano, did my sound check during the "fake" commercial break and waited for my cue. The sound equipment all seemed to be working fine, and I was excited about my song. Annie started counting down from the break, but then she suddenly stopped. I waited for her to resume, but for at least a minute, nothing happened. Finally, she came back on the intercom and said, "Hang on, the screen doors aren't working."

Apparently, the enormous video screens that closed over the retractable staircase and lined the back of the stage had gotten stuck in the open position. Technicians tried to close it, but nothing they did worked. There was no way to manually open and close the screen during a show, so it had to be fixed immediately. The crew scrambled to find a solution and a call was made to the technician responsible for the operation. He was on his way but it was going to take awhile.

Meanwhile, I was still sitting at the piano and the live audience was growing restless. Suddenly, Annie said over the intercom, "Scott, why don't you play something?"

It was the moment I had been waiting for. I realized I could play anything I wanted, so of course I chose one of my own songs. I started playing an instrumental version of a song I'd written in London called "Hard to Be Away." It was in the same key as the Billy Joel song. As my fingers danced across the keys of the chorus, I wondered what would happen if I started to sing too? The worst they could do was stop me, and I knew I'd likely never have another chance again. How many people ever got to sing their own songs in front of a live audience on the *Idol* stage?

As soon as I sang the first lyric, "I wake up every morning to a picture of you," the audience fell silent. It was one of the most emotional songs I'd ever written, and I figured many people could relate to missing someone they loved. I could feel them hanging on every word I sang. When I finished the first chorus, everyone started to cheer. Their response encouraged me, and I sang the second verse and chorus with even more passion.

With every word, my emotion built. When I got to the bridge, I landed on one long, soaring note and the audience went crazy. It was the first time I'd ever played my music and heard the audience cheer all the way through it. They acted like they did for all of the *Idol* songs, screaming each time they were touched by the music. But the difference was, this was *my* song. I had written the words and music that caused their excitement. It was an incredible moment for me. The door of opportunity closed as I finished the song—the retractable jumbo screen had been fixed—and rehearsal continued.

That night the judges loved my performance of "Just the Way You Are." But I was really excited when some of my online fans said it was my best performance yet because they could finally hear the piano. On elimination night, I sailed through and was safe for another week. Though I had spent the entire week worrying about the monitor, in the end, it worked out and I had my best week ever. By then we were into April and the finale was scheduled for May 20, so only a few weeks remained. I was hitting my stride and I couldn't wait for what came next.

~

Mom learned that Katelyn's surgery was scheduled for April 17, and as that date grew closer, it became obvious that Katelyn needed Mom at home not only for practical reasons like doctors appointments and testing, but also because her symptoms had worsened. She wasn't feeling well. We were all thankful that she held on this long and hadn't needed dialysis; we just hoped she could continue to make it until the surgery date.

The plan was to have Todd come and stay with me as my sighted guide while Mom went home to be with Katelyn. He was already familiar with *Idol*, since he was the one who escorted me on and off stage on show days. But now he would be with me during all the extra activities, too, like the Ford commercial shoots and iTunes recording sessions. To help with the transition, we planned for him to spend a day or two shadowing Mom before she left so he could learn his way around.

The theme for the top eight week was songs from our birth years. I decided I needed to do something to surprise the judges and the voting public. Everything had gone so well the week before that I figured this was the time to take a risk. Everyone knew I could handle a piano or a keyboard; now I wanted to show them I could also play electric guitar.

But as I prepared, I had trouble deciding between two songs—"Broken Wings" by Mr. Mister, or "The Search Is Over" by Survivor. I debated the pros and cons all week, even asking my fellow contestants for their opinions. I asked Adam Lambert to listen to the Survivor song, and after just a few seconds, he slipped off the headphone and said, "No, don't do that one. It sounds so dated."

I was struggling with the decision. I had done well until that point, but I didn't want to make the wrong choice. Each week there was more pressure to select the right song. I asked Kris Allen, who would go on to be the season eight winner, to listen to me sing both songs. "You should definitely do 'Broken Wings,'" he said. The vocal coaches also preferred it. Even Mom liked it better. It was more of an upbeat song, which was a plus, but every time I sang it, I felt like I was faking it. The melody just didn't click with me, and it didn't feel as organic. So against all the recommendations, I went with my gut and chose "The Search Is Over."

The title of the song should have been the first clue. The judges hated it. I thought it was a decent performance, and I loved doing it, but they criticized everything about it, including the guitar. I'll concede that it may have not been my best vocal night—I didn't sing with the guitar as often as I sang with the piano—but I didn't think it was nearly as bad as they said, and there was nothing wrong with the guitar playing. More than anything, I wanted to surprise them, and I felt I'd done that. But their words hurt.

Mom had doctors' appointments with Katelyn on Monday and Tuesday, so she hadn't made it to the show. When I got back to the mansion, I called her. I could feel my chances of surviving the week slipping away. I told her that Simon had said my guitar playing was awful, and then I said something I had never said my entire time on *Idol*: "I hate this show!"

"Don't say that," she said. Then joking, "They probably have microphones in the room. They might hear you."

But really she was right for another reason. That wasn't how I truly felt. *Idol* was one of the biggest blessings of my entire life. I was just tired and exasperated. By the next morning, I was over it and ready to do whatever I could to stay on the show.

Mom and Katelyn flew back to be at Wednesday night's elimination show. As the show began, I wasn't nervous. Even when I found out I was in the bottom three, I didn't worry. I'd been there once before, and it had worked out fine. But when I found out I was in the bottom two, suddenly things got very serious.

There was a commercial, and after we returned, either Anoop, the other contestant in the bottom two, or I would have to sing for our lives. A judges' save had been introduced that year, and if the judges chose to use it, they could keep their chosen contestant on the show for a week longer. I wanted to do everything I could to convince them to use it on me. During the break I warmed up my voice, ran through the words, and, since I'd be singing without the guitar, tried to improvise some movements that wouldn't seem stiff. As a blind person, hand gestures didn't come naturally to me.

The break ended, and Ryan announced that I had the lowest number of votes. Out of thirty-four million votes, less than thirty thousand had separated the two of us. I would be the one to sing, and now my only chance was for the judges to use their save.

Ryan introduced me. The music played and I started to sing "The Search Is Over," but as soon as the words came out of my mouth, I knew there was a problem. Once again, the monitor was either off or not working. I couldn't believe it! It was the most important song I'd ever sing on the *Idol* stage, the one that would determine my fate, and again faulty technology or human error kept me from giving my best performance. But as I stood alone center stage, the eyes of the world on me, I knew I couldn't let this beat me. So I pushed all of the negatives out of my mind and sang as I'd never sung before. If I was eliminated, I wanted to go down knowing I had given it everything I had.

The judges debated whether or not to use the save, and when they told Ryan it was a split decision, I was hopeful. They hadn't even considered using the save the week before. Ryan asked them to make a decision, and the audience cheered them on to use the save. Finally, Simon delivered the news. "Scott, it's the end of the competition. Sorry."

I was crushed.

Over the past few weeks, I had become comfortable watching other people leave, but now that it was my turn, I was totally caught off guard.

I hadn't seen it coming.

The show ended in the studio, and televisions across America began showing local news. The *Idol* contestants who had gathered around me began to leave. Some left me a few parting words; others hugged me before slipping offstage in a hurry to move on to the next thing. I knew how they felt; I had been them for so many weeks. Of course, they were sad to lose a friend, but I knew they were secretly happy to have made it through for another week. I wanted to find a quiet place, away from the exiting studio audience who I knew was still watching me. It was like being dumped by your good-looking girlfriend in front of a crowd of onlookers. I couldn't help but wonder what story my face betrayed to those who stared.

I just wanted to be alone.

But I heard the judges making their way toward me. Randy was the first to shake my hand. "You sang great tonight."

"Was it better? I couldn't hear myself. The monitor wasn't working."

"Oh, yeah. It was way better."

More hugs, handshakes, and words of encouragement were offered from the other judges. But my mind was spinning. I couldn't focus on what they were saying. *If it was better, why didn't they save me?*

Soon everyone except for my brother Todd had left the stage. Todd was my sighted guide that week, and he was waiting to escort me backstage. I heard him approach and turned toward him. He didn't say anything; he didn't need to. More than just a brother, Todd was also my best friend. Our ability to communicate went much deeper than words.

I reached for his elbow—my cue that I was ready to follow him. Todd handed me my cane, and for the last time, he led me across the stage, down the stairs, and through the dark scaffolding behind the set. I recalled the many weeks I'd walked this same path; only then, I was surrounded by the familiar voices of fellow contestants. Each week we had talked about how relieved we were to still be there and how sorry we were to see a friend go. But this time the only sound I heard was our footsteps and the occasional swoosh of my cane over the cold concrete floor.

Todd stopped suddenly, and so I did too. A woman's voice spoke, "All of this . . . it doesn't matter, because you inspire people." I recognized it as the voice of Kara DioGuardi. It seemed she had been waiting for me backstage. I was surprised; we'd just spoken out front.

She paused as she searched for the right words, and then while touching me on the arm she said, "You make a difference in people's lives, and that is the most incredible thing! No one does that!" I heard the urgency and passion in her voice.

Overcoming blindness had inspired the audience and the judges, but they had no idea about all the obstacles I'd faced in the past few years. At only twenty-three years old, I had already lived more life, overcome more obstacles, and dealt with more life-threatening situations than I would ever hope most people will encounter.

We parted ways and Todd and I exited the soundstage, passing through the door into the lighted hallway. Outside the door stood my mom and my sister, Katelyn. As the light of the hallway pierced the darkness of the soundstage, I blinked back tears. As I walked toward my family, the *Idol* reality show gave way to another reality as my public and personal lives collided. A thousand thoughts piled up in my mind before I could consider the first one. My knees felt weak and any remaining energy drained out of me like a bathtub drained water.

"Oh, Scott," my mom said, hugging me.

"Thanks for coming," I said, my voice cracking as I hugged her. I wanted to say more, but I couldn't get the words out. I didn't have to.

When I hugged Katelyn, I felt how thin and frail she'd become, and I sensed her exhaustion. In that moment, the reality show bubble of *American Idol* burst and I was reminded once again of the reality of my life. Reality was a catheter stuck in my chest while I endured months of dialysis. Reality was listening to Mom cry when she learned her daughter faced the same life-threatening illness that her son had just fought for two years. Reality was that Katelyn was just days away from her transplant surgery, and although we prayed for the best, we didn't know what would happen. Reality was Katelyn traveling to Los Angeles just to support me, despite how much it would take out of her physically.

Yes, it hurt to leave the show, but it hurt more to think about what Katelyn was going through. In my new reality, her recovery was the only thing that really mattered.

CHAPTER 32
Finale Follies

I can't let it end this way
So much more I wanna say
—FROM "THIS SONG," SCOTT MACINTYRE

"Not many know this," Don, an *Idol* producer said, "but before Scott tried out in Phoenix and made it through, he first tried out in San Francisco with his brother and sister."

"Ohh," said the people listening.

"But he didn't even make it through the first round. He was turned down by this lady right here."

Everyone laughed. He must have been pointing to another one of the producers. I wondered if it was one of the two evaluators who'd sat behind the table, or perhaps even the infamous San Fran swooper.

"But he came back to the Arizona auditions, and he made it through. And he kept making it through, round after round after round . . . and finished in the top eight, and we're so glad he did."

The room full of producers, staffers, and the top seven *Idol* contestants had all gathered in an upstairs room at an Italian restaurant called Buca di Beppo for a post-show dinner. The elimination-night dinners gave everyone an opportunity to say a few words to the person leaving. Next, Matt stood up to speak. He was a pianist, like me, and he'd become a good friend of mine. "I remember when me and Danny first saw Scott. He was playing the piano and singing. I looked over at Danny and I said, 'He can totally see, dude. He's not blind.'"

Everyone had another good laugh. I'd made some lifelong friends through my time on *Idol*, and their words showed me they felt the same way.

I was surprised at how much pain I felt at leaving *American Idol*. I was sad and disappointed and maybe even a tad angry that the judges had strung me along and then ultimately not used the save. And I was irritated at myself for feeling that pain—I should have known better. It was a reality show after all, a show where everyone except the winner eventually had to leave. I had already overcome so much in my life that being eliminated shouldn't have hurt that much.

But it did.

And yet, even then in the midst of the pain, I knew that it was just one more struggle I would overcome.

God had already saved me from so much and blessed me with so much more. In my darkest moments, I had realized that with every obstacle comes an opportunity to trust him. Getting eliminated wasn't the end. Although I couldn't see where I was going, I knew God was leading me and I was willing to follow. My reality has always been driven by faith and not by sight. This wouldn't be any different.

The warm feelings shared that night helped me get past the initial sting of being kicked off. Within hours, as I worked past the disappointment, I realized that *this* was the moment I'd been waiting for all season. Getting eliminated from *Idol* didn't end my music career; I'd had a growing career before the show. Instead, it had just propelled it to a higher platform. And now that I was off, I was no longer limited to its rules. I could sing any song I wanted to without worrying about someone else's approval or whether it matched a theme. And for the first time since the top 13 red carpet, I was allowed to talk to the media. I could fully be myself.

Over the next few days, media outlets across America would be focused on me and what I had to say. One of the *Idol* executives had given me some great advice: "In all your interviews this week, talk about who you want to be."

At three o'clock the next morning, I began another satellite media tour. I announced my plans for a new CD and told them I would also be writing a book. Most important, I let them know what kind of music they could expect from me as an artist.

Later that day, Judge Kara DioGuardi joined me on *Access Hollywood*. I had the opportunity to perform my original song "Who Am I" for her. When I finished playing and singing she said, "I love it!" She was surprised that it was so up-tempo since she usually pictured me singing heartfelt ballads. Then she offered some advice about making sure my voice was featured when I recorded the song, because as she reminded me, people wanted to buy my voice. Her words meant a lot. She was the only judge with extensive song-writing experience, and I appreciated her wisdom.

Todd stayed with me for the LA press while Mom flew back to Phoenix with Katelyn and got her settled. Katelyn's surgery was just over a week away, but by Thursday, Mom was back in LA to accompany me to New York for additional media events. Todd couldn't go because he had to stay in Los Angeles to sing at a church on Easter Sunday.

In New York I performed "Just the Way You Are" on *Live with Regis and Kelly*. After I finished singing, they asked me about my music and graduating college at nineteen. For the first time since *Idol*, I talked about my academic background as a Marshall and Fulbright scholar.

NBC's *Today* filmed my segment outside. A crowd of fans showed up carrying signs and calling themselves my "Wild Angels." One of the producers said it was the biggest turnout they'd had all season. It was encouraging to have such fan support. The other contestants and I hadn't been able to connect with fans during the show, so this was my first opportunity to meet and talk with some of them.

The media tour took a break during the Easter holiday, and since Mom and I had some time off, we spent some of it walking through Central Park and quietly reflecting on all that had happened during the previous few months. I'd received a lot of e-mails that week from people who told me they cried when I got voted off. It was wonderful to have impacted so many people I didn't know, but it was also strange to be separated from the rest of my family on a holiday that was so important to me. I wondered if this is what life would look like from now on—a sort of faux intimacy with people I didn't know, and a longing to be more intimate with those I loved most. While I had big dreams and they were all coming true, I realized there would be a cost to my dreams, and time away from my family was one of the prices I'd pay.

Mom and I were both worried about Katelyn, and we talked to her frequently. Her surgery was scheduled for Friday. We flew back to Phoenix late Tuesday night. I was looking forward to spending time with Katelyn before her surgery—not only to support her as a fellow traveler on the journey through a kidney transplant, but also simply because I missed her a lot.

We walked into the house around one o'clock Wednesday morning. Mom and I were both so exhausted that we went straight to bed, leaving our suit-cases next to the door. It was the first time we had all been under the same roof in months. Sometime around noon, the phone rang and I didn't pay any attention to it until Mom came over and said, "Scott, we need you."

"What's wrong?"

"We just got a call from Katelyn's doctor. They have a pediatric kidney for her."

"What?"

Mom filled me in on the details. Someone under the age of eighteen had died, and their kidney was being offered to Katelyn. The doctor wanted to know if Katelyn would rather have the deceased donor's kidney instead of Marianne's.

"He recommends that she take it, but we only have thirty minutes to decide or it's going to someone else. We're getting a couple of the specialists on the phone, and we'd really appreciate you being on the call too."

I had been home for less than twelve hours, and I'd barely talked to Katelyn, and now I was being asked to contribute to a decision that would affect her health and possibly her life. Dad, who was at work, got the doctors on the phone along with Katelyn, Mom, and me. The doctors explained that typically a live donor kidney lasted longer than a deceased donor kidney.

"Wouldn't we want to go with my live donor, then?" Katelyn asked.

"Well, in this case, your live donor is middle-aged and the deceased donor isn't even eighteen. We think the age difference trumps some of the other factors."

We asked if the kidney had been tested. It had, but not all of the results were back yet. The match was good, but Marianne's was actually better—she matched more of the protein antigens. But even with those differences, the doc-tors thought the young kidney might be a better choice. We hung up, and with only five minutes remaining in the half hour, we prayed together as a family. I think we were all leaning toward the doctor's recommendation, but the final decision would be Katelyn's.

After we finished praying, she said through her tears, "I think I should take the deceased donor's kidney."

"I would wait to tell your live donor just in case anything happens and you still need her," advised the doctor when we called to give him our deci-sion. Instead of getting the reassurance we would've liked, we had yet another reminder that the surgery wasn't simple—anything could go wrong.

The doctors asked Katelyn to get to the hospital in the next couple of hours so she would be ready when the kidney was ready. Mom, Dad, and Katelyn arrived at the hospital around three. Mom promised to call Todd and me as soon as she knew when the surgery would take place.

We waited all night.

I tried to sleep, but I couldn't. My mind was on Katelyn and what she was going through as they prepped her for surgery. I was tempted to cancel my radio interviews for the next morning, but I knew Katelyn would want me to keep them. I remembered her words before I left for *Idol* the first time: "I'd rather watch you on TV from my hospital bed than have you standing next to my bed."

Around five o'clock the next morning, they took Katelyn down to prep for surgery. The procedure actually started around eight that morning, the same time I was doing an interview for a morning television show. I still felt torn about being in the studio instead of the hospital with Katelyn. I had to fight the urge in that interview to just stand up, take off my mike, and go to the hospital. Todd had accompanied me, and I knew he was just as torn. But I knew there was nothing we could do differently for Katelyn even if we were there. It was at least comforting that Todd and I could be together.

We checked in several times during the day, and when we finally returned home, we called again and received the good news. The surgery had gone well. The kidney had started pumping immediately, and she was now resting comfortably.

Unbelievably, God had given our family a *second* miracle.

~

Because of my newfound "celebrity" status, Katelyn was moved to a private room in a secluded section of the hospital so no one would bother us. The first time I visited her, I could tell she felt better. She had more energy and her exuberant personality had returned. "Thanks for coming to my final show," I told her. "That meant a lot. I know it must have taken a big toll on you, but I really appreciate you being there for me."

"I'm glad I was there, but I'm sorry you got eliminated," she said. "Now tell me, how was New York? Did you get a picture with Regis and Kelly?"

I wanted to talk about what she'd been going through, but all she wanted to do was hear about *American Idol*.

I thought about all of those days I'd felt drained and unable to experience the joys of life, especially the joy of making music. I understood. What Katelyn needed most was for me to talk about something other than kidney failure and to help give her hope for the future. So we talked about *American Idol*, about my music plans, and about the music we would perform together once she got well.

Katelyn came home from the hospital a few days later, and her recovery was amazing. The same day she came home, she wanted to sit up and play cards with Todd and me. It had taken me several days to sit up for longer than a few minutes. I was so proud of her; I knew better than anyone how hard those first days of recovery were. I also knew how hard it was to spend those first weeks trapped in the house, only leaving for doctor's appointments.

I was only home a few days, and we didn't get to spend as much time together as both of us would have liked. She was often gone for medical appointments, and I was preparing for the *American Idol* season finale.

~

A few days before the finale, I returned to Los Angeles to begin rehearsals for the final show. In addition to announcing the winner, the finale would feature the top 13 contestants performing songs with celebrities. Each contestant was in a group number, or sang a duet, with a celebrity. I'd learned that Matt and I would be playing dueling pianos on Billy Joel's "Tell Her about It." I couldn't wait. There had never been two highly skilled pianists on *Idol* before, and the media had pitted us against each other all season. Now we'd get to bust loose in a battle of the keys to see who could lay claim to best piano man of season eight.

At one of our first rehearsals, Matt and I were told that although Billy Joel had been invited, he had declined because of his busy schedule. I was disappointed that I wouldn't be meeting or playing with him, but I was still so excited about the piano duel that it didn't dampen my spirits much. Even without the legend, I believed my performance with Matt would be one of the most memorable *Idol* moments of all time.

We showed up at the Nokia Theater for our dress rehearsal on Tuesday. The rehearsal couldn't have gone better. We had two gorgeous grand pianos facing each other on stage. As we played, we fed off of each other's energy, creating not only great sounds, but also an exciting energy in the room. According to at least one producer who saw the rehearsal, it was the most exciting and memorable number of the entire finale.

I slept well that night and woke up incredibly excited. It was like when I woke up the morning of my college graduation, all keyed up for the day's events. Our rehearsal the day before had gone well, and there had been no technical problems. I returned to the theater Wednesday morning expecting to have one of the best shows of my life.

Around nine thirty that morning, Matt and I were rehearsing in the basement of the Nokia Theater when Ken Warwick came in and sat down. "Guys, I've got some bad news. The show is too long, and due to time constraints, we are going to have to cut your duet."

I was stunned. "Is there any way we can just shorten it?" My mind was spinning as I tried to think of alternatives.

"I'm sorry, but the decision's final. Yours is the only number without a celebrity."

I was dumbfounded, devastated. It seemed so unfair.

"But I'll make it up to you. I'll have you back on next season to perform. And that's a promise." Some people would say you can't trust a Hollywood executive to keep his word, but I trusted Ken and believed he was being sincere. It was a twinkle of hope amidst some very dark news. But even the hope of next season didn't lesson the pain of having the performance cut.

The bad news didn't end there, however. During the next few hours, the producers surgically cut out other pieces of the show. A chorus here. A verse there. But unbeknownst to them, every solo line I was supposed to sing in the finale was cut. Once all the changes were finalized, I was the only one out of the top 13 finalists who didn't have at least one solo line.

I decided to ask Ken if he could help. I requested a meeting with him and told him what had happened. "Is there anything you can do? Anything that can be switched around?"

"I'm sorry, Scott. There's nothing I can do this late in the game. We're only a few hours from showtime. And you need to know, we didn't want to cut your duet with Matt. It's just that we couldn't cut a number that included a celebrity who is coming in for the show." I understood what he was saying, but it still hurt.

While I was downstairs waiting for the show to start, I got a text from Jerry Lindahl saying that he and Jason Mraz were waiting to see me. Jason was a guest performer in the show, and they'd been told I was too busy to meet with them. I laughed. Busy doing what? I had nothing to rehearse.

"No, I'm not doing anything. Let me see what I can do."

I texted a producer and asked if I could leave the basement because Jason was waiting to see me. The producer seemed surprised, but he came and escorted me to the VIP lobby where they were waiting. I always looked forward to hanging out with Jerry, and it was the first time I had seen Jason since his Christmas party a year and a half earlier. At the party, I'd never imagined the next time I would see him would be at my own *American Idol* finale. I talked with Jason and Jerry for over half an hour before heading back to the *Idol* holding area. As I said good-bye, Jerry leaned in close to me and said, "Just remember, Jason had to come to you this time."

The show went well, and Kris Allen was named the season eight American Idol. I was happy for him, but I was still bothered at how things had ended. So were my fans. After getting lots of frustrated messages in e-mails, postings on forums, and comments on MySpace, I wrote a blog about what had happened. The media then picked it up and started talking about it. I had started *Idol* with the high-five controversy and now I was ending it with this.

Although my fans felt I'd been treated unfairly, I didn't believe that was what happened. I wrote in my post that life wasn't always fair. "But I believe God is bigger than all of this and has a plan for my life that reaches far beyond the circumstances of today. I have dealt with these kinds of situations before and know that everything happens for a reason, and in time, I very well may look back on this and finally realize it was for the best. That something better was waiting just around the corner."

I believed that.

Only time would tell what that "something better" would be.

CHAPTER 33

Dream Tour

I have found a perfect world
That I go to in the night
—FROM "SWEET DREAMS," SCOTT MACINTYRE

I no longer had to dream about going on tour and playing in arenas. The summer after the show ended, I was doing that every night. From Portland, Oregon, to Portland, Maine, we played fifty-two arenas across North America. I'd never had more fun in my life.

Although the tour was called *American Idols Live*, the tour had a completely different crew from the television show. There was a new producer, new musical director, new band members, and new hair and makeup people. They were all a joy to work with. On the TV show, we had been treated like contestants, which was fair—that's what we were. But on tour, we were treated like talent. We could interact with the musicians, and they treated us like peers. When there was a problem, there was no all-powerful producer to run to, so we worked it out among ourselves. It was a collaborative environment, and more importantly, almost no one had an ego. Everyone wanted to create the best show they could, regardless of who got credit for the ideas.

For the first time we were able to use wireless in-ear monitors, which replaced the floor monitors. On the TV show, even with a monitor pointed back at me, it was still hard to hear my vocals above the five hundred screaming fans in the studio audience. But now, the sound was right inside my ears and I could work directly with the technician who did the monitor mixing to optimize the perfect combination of voice, piano, and other instruments. And there were no more problems with the sound system either. Finally, every night when I went on stage, I could completely depend on the sound system to support my performance. That was such a relief after my television experience where it was hit and miss for every rehearsal and performance.

But the best part was we no longer had themes. No more Motown or Grand Ole Opry weeks meant I was finally free to choose the songs that best showcased my artistry. For the tour, I wanted to do music I hadn't performed on the show—songs like "Bend and Break" by Keane and "A Thousand Miles" by Vanessa Carlton. As a group number, we all did "Don't Stop Believin'" by Journey.

For the "Bend and Break" arrangement, I had some specific ideas for the drummer and how I wanted other band members to interact musically. Although the musical director for the TV show was brilliant, he often seemed territorial and wanted to control the arrangements. But Dave, the musical director for the tour, was very collaborative. He took me over and introduced me to the drummer. Since I also played drums, I could speak his language. "I've been working out an arrangement in my head," I said. "I'd like to do something like this," and then using my body drumming, I demonstrated the kind of sounds and rhythms I was looking for in each part of the song.

"I'm totally into it," he said, and played it on the drum set just like I'd showed him on my body.

On another song, Dave and I were having trouble deciding how to end it. Should it end softly or go out with a bang? We had different opinions, but once we talked about them, I felt like his idea best served the song, so we went with it.

I always strived to create unique and dynamic arrangements for the songs I performed, regardless of whether they were my songs or not. A song is like a story—it has highs and lows, a beginning, middle, and end, and emotions and shades of color that can all be tweaked to create the best possible experience for the listener. It was exciting to collaborate with a musical director and musicians of such high caliber who could help bring my vision for each song to life.

With control over song choice, input on the arrangements, dependable equipment, and my in-ears, I could give my best performance every night. After hearing my performance, *Rolling Stone* said, "His rendition of Vanessa Carlton's 'A Thousand Miles'—and his gentle mocking of Ryan Seacrest's attempt to high five him at the auditions—drew some of the loudest applause of the night."[1] Throughout the tour, people told me that I "sounded so much better in person." I wanted to say, "Yeah, this is how I usually sound." But instead I just said, "Thank you."

~

1.   Susan Yudt, "Adam Lambert, Kris Allen Hit the Stage Again as American Idols Live Tour Kicks Off in Portland," *Rolling Stone*, July 6, 2009, http://www.rollingstone.com/music/news/adam-lambert-kris-allen-hit-the-stage-again-as-american-idols-live-tour-kicks-off-in-portland-20090706.

Several days before we opened the first show, we took the bus to Portland, Oregon, to rehearse on the new set. Todd was my sighted guide for the tour, and Mom was home with Katelyn. Though Katelyn's recovery initially seemed to be on a fast track, lately it hadn't been going as well. The doctors had over-suppressed her immune system, and as a result, she'd picked up a couple of viruses from the deceased donor's kidney. Now she was seeing doctors several times a week to help her maintain a balance between staying healthy and making sure her body didn't reject the kidney.

Todd had agreed to come on tour with me, but he had to pass up paying performance opportunities to do it. Since I was being paid for the tour, I paid him to accompany me. And I couldn't have picked anyone better. Todd got along great with everybody, and he was so much fun to hang out with.

Since none of the contestants had done an arena tour before, the crew planned a grand unveiling of the stage set for us in Portland. We entered the arena through the loading bays and walked down a long concrete hallway and then through a door that led to the arena floor. As soon as we had all walked in, they played the intro music and started the light show. It was unbelievable! The stage was directly ahead of us, and there was video, smoke, and so many lights. I tried to take it all in as I imagined the roar of the crowd. Todd described everything to me as he motioned my arm across the length of the enormous stage. It blew my mind to think that, in a few days, I would be on that stage, leading the emotional frenzy that would fill the arena. People were paying up to one hundred dollars a ticket just to sit in those seats and see us perform.

It was time to get to work, and as we walked backstage, Todd used a phrase I'd never heard him use before, but it summed up perfectly everything we'd seen: "This is legit."

～

In all my dreams about touring, the one thing I had never dreamed about was how I'd get on stage. But even if I had, I probably wouldn't have thought of something as cool as what they planned for the tour; it was better than my wildest fantasies. My piano rose up out of the stage amidst the smoke and lights while I played it! Every night, that moment was just like the first night—the crowd cheered and screamed as I rose up on the platform.

But the process of creating that illusion was harder to pull off than any-one would suspect. Each night, when Megan started her last song, "Put Your

Records On," I would put on my jacket and insert my in-ears. Then Todd would lead me to the back of the stage, where there was a tunnel that ran underneath it all the way to center stage where the moving platform lowered. Todd would put his hand on my shoulder to guide me, and we'd bend over and move as fast as we could through the passageway, ducking down the whole way.

As soon as Megan said, "Thank you!" the lights would go down, and a moving platform in the center of the stage would lower. We'd arrive there just as the platform stopped. The stagehands then had about five seconds to get the piano loaded onto the platform and situate the microphone and the bench before I had to crawl onto it and start playing. I had to stay hunched over so the audience couldn't see me at first, but the music started right away. That meant that while I leaned as far as I could to the right, I would have to stretch my arms to play from that hunched-over position. As the platform lifted, I slowly raised my body, giving the illusion that I was rising from a much deeper hole.

We had a few close calls—like the night I started the song an octave lower than I should have because my hands weren't in the right place. But I quickly found a spot in the song to seamlessly transition back to the right place. It was a very dramatic entrance, and though there was a lot that could go wrong, nothing ever did.

~

Our tour was one of the biggest tours in North America that year, and as a result, we had many responsibilities beyond just showing up to perform every night. Each day, before and after the show, we went to several private meet-and-greets—usually for employees of sponsoring corporations and their families. A hundred people or more would be at each one, and they all wanted pictures and autographs.

After the last meet-and-greet, usually around midnight, we would head out to the buses. Typically the buses were kept in a parking lot that was barricaded to keep fans away, but they always knew where we were. Although it might be an hour or more after the performance ended, there could still be a thousand fans lined up along the perimeter waiting for us, just hoping to shake our hand or get an autograph. It was up to us if we wanted to meet with the fans along the barricades. I always did. I felt like those were the true fans, the ones who really cared about us. And every night, they proved it by waiting outside—in the dark, sometimes in the rain—just to see us in person.

Todd would describe how the barricade line often stretched as far as he could see. As we approached, the fans would scream and press up against the barricades. It was never possible to get to all of them because they usually stood several people deep. Todd would lead me along the fence and guide my hand on where to sign each photo or tour book. People would shove things over other people's heads just to get them in front of us. Todd would grab the nearest item, and while I signed it, he grabbed the next one. It was pandemonium, but we eventually got it down to a method that allowed us to sign one item about every two seconds.

Though we tried, we never got through the whole line before the tour wranglers told us the buses were ready to go. No one made us leave, but you didn't want to be the person who held up the bus if all the other performers were ready. I cut it close several times, though, because I stayed until the very end—it was important to me to spend as much time as I could with the people who had watched and voted for me on *Idol*.

One night, when the barricade was long and time was running out, Todd had a great idea. "You stay close to the fence but hold on to my elbow. I'll run along the barricade, and you can hold out your hand and high-five everyone as we run by."

Since I told the Ryan Seacrest high-five story during the concert every night, Todd's idea made a lot of sense. We would run full speed along the barricades, Todd telling me when to turn or when to avoid extrusions. And as I raised my hand, everyone cheered and held their hands out to connect as we passed. It worked so well that we made it a regular part of our routine. It is one of my fondest memories from the tour.

~

Though I'd been on tour with the MacIntyre Family Singers, comparing those experiences to the *American Idol* tour was like comparing a black-and-white photograph to a 3-D, Technicolor movie. Everything was bigger, faster, louder, and more exciting. Most enjoyable was the fact that I didn't have to worry about any logistics—all I had to do was put my heart and soul into my music every night. I was extremely thankful to have been a part of the *American Idol* television show, but the tour meant more to me than anything. As a blind person, being able to hear ten thousand fans cheering under one roof was more stimulating than knowing thirty million were watching on TV. There was something about making music, people responding to that music, and my responding to them that lit me on fire.

The second anniversary of my kidney transplant took place during the tour, and it was an emotional day for me. It was hard to believe that I was singing before ten thousand people when just over two years earlier, I could barely open my mouth and have enough breath to support a single line. Then, I had wondered if I'd ever make music again. Now, I was doing it in the biggest way possible. And it was all thanks to the selfless gift of a friend. Without my new kidney, I knew I wouldn't be living my dream—I might not be living at all. That day I called and thanked her. I will always remember that tour as the celebration of a second chance at life.

Two-thirds through the tour, Todd left to move to Japan. He had been offered a yearlong contract to be the lead singer in several shows for Tokyo Disney. A friend of mine from Toronto helped me for a week, and then Mom took his place as my sighted guide for the rest of the tour. Meanwhile Katelyn had recovered enough to head off to college in California, and while Mom and I finished the final stretch of touring, Dad helped Katelyn move out. It all seemed to happen so quickly. Mom didn't get to see Katelyn off to college or Todd off to Japan. And neither did I.

The day the tour ended, the two of us flew to New York to meet with executives at several record labels. Initially things looked promising, but it soon became clear that, with the downswing in the economy and the unpredictability of the music business, they weren't ready to sign a new artist. I decided that as soon as I returned to Scottsdale, I would take matters into my own hands and begin work on another independently produced CD.

But first, I needed to relax.

～

As we walked off the plane, I felt the warm tropical air rush over my face. Mom, Dad, and I had decided to take a long-needed vacation in Hawaii to decompress from a crazy year. Between Katelyn's diagnosis and transplant and my time on *Idol*, it felt like we'd been running constantly. I couldn't remember the last time I had just slept in and not thought about anything. Just for a week, I wanted to forget about my career and let time slip away.

By the time we got to our hotel, it was getting late.

I was exhausted. The moment I left the tour, I felt like I was stepping back into an old dimension where time moved slower. I had been on over-drive for so long—first the grueling schedule of the *Idol* TV show and then the fifty-two-arena tour—I had completely lost my sense of time and place. After waking up in different hotels all over North America, I looked forward to sleeping in the same bed for more than one night. I had spent twenty-four hours a day with the same people for so many months, and leaving the tour and parting ways with my newfound friends was a sharp awakening that my *Idol* journey was now truly over. But I had my whole life ahead of me, and now I could wake up every morning and perform music for a living. I marveled to think that I was actually living out my dreams—dreams I'd had since I was a little kid.

By midnight everyone else had gone to bed, but I couldn't sleep. I walked out onto the balcony to reminisce. I couldn't believe how far God had brought me and how much he had blessed me with. I thought about my first TV appearance on CNN so many years ago, when I played for our neighbor's wedding, and how exciting it was to hear myself on TV. Now I had performed on TV for millions of people around the world. I remembered going around our neighborhood in Toronto with Todd when we were kids, shamelessly selling my newest CD door to door. Now people were asking me to autograph tour books, purses, iPod covers, and babies. Most of all, I thought of Patricia and how I wouldn't have been standing there at that moment had it not been for her sacrifice. What else could I ask for?

As I listened to the lapping waves, my thoughts turned to other things. Music had always been my dream, but I always thought there would be some-one there to share it with. I never pictured myself living the single life, but instead, I pictured my wife with me on the tour bus. I wanted to get married and have a family someday. Throughout my life, I had prayed that God would lead me to that person, but I had always been so focused on being the best I could be musically and academically that I had never had time for a serious relationship. I believed it had worked out for the best, but with my new celeb-rity status, it would be harder than ever to meet someone and know they were interested in me and not just because I was an *American Idol* finalist.

Suddenly, my thoughts landed on Christina. How long had it been since we'd talked?

Christina had never been able to see the tour. We talked on the phone while I was on *Idol*, and we'd even planned to get together one week, but it was the week I was eliminated, so I went to New York to do media instead. I didn't talk with her much once I went on tour.

I dialed her number, and then realized it was 3:00 a.m. California time. I almost hung up, but she answered on the first ring. "Hang on," she whispered. "I'm going outside so I don't wake my roommate." After a short pause she said, "Okay, I can talk now." Her voice melted me.

"I'm sorry, were you sleeping?"

"No, not at all. I'm starting an internship at NBC tomorrow, and I guess I'm too nervous to sleep. Where are you? Are you still on tour?"

I filled her in on the post-*Idol* details and told her about the incredible experience I had on tour. She told me about her new internship, and I was lost in the melody of her voice.

Sighted men and women are often first attracted to each other because of physical appearance. But for me, the primary attraction was auditory. I was attracted to girls who had melodious voices. Not only did Christina have a beautiful voice, but her tone was also very expressive. Her emotions came through in every word she spoke.

We had been talking for an hour when she said, "I've been thinking about you a lot lately and wondering what you're up to. I'm glad you called."

Before I let her go, I had to ask her one question. "So, are you seeing anyone right now?"

"No actually, I'm not."

"Really?" What started out as a whimsical call had turned into the most fortuitous call of my life. Christina was single, I was single, and I'd always been attracted to her. This was the moment I'd been waiting for.

"Would you want to go out with an *American Idol*?"

Without hesitating, she answered.

CHAPTER 34

Together by Faith

And we'll see the morning glory
Come to end the night
But the stars will tell our story
A hundred times

—FROM "STARS," SCOTT MACINTYRE

When Christina and I first met, I already had a wife. Well, at least within the context of the show we were both performing in. We met in a musical theater production of *The Music Man* at our church. I was seventeen, and she was fourteen. I played Mayor Shinn and she was one of the "Pick-a-Little" ladies. Whenever there was a break in rehearsals or we had time backstage, we would hang out. Other cast members noticed and joked that their mayor shouldn't fraternize with the young ladies. But we enjoyed each other's company. We talked, and laughed, and I even taught her how to swing dance.

I liked Christina, but I wasn't sure how she felt about me. I knew she confided her feelings to one of her girlfriends, so when I couldn't stand not knowing any longer, I cornered Helen and asked.

After much cajoling, she finally said, "She likes you, but she doesn't want you to know."

I was overjoyed. After the show that night, I went into the bathroom to change out of my costume, and as soon as the door closed behind me, I threw my arms up in the air and said under my breath, "Yes! She likes me!" I had totally fallen for her, and as I hung up my costume, I felt warm and happy inside. I peeled off my Mayor Shinn moustache, which usually burned as I removed it, but not that night; I only had feelings of jubilation.

After the run of *The Music Man* ended, we held a huge cast party at the community center in our gated community. People sang, danced, and swam in the pool. Music played over the speakers, and when a great song came on, I asked Christina if she wanted to swing dance *in the pool*. It seemed like a good idea—until I decided to dip her. Not only did I get her hair wet, something she didn't want, but she had been wearing contact lenses, so she didn't want to go under water. Not my most romantic moment.

When she came up coughing, I said, "I'm so sorry, I didn't know."

"No, no. It's okay. Next time I'll be ready," she joked. It seemed despite the inconvenience, she hadn't minded.

Fortunately, we remained friends and continued to talk. That fall, our families and some friends went to see a production of Shakespeare in the park. During the first half of the show, I was sitting next to Christina. As an awkwardly romantic teenager, I decided I was going to put my hand on her knee. It took me forty-five minutes to work up the courage, as I slowly inched my way from the center of my seat to the side closest to her. Finally, I reached over and let my hand fall.

It was there for two seconds before I chickened out and removed it.

I didn't know it at the time, but I had totally caught her off guard. At intermission, she went to sit by her mom and said, "Scott tried to put his hand on my knee!"

"Maybe he was just trying to know if you were still there."

But Christina knew it was more than that, and she never came back to sit by me.

A few weeks later I ran into Christina and her friend Helen at a local restaurant. They had just been to a church conference that focused on marriage. I was just listening politely until Helen said, "One of the things we learned is to keep your hands to yourself until you're married."

I kept a straight face, but I could barely keep myself from bursting out in laughter at the irony of the situation. I wanted to crawl under the table and hide. I didn't know if Christina had told her about the other night.

Through all of it, Christina and I somehow remained friends and continued to do things together. What started as a crush grew into a beautiful friendship, but there were lots of mixed signals. One night, when we were driving home after a concert, she reached over to take my hand and held it the rest of the way.

A friend later told me that Christina had always liked me, but she was afraid that if we started dating, it would quickly turn into more and there would be no turning back. Apparently I was the one guy she always compared everyone else to, but at the time, she wasn't ready for a serious relationship.

That wasn't the only thing that stood in our way. For several years, we lived in separate cities. I was in London for a year, and then I got sick. But once I recovered from the kidney transplant, she went to school in Los Angeles. I went on tour with the MacIntyre Family Singers, then it was off to *American Idol* and the *Idol* tour. It had been a long time since we'd both been in the same place, physically or emotionally. But now the timing seemed perfect.

⁓

As I stood on the second-floor balcony, phone in hand, the waves crashing in the distance, I was frozen in disbelief. It was obvious that we had not only a great friendship but a strong attraction. *Maybe she didn't hear the question? Would it be wrong to ask again?* It was my only hope. "Would you want to go out with an *American Idol*?"

"No," she said plainly. But then her voice warmed up when she added, "I want to go out with Scott MacIntyre."

Those simple words overwhelmed me—not only because she finally wanted to go out, but because she wanted to truly know me, my celebrity status aside. With her simple response, Christina proved that none of that mattered to her. Immediately heat rose in my face and warm butterflies filled my stomach. After we got off the phone that night, I once again celebrated by saying, "Yes! She likes me!"

She was still in school and working in Los Angeles, so we set our first date to coincide with a meeting I had in LA. We spent the day together at Disneyland and made lots of memories. By the end of the day, I was love-struck. God had answered my prayer and the relationship void in my life was being filled.

⁓

That fall, Christina and I continued our long-distance relationship. It was an incredibly busy time for me as I was also working hard on my new CD, *Heartstrings*. Since a record label hadn't picked me up, I did what I always did—I produced it myself. Fortunately, I had already independently produced seven CDs, and I knew the right people to hire to help me create a professional CD and packaging.

Out of dozens of original songs I had written, I felt I had chosen a great collection for the CD. The instrumentation and drums for "The Good, the Bad, the Ugly" had been recorded in the weeks immediately following my transplant. In fact, many of the songs had elements that had been recorded during the six post-transplant weeks when I couldn't leave the house. When I revamped a song called "Never Tired," that talked about a longing to devote all your energy to loving someone, it reminded me of how tired I'd been through those long days when I didn't feel well. And of course, "View from Above" made the cut. More than any other song, that one described my journey during the previous couple of years.

I worked hard to get the CD ready quickly for one reason—I hoped Ken Warwick would keep his promise and have me on as a guest performer. I truly believed he would, but I wasn't going to expect it would just happen. I sent him a couple of reminder e-mails—nothing to pester him—but just to let him know I hadn't forgotten. I didn't hear anything back, but I had continued working on the CD so I'd be ready to promote it if the opportunity came up.

Sometime in January I received an e-mail from an unknown, non-professional looking return address. I figured it was probably junk mail and almost didn't open it. I listened as my screen reader read the message: "Simon Fuller and Ken Warwick would like to invite you to come back on to *American Idol* and perform." Ken had kept his promise! I was ecstatic to be returning to the world's most popular television show, and this time, I would be a guest artist.

As soon as I learned the date, finishing my CD as quickly as possible suddenly became my top priority. I hired a high-profile publicity company I'd worked with in the past. I interviewed radio promoters and hired one to help me get radio play for singles off the new CD. For several months, Mom and I worked eighteen-hour days, proofing artwork, shipping CDs to radio stations, creating promotional materials, and taking care of pre-sales. I was going to bed as late as four o'clock in the morning.

I hoped our efforts would pay off. But the one thing I hoped for most—to announce the album on *American Idol*—was something I didn't have control over. I knew that having an opportunity to introduce my album to the television audience would be huge. Tens of millions of people would be watching. There wasn't another promotional opportunity like that in the whole industry.

I wouldn't be playing anything from my new CD; Matt and I were set to play the Billy Joel duet that had been cut from the finale. While I hoped that Ryan Seacrest would mention that I had a new CD, I knew that *Idol* rarely did much promotion, even for high-profile celebrities. And Matt didn't have a CD. They might not want to seem unfair by promoting something I'd done if he didn't have something similar. But I didn't give up hope. As soon as I finished the CD, I sent Ken a copy and let him know I'd be releasing it on iTunes the same day I was on the show.

Mom and I went out to Los Angeles the day of the show to rehearse. It was great to see Matt again, and we laughed about all the jokes we had made about each other on tour. We also brought Christina along. By now I'd told her a lot about *American Idol*, but she hadn't experienced it for herself. It was amusing to see how different things were now that I was a guest artist. I finally had a nice dressing room. When I was on the show, they kept contestants separated from the guest artists, but now I could roam the hallways and talk to whomever I wanted.

Everyone seemed happy to see Matt and me, with the possible exception of the music director—he still treated us like contestants. But I felt very comfortable. All of the stress was gone now, or maybe I was just relaxed because no one would critique us after we played.

Annie the stage manager was still there counting down the commercials. During a break in the rehearsal, she stopped by my piano and we chatted for a few minutes.

"What are we doing after the piece?" I asked, hoping that Matt and I would have the opportunity to talk with Ryan and maybe I could sneak in a mention of the CD.

"You guys will just stay seated at the pianos. We'll go straight to commercial break, and then we'll get you off."

"So we won't get to talk with Ryan?"

"No, we're going straight to commercial."

I was a little disappointed. I had really hoped for the chance to promote my CD. But I quickly realized how fortunate I was to once again perform on the *Idol* stage. Though I didn't get to sing a solo in the finale, Ken had kept his word and given me an even larger spotlight. Now it was up to me to shine.

Thirty minutes before the show started someone came into my dressing room and gave me a wireless mike pack to clip on my belt.

"What is this for?" I asked. The wireless packs were only used to talk to the judges or to Ryan. When we sang, mikes would be at the pianos to pick up our voices.

"We're not sure if you're going to be talking with Ryan or not, so wear it just in case."

I didn't want to get my hopes up. It was a long shot, especially after what Annie had said. But still, hope bubbled up in the corners of my mind.

The show was already on the air when someone came to escort us to the stage. We went down the elevator and walked to the back of the audience as they went to commercial. Over the intercom, Annie said, "Forty-five seconds." And then to me she said, "You're going to talk to Ryan after your song."

Yes! Maybe, just maybe, I could announce my CD. Just then, Ryan came up behind me. "Is it a full-length release, Scott?"

"It's a full-length," I said proudly, knowing that a full album was a much bigger deal to pull off in such a short amount of time than an EP or a single.

"Thanks," Ryan said. "I just wanted to check."

"Ten. Nine. Eight . . ."

As I sat down at my piano and Annie's voice counted down the commercial break, those old butterflies stirred up once again. I wasn't nervous exactly; it just reminded me of all those feelings from when I was a contestant.

The song went great. Matt and I tore it up. The audience loved it and was clapping along and cheering as we played and sang. When it ended, Ryan came over and made a few comments and then said, "Scotty the Body has an album out."

As we talked, not only was I able to plug the CD, but I was also able to give my website address. I knew they might bleep that out, but at least I tried.

After the show, I attended the red carpet event with the top 12 contestants from that season. While I was there, I ran into Rick, one of the producers I'd become friendly with during my time on *Idol*.

"Nice going, plugging the website there," he said, smiling and poking fun at me.

"Did it go through?"

"Oh yeah. I was in the booth. It went through."

I knew they had done me a favor. I've watched countless shows, and there were many times when the mike was muted and the audience at home had no idea why—usually because some artist had plugged their website. But for whatever reason, they let mine go through. It was a huge promotional opportunity for my music, and it never would have happened if they hadn't cut me from the finale.

I marveled at God—how he had worked something so disappointing into something so good for my career. But I shouldn't have been surprised. Hadn't he done that my whole life?

During the afterparty, we were all hanging out when Matt happened to look at something on his iPhone. "Scott! You're number 18 on the iTunes pop album chart!"

"Really?" I was stunned. It was better than I had even imagined.

"That's amazing," Matt said. "You've got to compete with everybody to get on that chart. That's legit!"

I was speechless. Matt handed me his iPhone. The screen was well lit in the dark room, so after a minute of scanning, I saw my album cover right there among contemporary pop's best-selling artists. I was above Lady Gaga, and I hadn't even had to wear a meat dress. It was hard to believe how far I'd come.

～

I celebrated the success of my album, but I knew it wasn't something I'd done myself. It had all started with a piano my mom unexpectedly inherited. She had made every effort to get me the best educational opportunities and to find music teachers who could bring out the best in me. My whole family supported me, even when it was hard on them—like when Katelyn was sick at home without Mom because she wanted to see me succeed on *Idol*.

There were other people, like Laurie Z., who taught me how to promote myself and not wait for a record label to do it for me. People like Gregg, who taught me to take risks at the keyboard, and in life. And my O&M instructors who taught me how to take those risks safely. Dad, who paid for my piano lessons, listened to pop music with me, and told me I could do it, was so influential, as were people like Yonty, Jerry, and Jason Mraz, who offered me encouragement when I needed it most. Of course there was also Walter Cosand, who gave me an incredible training and education in classical music. I still use the things he taught me every day as I write and play—even if my style is different than his.

But if I'd been too sick to use my God-given talents, none of my recent success would have happened. It was Patricia who gave me life through the unexpected gift of her kidney, enabling me to get off of dialysis and back into the music business. She literally gave me a piece of herself so I could continue to give myself to others through my music. How do you thank someone for that?

Though Marianne never had to give up her kidney for Katelyn, the hope she gave my family through her offer was also a huge gift to us during that very dark time. And though Katelyn's healing came from another family's pain, as they graciously gave up the kidney their child would no longer need to restore the life of someone else, it was also a sacrificial gift. It's likely one or both of us wouldn't be here today—we certainly wouldn't be thriving—without that kind of extraordinary generosity.

Looking back over my life so far, I realize that many times when I was on the verge of experiencing incredible success, that's when the trials came to knock me down. I don't think that was a coincidence. God works through us during the good times and the bad—when we are on the mountaintop, and when we trudge through the valley. I have experienced both extremes in my life, often at the same time. But I learned that he used the worst days of my life to bless me the most. And he's not done with me yet. I continually find myself in new places, doing things I never imagined I'd be doing. Like motivational speaking. Or writing this book. Although my gratitude is given to many, the glory is all his.

For as long as I can remember, I have dreamed of being able to share my music with the world. Though I was faced with seemingly insurmountable obstacles, and at times felt like giving up, I am now living that dream every day. I didn't know how I was going to learn to play the piano when I couldn't even read sheet music. I didn't know how I was going to live and study overseas in London as a blind person whose health was also in danger. I didn't know how I could share my God-given talents with those around me if I was too sick to play the piano in my own living room. And I didn't know how in the world I was going to connect with viewers of *American Idol* if I couldn't even see the cameras. But none of that mattered to me. Every time I faced a new obstacle, it was another opportunity to take a leap of faith. I believed it was possible to realize my dreams, even when I couldn't see how to get there. And I knew if it was God's plan, he would bring it all to fruition in his perfect timing.

I can only imagine what trials and what triumphs I will face in the years to come. But with a grateful heart for all that I've been given, I will face them boldly. And wherever I go next, I know I won't go alone.

Not only has God always been there for me, and with me, but now he's also given me another very special gift. On August 18, 2011, Christina became my wife, and joined me on this journey. And together we will move forward into whatever our future brings.

For we live by faith, not by sight.
(2 Corinthians 5:7)

August 18, 2011

Acknowledgments

First, I would like to thank God for blessing me with such a wonderful life. Special thanks to my loving wife, Christina, for her tenderness and devotion. My mother, Carole, for her invaluable support through the years and for riding on the guys' *AI* tour bus. My sister, Katelyn, for allowing me to share a part of her incredible story. My brother, Todd, for his selfless attitude and always wanting the best for me. My father, Douglas, for his shining example of humility. And the Cosand family. Thank you to C. Corzine, F. Breeden, D. Ward, M. Baugher, D. Fleming, C. Nagelson, S. Fuller, K. Warwick, M. Darnell, P. Abdul, K. DioGuardi, T. Vinciquerra, W. Fong, H. Froget, S. Green, J. Bozeman, M. Cilnis, J. Lembo, R. Mills, M. Dixon, F. Bronson, E. Leonard, M. Ravenhill, everyone at Thomas Nelson, Premiere Speakers, Donate Life America, Women of Faith, 19, Fremantle, FOX, and *American Idol*. Thanks also to G. Gilbert, J. Lindahl, B. Silva, M. Kahn, J. Burke, R. Moody, P. Baack, L. Fletcher, Y. Solomon, S. Roberts, K. Burley, J. Rink, VSA Arts / Kennedy Center, C & A Faloona, M. Crum, British Council / Marshall Commission, M. Smith, A & C Cooper, D. Foster, M. McDonald, J. Vellutato, S. Kling, B. Okrent, D. Koz, J. Mraz, E. Hurt, C. Oglesby, L. Phelan, B. Baker, B. Cakmis, C. Morgan, L. Smith, S. Sharp, P. Aiken-O'Neill, R. Seacrest, R. Jackson, S. Cowell, J. Rasmussen, J & T Politan, L. Anderson, and all my friends and supporters at Scottsdale Bible Church. Thank you to the countless venues, companies, charities, churches, and media outlets around the world for inviting me to speak and perform throughout the years. Thank you to D. Kinnoin who had a profound impact on my music but was not mentioned in this book. Last but not least, thank you to my amazing fans. You inspire me to make music every day.

All songs are available on iTunes.
www.scottmacintyre.com
www.twitter.com/ScottDMacIntyre

Be
HOPE
to someone in need.

Over 112,000 men, women and children
are currently waiting for a lifesaving organ
transplant. Hundreds of thousands more are in
need of a tissue, bone or corneal transplant to
resume normal life or restore sight.

**You can provide HOPE to those waiting by registering
today as an organ, eye and tissue donor.**

Register Now

Find out how by visiting:
www.donatelife.net